From Rags to Bitches:

AN AUTOBIOGRAPHY

by
MR. BLACKWELL
with
Vernon Patterson

GENERAL PUBLISHING GROUP, INC.
Los Angeles

Makeup by Dominique Graham

For information:
General Publishing Group, Inc.
2701 Ocean Park Boulevard
Santa Monica, CA 90405

Library of Congress Cataloging-in-Publication Data

Blackwell, Mr.
   From rags to bitches : an autobiography / Mr. Blackwell
Vernon Patterson.
     p. cm.
   Includes index.
   ISBN 1-881649-57-1
   1. Blackwell, Mr. 2. Fashion designers–United States–Biography.
I. Patterson, Vernon. II. Title.
TT505.B53A3 1995
746.0 ' 2 ' 092–dc20   95-12007
[B]   CIP

Printed in the USA
10 9 8 7 6 5 4 3 2 1

General Publishing Group
Los Angeles

Table of Contents

I was born into this world in a cocoon of mystery, lies and deceit...I have lived my life in that cocoon, often incapable of sorting out reality from illusion, always living on the edge between them...perhaps I created for myself the world of fantasy in which I wished to exist...I don't know...I really don't know...but now, in my later years, I realize it worked for me...so everything in this memoir is true—at least to me it is.

Only the gods and my mother
knew more than I did...

For

Eva Pauline Ellenson-Selzer

…my mother…

who taught me about surviving…

even in the bleakest of times

I feel as though I'm standing on a high mountain and I look down and there is thunder and lightning and the earth opens up beneath me...

That's life.

I've always been afraid of falling off that mountain. So I hang on...

I hang on to the sky.

Prelude

I awoke suddenly, suffocating from anticipation. My hotel suite looked dreary and dismal. Outside, under gray skies, Manhattan was dark and silent in the early morning haze that crept over the city. Today would mark the end of my career as a designer. My final collection would soon be unveiled—a glittering, dramatic swirl of chiffons and silks that symbolize the Blackwell attitude toward feminine fashion. My collections have always contradicted the passing trends and frenetic fads the fashion industry has embraced with reckless abandon. Memories of painful decades assaulted me. The price of success was high. Too high. I felt angry, confused. I had given too much to this frivolous industry called fashion. For what? It was all a meaningless farce, devoid of any real achievement or accomplishment. But I planned to orchestrate this grand finale with great care and dignity.

As I stood looking into the mirror, I thought about my appearance. Dark suit, dark tie—no jewelry. I will dress as unpretentiously as possible. My trademark, a mass of heavy gold chains, lay untouched on my dresser. I stuffed them into an open drawer and laughed—an open, almost hysterical sound. For the first time in years, I felt free. My facade as the outrageously outspoken man of many faces was really only a weapon to publicize my ultimate purpose: to succeed in fashion. My preoccupation with facades was ending, and so, too, was an era in my life.

In the street below, the black limousine resembled a luxurious hearse as it waited to take me on my last ride as the flamboyant Mr. Blackwell. The phone rang.

"The car is here, Mr. Blackwell. Are you ready?"

"Yes," I replied softly. "I'm ready."

As I descended to the lobby in the elevator, two aging fashion victims stood next to me like ancient soldiers. Seventh Avenue at its absolute worst, I thought. Dull, boring, impassioned. Tinker toys have more shape and style. I watched them arrogantly, realizing with a touch of sadness that these women were hopelessly enslaved to the dictates of *Women's Wear Daily* and the ineffectual designers who littered Seventh Avenue. As the doors slid open, I rushed past them and raced through the lobby. Voices echoed around me in the mirrored foyer.

"Good morning, Mr. Blackwell."

"Your car is waiting, Mr. Blackwell."

"I loved your list, Mr. Blackwell."

"Flowers, Mr. Blackwell."

I ignored them all.

The gray skies turned black as rain began to fall, creating murky, iridescent puddles as it mixed with the oily grime from the avenue. The chauffeur nodded with respect as he opened the polished limousine door. I couldn't nod back. I was lost in thought as I nestled into the corner of the car, sinking into the tufted ebony leather. I felt my life flash before me as we drove past Park Avenue, Lexington and Third. A thousand neon lights bled through the rain and reflected color across my face and hair, now streaked with gray. Looking out the window, I saw a young man molded to the corner of a building. He turned on a soft smile as he glanced toward the limousine. I knew that smile well. Cold sweat coated my brow. I turned away. I, too, had used that same insincere expression on this street so many years ago. I, too, had lived on the desperation, not kindness, of strangers. I, too, had possessed the same hard, sculpted body, jet black hair and hungry brown eyes. I, too, had been for sale. I remembered walking into dark hotels, climbing endless stairs to dingy apartments. Dirty money would exchange hands and the performance would begin. Looking back, I realized that many of my customers brought me a strange sense of satisfaction, power, even fulfillment. I wondered what they were like now, if they remembered, if the years had been kind to them. I felt foolishly sentimental and suddenly very old.

"Nothing really changes, does it?" I asked my driver quietly.

But the glass between our seats was closed and he couldn't hear me. Nothing really changes. I was still alone.

As we crossed the bridge, we entered Brooklyn. I felt oddly peaceful, disconnected from my childhood streets and buildings. Like an artist creating a portrait, I had managed somehow to erase the early failings of a now-celebrated life. But I saw myself in the pleading expressions of the young faces that peered in my window. Forgetting about my collection waiting to be shown, I rolled down the tinted glass and reveled in the sounds and smells of these streets on which I had traveled too many times. And I thought about my life, a life that began in the black alleys and tenements of my childhood here in Brooklyn. It still hurt inside.

Inside the womb-like walls of my limousine, I saw it all, for the first time.

This was and is my life.

And now it's time to tell my story.

It's been one hell of a ride.

With...

No apologies.

No regrets.

On October 29, 1929, America's great party ended—that infamous day the stock market crashed. Suddenly our nation felt the shattering disaster. There would be no jobs...no money...a maniacal surge of mass suicides...homes lost to banks...everything and anything repossessed by the lenders. Anarchy gripped the streets. Mass bedlam, terror and fear shot through America. How could this have happened? I was only seven. I didn't know or even understand. Everyone was thrown into a maelstrom of hysteria, bitterness and frustration.

Beginnings

The sunlight slipped through my fingers, hit my drowsy eyes and woke me with a start. In the alley, behind the fire escape, beside the smoking ashcan where I sometimes rested to keep warm, I was too scared of my father to go home. The sudden sliver of light announced another lonely day in Bensonhurst, the tiny, overpopulated section of Brooklyn that seemed to grow uglier and more desperate by the hour. I felt the cold. The bitter sting of winter sliced through my ragged cotton shirt. I wiped my eyes and shivered. As the rays of light filtered, ghost-like, through the dust and dirt, the alley emerged from darkness. In the daylight, shapes became clearer, shadows more defined, fears more real. Here, the rats grew as large as cats, and scampered across my body. Here, the sick stench of garbage, rotting in forgotten heaps, made me retch. I was hungry, tired.

Time to go home. Mother would worry not seeing me, I thought. Henry Selzer's heavy, black-browed face flew into my mind. He was tall, terrifying, explosive. His hands hurt. Not only me, but my mother as well. He was, to my great regret, the man my mother married, the man I forced myself to call Dad. It was a hard word for me to say, and the word stuck in my throat every time I saw his face. There was little between us.

I stood up, brushed off my brown wool pants, tied my leather lace-up shoes and walked out of the alley. A horse-drawn vegetable cart filled with fresh corn, radishes, potatoes, cabbage and apples, caught my eye. My stomach lurched. It had been too long since I had been home to eat, and even then I couldn't take more than a few bites of the stew meat Mother bought from the butcher. A nickel's worth, I think. Enough to feed us that night, but like always, Dad got angry about something and it all began again. That was when I'd leave and go to the alley—like I had a dozen times before.

I learned how to survive, living day to day. I often would fill my pockets with heavy rocks and take any large glass jar I could find and whack it against the fire escape to create a jagged edge. I would sit, clutching my makeshift weapon, feeling the weight of the rocks at my sides, giving me a false sense of security. When groups of street kids threatened me, I'd lash out and defend myself. I looked around to see if any gangs were in sight as I walked home. The dusky streets were empty as I drew closer to the tenement building where we lived.

They were all gray, dark, battered, with rows of windows that were empty and cracked, with broken glass glistening on the ground crunching beneath my feet.

"Please don't let him be home." I repeated the phrase over and over again.

I was scared—hate roared silently. Down the hallway the front door loomed like a silent monster, waiting. Through a thin, serpentine split in the wood, I put my face flush to the door to see who was going to answer. A splash of blue, the raveled edges of Mother's threadbare rug, and then the sound of footsteps. Mother was coming. I smiled, relieved, excited to see her. Mother's face made me forget the alley. Her dark hair was swept off her neck and shone like wet licorice as she held me in the doorway. I liked the way she tousled my hair, the sweet exasperation in her voice when she asked where I had been, the sudden, tight-lipped seriousness when she begged me never to run away again.

For the rest of the day, Mother and I were alone. My older brother, Benson, who was as much like Dad as I was like Mother, had gone to Grandmother Selzer's house, as was his usual custom. Dad's parents were strict, old-world Jews. Orthodox, devoted to study, wary of change. After Benson started first grade, he often went to their house to read, which was fine with me. I knew Dad would be home soon. I always knew when to expect him: The skies grew dark with nightfall and small lamps appeared in the neighborhood windows. It was as if he alone blocked out the sun. His arrival was signaled by the stomping of his shoes on the rotten wooden floorboards that led to our apartment, and by the harsh, cold voice that barked, "I'm home," when he flung open the door and barged in.

I hated seeing him kiss my mother. I hated seeing him, moments later, curse at her, with his furrowed brow and ravaged eyes. Poverty brings pain and sudden, swift violence. I hoped tonight would be different.

Mother raised our family the best she could. She always managed to provide for us somehow. We moved frequently, often being evicted and finding our furniture on the street, but she always seemed to find us someplace to stay. During those early years, our family, from what I remember, endured a never-ending series of makeshift shelters—one and two rooms that weren't much of an improvement over the alleys I roamed. But Mother always did her best to try to capture moments of togetherness. But our poverty was so stifling that no matter how hard she did try, I would retreat into myself, frightened and alone.

I became an expert escape artist, slipping out of my mother's hands with ease. Often, the East River, three blocks from home, became my refuge. For hours I retreated to its rocky banks and watched the murky brown water rush toward the sea. I loved the river. Its endless moods and rhythms mesmerized me. I felt safe there, watching the skies change from deep blue to amber to fiery red and then to black. I often sat by the water under a fortress of corrugated tin, safe beneath inky skies.

Food was always my first priority, and I was always hungry. So I took whatever I found. I never reasoned whether it was right or wrong. I was often chased out of Bensonhurst's General Store by a pack of shrieking, finger-wagging women.

Poverty also brings violence. Large gangs roamed the streets, guarding their turf with knives, rusty razors and wooden clubs. As dusk approached one day and the streetlights began to cast long shadows all around me, I had my first experience with gang violence. I was alone in an alley, scratching the hard dirt with rocks, oblivious to the six older boys who saw me as they passed by on the sidewalk. Lost in my daydreams, I continued scratching at the dirt until I heard a hard, short laugh. I was surrounded. Sudden, swift shouts shot through the air.

Suddenly clammy with fear, I looked up with as much nerve as I could muster and saw them. Greasy hair hung in matted curls around their blotchy faces. Lips curved into a frieze of mocking smiles.

"We're gonna mark you now, boy," the leader snarled.

He must have been sixteen or seventeen. Tall, powerfully built, dressed in torn street rags, he stepped closer. I felt the tip of a shoe being pushed into my chest. I jumped up and dove under their legs while my hands scrambled against the ground like a dog burying a bone. I heard my shirt being ripped down my back as fingers tore my collar. Someone grabbed my feet and twisted my ankle. White hot stabs of pain blinded me.

They hurled me against a brick building. My head snapped back, slamming into the hard wall. I lost my balance and fell to the dirt, begging them to stop. The leader grabbed my shoulders and pushed me toward a fire escape in the corner of the alley. My nose hit the steel railing with a sickening crunch. Salty warm blood dripped into my mouth. Hands shot out and pulled my arms, holding them taut while the others punched my stomach until I buckled over, gagging. As they bludgeoned me with their fists, I cried as loud as I could for help, but in Bensonhurst screams for help punctuated the streets every day. Immune to the sounds, no one bothered to listen. It was easier not to care.

The leader enjoyed the assault. He laughed again; his throaty chuckle chilled me. He pulled a small knife from his pocket and sliced the steel across my wrists. The knife entered quickly, like a razor through butter. Blood spurted up and dripped down my chest. Seeing the blood, my attackers quickly fled to the shadows. I doubled over in pain, pressing my wounds tight to my body, until finally I collapsed, weak and hurting.

I was living like an animal, and it tormented Mother that there was nothing she could do to protect me from life in the streets. There was only one way out, and she told me how important it was for Benson and me to attend school. I had never seen her happier than when Benson entered first grade and, a year later, when I started grade school myself. However, according to the New York Board of Education, one must have a permanent address to be a student in the public school system. The closest Benson and I could get was "Brooklyn, New York." Off and on we managed to get by—changing our address every other month on the school forms—until finally, in my third year, I was expelled. I always knew my expulsion had less to do with where I lived than with my rebellious behavior in the classroom. Though she was devastated by my dismissal, Mother refused to give up and did her best to educate me herself. Sitting beside me at the kitchen table for hours every day, she tried to teach me reading and writing—but she knew it was a lost cause, and it had to come as a relief when I was finally accepted back to school.

But I still never really felt accepted, and I hated being confined to the classroom. Wandering off, I would roam aimlessly or return to the river's edge to reflect, often being found by truant officers who would take me to the boys' home, where hundreds of homeless boys were crammed in tightly packed dormitories. Being locked inside those cold stone walls became a common childhood experience. At first, I learned to endure the entrapment; free meals were always welcome. But as time passed, I grew to openly despise the rules and the senseless humiliation all of us endured.

At night, I remember staring at the mottled brown ceiling as the rest of the boys slept, watching the moths flutter around the lights that swung from chains. I'd close my eyes and dream dreams that eliminated the rows of sad-eyed children who hated me as much as they hated themselves, the memories of daily beatings, the self-conscious embarrassment of standing naked under icy showers. I was ashamed of my undernourished body, and my near pathological shyness created a feeling of desperation. I felt separated from the rest of the kids and I feared the guards, who seemed cold, callous and cruel. Kept like a caged animal, I learned to hate—and to shut out the world even further than I had before. I had no one but myself, and that, I soon learned, would have to be enough.

Unlike the other, less streetwise youths locked away in the darkness, I was shrewder than the guards. Under the guise of offering to help with washing windows, scrubbing clothes or working in the kitchen, I was left unattended. Slipping past the guards was easy; most of the time they were asleep anyway. But eventually, like an endless circle, I'd be picked up again. It didn't really matter anymore.

I always managed to run away.

We struggled desperately day after day to make ends meet. The work was hard, demanding, never-ending, and the money was pitifully inadequate. Despair, disappointment and despondency were constant companions. Nerves were raw, tempers were short. The air was thick with turmoil. The fine threads that hold a family together were stretched taut, about to snap.

These fragile bonds could not possibly withstand the weight of the revelation of the secret Mother had kept for years.

Although I was too young at the time to fully comprehend what was happening, the course of events to come was so traumatic that it was to leave an indelible mark on us all.

The Bastard

Mother, Benson and I were sharing one of our rare evenings together when we heard shouts that grew louder and louder as they filtered down the hall. The unmistakable boom of Dad's voice ripped through the thin wood door; I ran to Mother and grabbed her hand. I saw her frightened eyes. Benson ran into our dilapidated kitchen. Something was suddenly, terribly wrong. I felt instinctively that Dad's rage revolved around me. I was right.

The door swung open, violently hitting the wall in one quick, deafening crash. Dad lurched through and barged into the room. I had seen him angry—even abusive—but never, ever like this. His eyes looked empty, haunted. His voice cried out as he moved toward Mother, shaking his fists in the air.

"Why didn't you tell me, Eva? Why the hell didn't you tell me?"

His voice pierced the room with steely, bitter force. I sat by her side, staring at him with fear and bewilderment. I didn't understand what he was shouting about at first, but as the battle began, a horrible realization became chillingly clear.

As his black eyes stabbed me like knives, a sick churning began in the pit of my stomach. Hands raised, he came toward me—but Mother jumped between us, crying, "Please, Henry, don't bring him into this!" which gave me the chance to run to the bed and crawl under its rickety frame.

"He's not even mine! Not mine!" he yelled through Mother's hysterical shrieks.

And then he said the unthinkable.

"I hate him—and I hate you, Eva! This marriage is over. Damn it…it's over!" Dad's voice was strangled with pain and rage.

Lying on the hard floor, I felt my heart burst in my chest. And then, horribly, the sounds of hitting. I inched over and looked up. Her sweater was torn, his lips split from her sharp nails. He flew at her, fists waving. I cowered, covering my eyes as the sharp thuds of his hands on her body echoed. Then, excruciating silence. I was too scared to breathe. Clammy sweat crept over me as I watched his feet stop at the corner of the bed.

"Richard! You damn bastard! Come out here!"

Terrified, I crawled out from my hiding place and stared into his mutilated face. He looked as broken and battered as Mother, who lay sobbing on the bed. Her hair hung in wet, stringy clumps; her face red and streaked from crying. Benson stood mute beside Dad: The battle lines had been drawn.

He grabbed me and pummeled my face and body. I fell to the floor, writhing. When I looked up, he was staring down at me with a hatred I had never seen—even on the streets, where such emotions are common. He made a point to kiss Benson on the forehead, pulling him close, and only then did he storm out, slamming the door behind him.

Time suddenly stopped. I felt a burning jealousy. I could not forgive.

Mother sat crumpled against the wall, tears streaming down her face. I lay curled in a ball on the floor. Benson stood mutely in the middle of the room, staring at the door as if at any moment it would fling back open and the whole terrible scene would replay. The clock ticked quietly in the background, soon growing louder, louder with each passing second. Several minutes slipped by, making the sound of the clock almost unbearable, when Benson suddenly turned and ran to the window, climbing out onto the fire escape to sit and silently watch the darkening city that was oblivious to the events that had transpired in that room.

Mother crawled over to me and held me in her arms. She told me how sorry she was for everything, and then she began her story. She knew I wouldn't really understand, but the sound of her voice soothed me and she needed to tell someone what she had kept to herself all these years. Everything flowed out like a river. She talked for hours.

She told me of her childhood—how hers, too, had been tough. Growing up in a Russian immigrant family who had come to America seeking the land of opportunity, only to find crowded streets, dirty apartments and sweatshop working conditions. She grew up learning that life was hard, not meant to be enjoyed, and dared not even to hope or dream that it could ever be different. So she was taken by surprise when she met and fell in love with a young man who brought joy to her life. They married and she was deliriously happy. But it was not to last. His mother violently objected to the marriage—since he was an Italian Catholic and my mother was a Russian Jew—and within a week she had the marriage annulled.

This man was my real father, and although he couldn't stand up to his mother, neither could he bear to be apart from mine. So they continued to see each other secretly for years. My mother's marriage to Henry Selzer had been arranged for her, and she tried to be a good wife. But she found herself constantly comparing Henry to her first husband and found him rough and lacking warmth. My real father was still waiting for her—to comfort her and give her the love she needed.

She explained to me that Benson was Henry's child, but she had longed to show outwardly her love for my father, if only for herself. I was the proof of that love.

This story stirred strong emotions within me. I wanted to know who my real father was, and I was angry that the only father I had ever known had turned his back on me—hated me. I, in turn, hated him for not loving me, because it wasn't my fault. Since he was no longer living at home, I couldn't show him my anger, and it built up inside until finally my hatred turned to the one who had received his love—Benson.

Although I was younger than my brother, I was as worldly as any boy twice my age. I began my plan simply. After I managed to steal a pair of boy's cowboy chaps from a local store, I told Benson we were going to play cowboys and Indians. I gave him the chaps and led him into an alley, where I had built a large pile of brittle wood, rags and newspapers. He naively stood in the center of the pyre, playing the captured cowboy, haphazardly roped to a metal pole that dropped down from the fire escape. With the flick of a match, I set the wood on fire and watched my brother, too frightened to pull away from the makeshift shackles around his wrists, become engulfed in a blaze of smoke and rising fire.

Benson's fiercely frightened screams signaled the entire neighborhood, and hysteria swept the streets as quickly as the fire spread over his burning body. I backed into the shadows of the alley and broke into sobbing tears. I had never hated or hurt anyone in this way. I had no right to be so savage. An ambulance was there faster than the flames were spreading. Many feared for their lives and possessions, thinking the flames might torch the building itself. I stood paralyzed with fright. What had I done? I couldn't stop sobbing. Mother went with Benson, who was rushed to the nearest emergency room. He was placed in a large tub of cold water with crudely broken pieces of ice, and ointments and lotions were poured over his legs and body. He was in a state of shock, staring at the ceiling and then at Mother, asking with his young sad eyes, Why? Why?

After several hours, Mother began to gain strength, determined not to let people see her destroyed by grief and sadness. Benson was her son, and although he too often rejected her affections, her love for him was strong. I ran and hid from the crowd in the neighborhood, for fear of hysterical retribution. I knew that I could never be accepted or looked at without the kind of hatred that drove me to this madness. I learned, then—too late—never to physically hurt anyone again.

I made my way to the hospital to find a silent mother and a brother whose face had become ashen with fear. He was, after all, only a boy. After hours of treatment, Mother was told that he would need daily therapy when the healing started. There was no charity for poor people in a neighborhood where crippled men and women roamed the streets, looking blindly into nowhere. Mother was determined to take care of him, doing the daily massaging and caring for his wounds that the doctor had informed her would need to be done. She knew this would be the only way to keep his leg from shriveling up when the scars healed. She had feared he would be deformed for life.

The next months were spent totally devoted to Benson's needs. Did mother have resentment for what I had done? Could I ever regain her love and possibly Benson's forgiveness? Dad reappeared and, strangely enough, asked me to forgive him. He knew he had driven me to this because of his own behavior some months before. We all learned that we could not survive with any more hate and fear. Perhaps in some strange way, this horrible thing became a lesson for us all. I knew Benson's wounds would heal...mine would not.

It was possible to understand the terrible pain behind Henry's actions. Benson's suffering would tie us together, but Henry and mother could not and did not reconcile their personal differences. Mother became a woman with the strength of an entire army.

I felt that by looking in the darkness,
we might find some light
at the other end.

Henry left to start a new life for himself. Mother, Benson and I were starting over, too, trying to put the events of the past where they belonged—in the past.

Mother was searching continuously for a better life for us, and one summer she thought she had found it by accepting a job as a camp mother at a popular co-ed summer camp—Harlee for Boys, Mitchell for Girls—located in the countryside of Tyler Hill, Pennsylvania.

It all started innocently enough...

Surviving

A menagerie of wealthy youngsters from seven to seventeen flooded camps like Harlee and Mitchell every summer. Harlee was situated on a knoll dotted with forest green canvas tents and wood cabins, each sleeping six, including the omnipresent counselor assigned to keep us out of trouble. Invariably, he failed at that impossible task. Beside the row of cabins, on a sloping, rocky path, was a large, man-made lake filled with bright yellow canoes for racing and rafts for relaxing, and lined with whitewashed lifeguard stations for sunning on the shore. It stretched for miles. The dark blue-green water, cold and refreshing, reminded me of the East River back home. Naturally, I spent as much time as I could sitting by the edge, trying to figure out why Mother had taken this job. I hated Camp Harlee at first. The structured, forced interaction with boys my age—around eleven—along with the unfamiliar surroundings, filled me with anxiety. I didn't have any idea how to act with the other children who were laughing and splashing innocently in the lake. I had never had a childhood friend. But I had nothing to defend or fight for here. Everything was given freely, without anger. I was lost, trying to fit in.

Mother's job—as camp mother and hostess of the packed-to-the-rafters mess hall—required patience, which she held in vast reserve. Instead of giving her a salary, Benson and I were allowed to go to camp free. However, she did quite well by summer's end. Parents of the other, more privileged children always had a gift at the close of the season. With over 200 children, the rewards were quite sizeable.

She wanted us to be around a different group of kids, kids we could learn from. But, of course, I rejected that idea. Resorting to my tried-and-true street habits, I stole every piece of candy, every carton of cookies, every trinket lovingly mailed to my naive bunkmates from their adoring parents. My small-scale larceny lasted only a few days until I was caught with contraband Tootsie Rolls, brought before the head counselor, dramatically reprimanded with threat of expulsion and, to add insult to injury, forced to return every item I had taken. (That was pretty difficult, since I had eaten most of the evidence by then.)

Benson loved my humiliating predicament. Mother didn't. She was thoroughly incensed, especially since my behavior reflected not only on me but on her child-rearing abilities as well. With her job—and my future—on the line, I forced myself to adjust, although I still wasn't quite sure why the camp continued to buzz about my activities. I didn't think I had done anything terribly wrong. I didn't realize that life on the streets had its own set of rules that were unheard of in the Waspy world of Camp Harlee. I tried to be civil toward my fellow campers, but I still steered clear of the crowd whenever I could.

Benson and I shared a room with several other campers. It was a fairly small room, but somehow they managed to pack in three sets of bumpy two-decker bunk beds and two large dressers. Each well-worn dresser had four drawers apiece, so everyone had their own private space as well as two extra drawers to fight over. There were four rooms in each cabin, with a large common bathroom and shower area in the middle. Benson took the lower bunk and I had the upper—an arrangement that suited me just fine. I was able to retreat into myself just by turning my back.

One evening I awoke to hear teeth chattering beneath me. I leaned over my bunk and peered below. Benson had buried his face and body under the thick folds of his blanket, trying not to make any noise. I quietly climbed down my ladder and gently touched his back.

"Are you all right?" I whispered.

He turned toward me, moaning and shaking. His mouth

twisted to one side, contorted into a horrifying, pathetic mask of pain. He shook violently. His back stiffened, his legs arched and his hands clawed his side. I held him down. I didn't know what was wrong, but as the shaking and moaning grew stronger and his mouth opened wide, I thought he was choking. Scared, I forced my small fingers inside his mouth; his teeth bit but I held on. Then suddenly the movement stopped. Sweat coated his body and ran down his face in dirty streaks.

"Don't tell," he whimpered, crying softly into his hands.

I looked around me, thinking that all the commotion must have awakened someone, but no one stirred.

"Tell what?" I was confused. I had never seen anything like this before.

"These terrible things. I can't stop them. I can't."

I kneeled beside him, wondering if I should keep his secret. I did—but it terrified me. I'd stuff cotton rags in his mouth when he experienced his attacks, hold down his arms—and most importantly, keep his secret. He hated needing me, but I truly wanted to help: I desperately needed to be needed. (It wouldn't be until we moved to California several years later that Benson's mysterious malady was diagnosed as severe epilepsy.)

Loneliness, especially in the midst of the kind of free and easy merriment at camp, is the cruelest emotion. I decided to let my guard slip and participate in the Saturday-night talent show—my first taste of "show business." Much to my surprise, considering how shy I was, I loved it. I felt strangely at home. Even then, applause was the most exciting sound I'd ever heard. As the weeks passed, I appeared in numerous amateur productions, belting out typically dreadful camp songs and dancing typically boring dances. The pleasure of it all was a welcome relief. I forgot the bad times and I was doing my best to succeed—until I met Ray.

One rainy evening after the weekly show, a thin, pale, even-featured man approached me through the maze of a hundred kids who were slurping ice cream and popping soda bottles. His face—plain, dark-browed, seemingly kind—made me feel at ease. He introduced himself as Ray. Smiling broadly, he congratulated me on the show. Saturday-night activity in camp was always some kind of theater program, and was the most popular night of the week. He asked if I wanted to be an actor. An actor? I didn't really know what an actor was, but if being one would bring me the satisfaction I'd gotten out of the camp talent shows, it sounded good to me.

I thought for a while and answered, "I think so."

Soon, Ray began reeling me in with invitations to visit his hideaway, a short walk from camp.

It was a tiny, primitive cabin, surrounded by a thick forest of pine and oak, nestled at the bottom of a flat, rocky path. It was totally disarming. A place, he assured me, I was welcome to visit anytime. When he asked me the following night, I did, without hesitation. Camp curfews meant nothing to me. Slipping out of my cabin, I wandered down the dark moonlit path to Ray's. The hot afternoon winds that blew over Tyler Hill had grown colder as the evening arrived. I shivered as a breeze passed by me and rustled through the huge trees lining my late-night route.

The lamp in Ray's window beckoned in the darkness as I walked to the door and timidly rapped. He answered immediately, ushering me in with a casual smile. Gently, he took my coat and threw it over a worn chair. A small fire burned in the stone-capped fireplace and threw sinister shapes across the walls and onto the rough wood beams. The cabin was nearly empty—a bed, several chairs, and a large handmade table decorated the sparse interior. Ray walked to the fire. Flames danced and darted over the huge log, now scorched and blistered to dull black by the heat. I continued to stand by the door, watching him from afar. He seemed nervous, detached. He turned around and stared at me. His eyes, like magnets, bored into mine. It might have been the devil's chamber.

Slowly, he walked over to the door and stood in front of me. I looked up at his face. I tried to smile, but he tilted his head away, embarrassed, and glanced over my shoulder. I stood in front of him, frozen with curiosity. Suddenly, his hands touched my shoulders, and they slipped down my body. His fingers quickly unbuttoned my shirt and, piece by piece, my clothes fell in a pile on the floor. His touch felt rough. He pulled me toward him and I shut my eyes, frightened. Only the muffled sound of Ray's breathing disturbed the heart-stopping hush of the moment.

I convinced myself that this was all perfectly natural, that this is the way people act. So I let him do what he wanted and needed to do, without any sort of protest. It actually felt good to be really wanted by someone. I visited him several more times that summer, but my indifference slowly turned to anger. Soon the pleasurable heights he was enjoying repulsed me. Yet I was afraid to ask him to stop. As the molestations grew increasingly violent, I withdrew. I felt shattered. It was a new kind of pain, a feeling I couldn't and didn't understand. Walking back to Camp Harlee from Ray's cabin often took hours, as I wandered aimlessly through the dark thickets beside the rutted roads. Above, the moon, masked by clouds, seemed to mock me in the surreal light, and for the first time in many years, I broke down and cried. All the anger and resentment over Ray's violation swept over me like a kind of death.

I told no one. I couldn't. Bewildered over his actions—but subconsciously intrigued with the motivation behind it—I withdrew into a private world of secrets and late-night excursions into the woods. I was embarrassed to look at the other boys when we skinny-dipped in the lake, afraid of the confused interest they might see in my eyes. I didn't know what to think, what to feel. Ray had turned me into a mass of contradictory feelings and emotions. But I'd survived Dad's abuse, and I would survive Ray's sexual advances. Often out of degradation comes regeneration, and that's what eventually happened to me. I felt stronger after I'd gotten over the initial shock; I knew I had the power to learn from the experience, however terrifying the road to understanding myself might be. And understanding was the key: I wanted to reconcile my emotions and move forward. As a kid, I was tough; no one was going to destroy me. Through a renewed sense of determination and hope, my final days at Harlee were markedly different. I began to appreciate the unconditional kindness of my fellow campers, and I began to share and relate. Finally, after years of being on the outside, always looking in, I was beginning to feel accepted from within.

That summer I began to grow up—partially by choice, mainly by force. Being exposed to new kinds of emotions and hidden feelings made me begin to see people differently. Camp Harlee remains a deeply joyful but somewhat painful memory. Under those sweeping auburn skies, I found my youth and lost it...discovered closeness, and fought against it...searched for love, and rejected it.

We returned to Bensonhurst and entered into a period of relative stability. Mother's family, a family I had known only in distant, hazy memory—for we rarely saw them when I was very young—began to visit us more often, especially her sister Bertha, whom I immediately loved. Short, full-figured, with heavy eyebrows that arched dramatically over her warm dark eyes, Bertha was several years older than Mother, and looked it. Her thick black hair, brushed off her face, was tied tightly in a bun. Unlike Mother, Aunt Bertha spoke very little. But when she did, we listened. She was devoutly religious and, I soon discovered, incredibly creative. Despite her outwardly prim veneer, she was also warm and wonderful. I loved being with her. Like so many post-Depression families, we banded together for comfort and strength. During those precarious years following the crash, my devotion to Aunt Bertha grew, and she soon became a surrogate mother.

Starting Again

Mother, Benson and I began to grow restless. We knew we had to leave Brooklyn. I was more than ready. The only way all of us could permanently move was to persuade Aunt Bertha to move with us. This way we could pool our resources, as meager as they were, and go to Manhattan. Aunt Bertha, who felt as trapped in Brooklyn as we did, excitedly agreed, and even decided to take a chance herself and open a one-woman millinery shop on 75th Street and Broadway. We found an apartment at 315 West 94th Street, which made even the notoriously negative Benson smile.

I dreamed of acting, but had to settle for Off-Off, Far-Off-Broadway—and I was lucky to get that. The parts were little more than walk-ons so brief they should have been called walk-offs—weeks of cattle calls for a few glorious seconds in the spotlight, usually as the Western Union boy or the skinny kid in the back row of a crowd scene. And the money was minuscule—nickels for a day's work—but at least I was helping Mother out, and she often watched me proudly from the back of the theater.

I wish I could say that it kept me out of trouble and off the streets. But when I couldn't find work, I'd feel restless and, in the early evenings before I went home, I found myself drawn to an area between Amsterdam Avenue and Central Park West that was filled with the worst dregs of humanity. I used to walk those streets looking to get picked up. I would sell myself for a quarter or even a dime, and sometimes they wouldn't pay me at all and just push me away when I asked. It wasn't the money. I was trying to see if I could make somebody want me. Somebody always did.

With their whiskey breath and their rough hands, these anonymous men would take me beneath the stairs of a brownstone walk-up—where it was too dark to see the sadness in my eyes—and stand me up against the wall. And five minutes later I'd be back on the street. Many of them wouldn't even say goodbye.

I guess it served its purpose for me, though, and gradually I grew out of it. New doors were opening for me, and one day I heard that a radio show, "The Children's Hour," needed actors. I auditioned for the show's producer, Nila Mack, and miraculously was accepted. I had no radio experience whatsoever, but I winged it with such nerve that the staff was fooled and the director dubbed me a natural. Part by part, step by step, I crawled up the ladder, occasionally faltering, until I heard about a role in an upcoming summer road show that would, as the old cliché goes, change my life forever.

During one of my daily neighborhood excursions, I heard from a street vendor that a "big-time" producer was looking for kids for a show about "immigrants." With nothing to lose, Mother brought me to the tiny dump of a theater where the auditions were being held. I took my place in a row with boys my age: They were a filthy collection of stringy hair, dirt caked slum kids. I was nervous, even though I had been through events scarier than this almost every day of my life. A tall man stared at me over the pages of a leatherbound script.

As he motioned for me to step forward, he turned to his assistant and, pointing at me, said smoothly, "Him."

He commented on my "dark hair" and "painful eyes," the perfect image of an immigrant. I was ushered into an adjoining room, where I met the others who had been cast. None of us needed to dress the part: We all fit its shoddy demands perfectly, down to our scraped knees and well-worn shoes. I was going to be in an honest-to-God theatrical production, and for a moment, the cruelty and callousness of street life faded away. It felt great.

The part was "Tommy," leader of the street kids in Sidney

Kingsley's Broadway smash hit, *Dead End.* Tommy, brash and outspoken, with piercing eyes, was sensitive and shy beneath the bravado. I was drawn to Tommy because I was a lot like him myself. After auditioning, the group of producers bellowed over the footlights that I had the part. Mother, who accompanied me to the audition, was elated. We practically flew home to tell Aunt Bertha the great news. *Dead End* would tour the non-equity summer-stock playhouses in 1936. I was more than ready and Mother could go with me. It was perfect. Benson decided to stay with Dad.

During those months I found myself learning, growing, changing—although I occasionally reverted back to my old, anti-social ways. My "aloofness" wasn't egomania; I worried that the other actors would discover my background and might reject me for being from the streets. They would brand me a fake for try-ing to fit into their close-knit, theatrical world. I was scared, but determined to make it work. The first half of the tour I watched and learned, separated from the rest of the youthful group by my lingering insecurities. But my performances improved—and so did my attitude. I softened the shell around me. It felt like I was falling into the swift mainstream of an entirely new life.

When I heard the original *Dead End* Broadway troupe had received an offer to reprise their roles in a film version, to be shot in Hollywood for Sam Goldwyn Studios, I fantasized that the show might lead to a job in Hollywood. But I quickly woke up to the fact that I was just one more struggling actor. The *Dead End* kids from the Broadway show left for California to star alongside Humphrey Bogart, Sylvia Sidney, Joel McCrea and Claire Trevor at the Sam Goldwyn Studio. I was still stuck in Manhattan, still dreaming.

I was impossibly impatient. Impatience has always been one of my most difficult but rewarding traits. Although people com-plain about my drive to succeed, and how quickly I want to real-ize my goals, impatience has always worked for me. For without that burning need to hurry up and get on with it, I might have been like the rest of the people who drifted through the streets, people who lived and died, people who accepted their lives as a simple matter of circumstance and never dared to ask why.

I continued auditioning for every bit part and sporadically landed small roles. Mother was hired by J. Thorpe on 57th Street, just off Fifth, one of New York's most exclusive stores. Fur-swathed socialites, drenched in perfume, swept through the elegant glass doors and bought J. Thorpe's exquisite dresses as quickly as they could command "Charge it!" To them, poverty was an unfortunate headline in a newspaper, or a lyric from a popular song: "In the morning, in the evening, ain't we got fun? The rich get richer and the poor get children." Mother's clientele, circulating in a different stratosphere, fascinated me.

As always, Aunt Bertha provided a steadying influence over us in our new home, and through her keen business sense, even-tempered nature and innate artistic abilities, her hat shop blossomed into a remarkable success. The location of her brain-child was equally advantageous: directly across the street from the ritzy Ansonia Hotel. Her shop attracted an eclectic blend of wealthy dowagers and an occasional movie star. In a short time, we all managed to hoard enough money to change our destiny.

Aunt Bertha decided to move to Los Angeles and design hats for the motion picture industry, and she begged us to join her there. Afraid of being disappointed, afraid that it might be just a dream, we dismissed the thought. But when Aunt Bertha actually packed up her belongings and waved goodbye on a west-bound train, I knew it would only be a matter of time before Mother, Benson and I followed.

Mother adamantly resisted leaving New York, sentimentally holding onto her memories, refusing to part with them. California was too far away, too different—an alien state she had no interest in knowing. But all the flimsy excuses were shot down one by one by a very persistent Aunt Bertha, who now owned a successful millinery shop on Sunset Boulevard in Hollywood. She felt, as I did, that Los Angeles would be the best place for us. She refused to relinquish her crusade until Mother relented. Finally she agreed, quitting her job at J. Thorpe and purchasing three train tickets on the Super Chief. We were on our way—next stop Hollywood, factory of dreams.

Hollywood 1937

The train lurched to a stop in downtown Los Angeles. It had been a long and dreary trip. As Mother, Benson and I disembarked, the hollow echoes of railcar whistles filled the enormous depot and a sea of travelers moved toward us, looking very different from the ragged inhabitants of my old neighborhood. Outside the station, the blue skies blinded us as a porter led us to a waiting cab with more than a dozen well-worn travel bags. We were headed toward Aunt Bertha's Hollywood home.

On our way, I watched the busy streets, bordered by rows of one- and two-story buildings. Up ahead in the distance, HOLLYWOODLAND was spelled out in huge white letters on a hillside. It wasn't long before we arrived at Aunt Bertha's Selma Avenue apartment in a four-story, red-brick building, not unlike the dwellings we had often been evicted from back home. As the taxi wheezed to a halt, she appeared on the front steps.

"Finally!" she cried almost impatiently. "I thought you'd never get here."

I watched Mother's eyes fill with tears.

It was good seeing them together again. To my surprise, Aunt Bertha even hugged Benson and me, an unusual emotional display for such a reserved woman. Then, she led us upstairs and opened the apartment door, motioning us to join her inside. We gathered up our suitcases and walked into a sparsely furnished but spotlessly clean two-bedroom apartment. Mother beamed with delight as she strode across the hardwood floors and peered into our newly decorated blue and white bedroom.

Her glistening eyes said what she couldn't. Finally she had a home all of us could be proud of. It had been a long time coming. Too long.

We soon fell into a regular routine. Benson was usually gone, entertaining friends or going to school. In order to work at the studios—not to mention the fact that I was determined to begin a new way of life in California—I had to attend school, too. To say that I was not thrilled about spending hours in a claustrophobic classroom is a gross understatement. Learning math with a bunch of nine-year-olds was not my idea of a glamorous day in Hollywood. My hopelessly sporadic educational pursuits in Brooklyn had cured me of ever wanting to be a bookworm. Returning to the schoolroom was an idea I absolutely hated. Mother, on the hand, was delighted.

Of course, there was a problem. Due to my less than stellar past in the New York school system, there were no records of my having attended classes at all, and if there were, I prayed no one would find them. I was not what anyone would call an exemplary student by any stretch of the imagination.

My miniscule amount of grade school education placed me on a par with a pre-teen—if that! Since I was now fifteen, I was way behind in every subject, with the possible exception of street smarts, which didn't count for an awful lot with the California Board of Education. My inability to provide any kind of documentation on my previous schooling caused untold problems. School after school demanded that I be tested, a painful procedure I wanted to avoid at all costs. In utter desperation, I even tried saying that I had attended a private school in upstate New York that had tragically burned to the ground. This got me nowhere—fast.

After searching from Malibu to Mar Vista, Mother finally located a school, called Mar-Ken, for professional show business children. It was situated in a small house on Franklin and Gower in the heart of Hollywood, just a few blocks from our apartment on Selma. The school was run by a wonderful woman named Mrs. Brassiere, or some such thing. Actually, it was more like Mrs. Bassiere, but being the irrepressible kid I was, I thought Mrs. Brassiere was more amusing. We all giggled like gnomes behind her back; I know she heard us, but she didn't crack a smile.

I approached attending Mar-Ken with trepidation. Despite my lack of enthusiasm, Mrs. Brassiere and her group of devoted teachers were able to untangle my woeful web of educational deceit with a minimum of fuss. I had to apply myself in the classroom for the first time in my life. Catching up to the accepted level of a fifteen-year-old was a tough challenge, especially for a rebellious kid like me. I would rather have been loitering outside the candy store across the street—which, on occasion, I did.

Unlike more traditional learning establishments, Mar-Ken was show-business savvy. Interview and casting call absences were tolerated as long as we made up the missed work. As far as a set-in-cement code of decorum went, Mar-Ken was easier than most. To be honest, many of my classmates attended this kind of professional school to avoid the rules and regulations of regular high schools. As I look back on those less-than-rigid days at Mar-Ken, I often wish I'd been more disciplined, but at the time I certainly wasn't complaining.

Eventually, Mother received my diploma in the mail. Not the most dramatic way of matriculating, but she cried anyway. Her son was a graduate! No more running away...no more lying just to get by. It felt good to be a legitimate member of society. Of course, I was never a conformist by most standards, and sometimes I wonder what would have happened to me had I obeyed all the rules all the time. I probably wouldn't have made it in life.

Mother had worked hard to put me through that school—and get me into show business—and she was perpetually exhausted from her six-day, eight-hours-on-your-feet job at the May Company department store at Fairfax and Wilshire. So I spent most of my evenings alone, climbing out onto the fire escape that hung tenuously from the side of the building. There, I watched the boys who loitered in front of the YMCA next door. Often they stood under the streetlights, silhouetted in the harsh glow, and used their bodies to pay the rent. Others huddled, whispering in the dark, only to disappear around a corner, lost in the shadows. Their mystery attracted me, although I tried to suppress the feelings that blurred my mind. But for how long? A part of me wanted to join them—I knew sooner or later that I would, but a part of me was too afraid to abandon my safe solitude.

In Hollywood, I knew I could make it. After months of frustrating auditions, good fortune materialized in the form of a prized customer of Aunt Bertha's hat shop—the Andrew Sisters' mother, Ollie. She had heard endless stories of my goals—and stepped in to help. As fate would have it, Universal Studios was in the process of casting a new *Dead End*-type series of films, beginning with *Little Tough Guy*, directed by Harold Young. An audition was arranged for me, and in the summer of 1937, at the age of fifteen, I was signed to a Stock Play Contract, which meant lots of minor roles in a multitude of major, and not so major, movies. I appeared in over a hundred films, in a plethora of parts, but too often my "moment of glory" would be relegated to the cutting-room floor. My studio status didn't bother me in the least. I was thrilled to be counted among Universal's stable of stock players.

It all began with *Little Tough Guy*, starring the original Dead End Kids, including David and Leo Gorcey, Gabriel Dell, Billy Hallop, Bernard Hunsley, Bobby Jordan and Huntz Hall. Working with them made me an official member of the Dead End Kids—a real coup, especially after Goldwyn's original *Dead End* film, directed by William Wyler, was nominated for Best Picture at the 1937 Oscar ceremonies. I was now part of an extraordinary world; everything was finally going my way, minor as it may have been.

The back lot was an ever-changing carnival. Walking down the studio streets past plyboard illusions of Victorian houses, Wild West saloons, European opera houses, stone castles and dozens of other perfectly detailed sets, I was constantly amazed. Clowns, cowboys, soldiers and fairy-tale princesses flew by in fantastic droves. Occasionally, two of the studio's biggest attractions, Frankenstein and Dracula, sauntered into the commissary and smiled through their inch-thick makeup. In contrast were two infinitely beautiful teenage singing stars I met shortly after I arrived in town.

The first was Deanna Durbin. Like me, Deanna had recently signed with Universal and completed her first film for the studio,

Three Smart Girls. Unlike me, Deanna was box-office magic. With her brunette beauty and her lyric soprano voice, she turned *Three Smart Girls* into a great success, literally saving Universal from declaring bankruptcy.

Although the class system was a stringent way of life on the lot, Deanna and I developed a wonderful friendship. When we weren't working, we often met at her cottage—she was one of the few to be privileged with a private bungalow—or we would meet in the Sun Room at the commissary, where I dreamed dreams under the photographs of Jon Hall, Peggy Ryan, Jack Oakie, Turhan Bey and the gifted Donald O'Connor, who was Universal's most dramatic claim to fame. Deanna's dreams were, for the most part, realized. She went on to make quite a few films, literally growing up on camera with the world watching and waiting for her first kiss. She retired at the ripe old age of 27 and married French film director Charles Henri David. Our paths have never crossed again.

I never got to know the other teenage singing star as well as I did Deanna, but that didn't stop me from developing a crush on her that I would never quite outgrow. Her name was Frances Gumm, but the world soon knew her as Judy Garland. I met her at MGM while she was still working as a young contract player, languishing as an ingenue in such forgettable fare as *Pigskin Parade*. It would be two years before she'd be cast in the role that would make her famous—as Dorothy in *The Wizard of Oz*—but from the moment I first heard her singing backstage for her gifted coach, friend and mentor, Kay Thompson, I knew she was going to be a tremendous star. I watched for hours, hiding in the shadows, as Kay shaped her patiently into a polished performer. Judy was only twelve or thirteen years old, but by the time Kay was through with her, it was all there: move for move, tone for tone, breath for breath, a voice like none I've ever heard before or since.

Judy was sensitive, warm and vulnerable. She touched my heart, and I longed to get to know her; however, she was surrounded constantly, by everyone up to Louis B. Mayer himself, and the Hollywood caste system made it impossible for us to do more than smile and exchange the occasional pleasantry. But even from a distance I could feel the struggle she was already waging with her own inner darkness, and with the pressures of being thrust into stardom while she was still a child; a struggle that she masked with self-deprecating humor and an effervescent charm that became increasingly poignant and desperate as the years passed.

I knew just how she felt. My new "family" were the other kids who were working just as hard as I was to break into the business. But as a kid from the streets with no training and a more than questionable education, I never felt like one of them.

I was captivated with the business of making movies, but also absolutely exhausted. Long hours, hot lights, lengthy delays and temperamental actors soon took a lot of the magic out of the movie myth for me. Of course, I was at the bottom of the celluloid staircase. High above, Garbo, Clark Gable, Fred Astaire, Ginger Rogers and Bette Davis ruled, even though child stars like Mickey Rooney and Shirley Temple were America's most popular box-office attractions. Below the legends stood the supporting actors and actresses, who lived in a world of little power. At the very bottom languished the stock players. Since most of us never made it any higher, it's not surprising that we began to feel disenchanted with the studio system.

After *Little Tough Guy*, I felt abandoned when the rest of the Dead End Kids left the lot to film *Angels with Dirty Faces* at Warner Brothers. But it wasn't long before my spirits were considerably raised when I was "loaned" to Columbia for *Juvenile Court*, starring Frankie Darro, and co-starring Rita Hayworth, still in her brunette days, and Paul Kelley. Although Harry Cohn, President of Columbia Pictures, treated all of his stars with unmitigated arrogance, *Juvenile Court* remains a wonderful memory solely because of Hayworth. She possessed a vibrancy that couldn't be duplicated, and had the face of an angel.

Life at home had changed—but not for the better. Mother's salary, meager at best, couldn't cover many of our growing expenses. And Aunt Bertha, always so strong and full of courage, had been diagnosed with stomach cancer. She didn't have long to live. Watching her suffer through a fate so undeserved devastated us. I loved her like a second mother, and had always turned to her for the support I needed. Now, as she dwindled into a ghostly shadow of the woman I once knew, I had to face her inevitable death. I watched her hide the pain I knew she suffered. I suffered, too. I felt powerless. To pay for Aunt Bertha's care, I worked as often as I possibly could—and I played the Hollywood game, knowing my family depended on me to win. Aunt Bertha's eventual death was, in retrospect, a blessed relief from the unhappiness she endured, but I cried endlessly, shattered. She had provided the first link to my new life, the first step in my still unfolding future. I have not forgotten her.

The financial storms continued to pour down on all of us, and Mother, after Aunt Bertha's passing, relied on me more than ever for support. With Henry Selzer long out of her life, and Benson requiring extensive medical attention for his epilepsy, I paid most of the bills, rather blindly. The majority of his medical costs were kept from me. Supporting him became a perverse sort of poetic justice. Throughout our lives he had labeled me the weak, useless dreamer, unable to cope, always running away. Now I was coping for all three of us. His resentment hung over us like a black cloud. The tension was enough to depress anyone, but I found it infuriating. I despised paying for a lifestyle that, as far as I was concerned, surpassed my own, and although I knew his dream of attending college depended on my success, he accepted his weekly allowance without the slightest show of gratitude. The irony was that I had no alternative but to continue supporting him—or risk alienating Mother—and so his dream of achieving a college degree was fulfilled. Somehow, though, it drove a wedge between Mother and me. And then, almost the day he graduated from UCLA, Benson left our home to join Dad in New York.

If my home life was in a constant state of uproar, my "career" was decidedly dormant. As much as I wanted to break away from the Dead End image, it wasn't easy. The waiting went on and on—it seemed endless—until I received a phone call from New York. It was from Mayor LaGuardia's office. The mayor wanted a movie "roughneck" to star in a radio series titled "Why Children Come to Court," broadcast on WNYC following his reading of the Sunday comics. I happily agreed and left Hollywood to go back to New York, back to the familiar city sounds, back to the bustling streets. It looked the same, smelled the same, even rained the same. In an odd way, it felt good. I even caught myself wondering if Henry would hear my voice on the radio. I hoped he would.

As part of my agreement with the show, it was understood that I could revisit those very same shelters that often held me in my youth. I had traveled many miles in my short life, and as I began to talk to the kids about my own experiences, I felt elated. I had made it out. I tried to give them hope. I told them, often to deaf ears, there was a way out. I hoped even one would hear me and listen, just one.

"Why Children Come to Court" was a big success, and instead of returning to Hollywood to face the wolves, I decided to stay in New York to see if my luck would last. It did, in the name of Gypsy Rose Lee, the legendary Queen of Burlesque. Gypsy had been signed to appear in Mike Todd's elaborate theatrical spectacle, *Streets of Paris*, held at the 1939 World's Fair on Long Island. Working with Gypsy, whose jeweled hand I led down the runway to a symphony of shrieks, whistles and applause, was a brief stint in the world of fantasy and excitement. I had never seen anyone like her. Every evening as I escorted her on stage, the reaction was the same—bedlam. Under the twinkling spotlights, wrapped in scarlet silk and crystal beads, she glittered with supreme sensuality as she walked into the roar of applause. I stood in her shadow.

After Gypsy's entrance I went back to the wings and watched. Every slight smile, curved hip, raised arm and seductive thrust created a frenzy among the wide-eyed, open-mouthed men. She loved her audiences, as animalistic as they were, and as she slowly peeled away her layers of carefully applied clothing—although never completely—the phrase "stopping the show" became the understatement of the decade. With her long, white fur slung across the stage, she offered one last privileged peek of pale, tempting thigh—and disappeared backstage.

In private, I saw little of the beautiful lady, but by watching her work, I became fascinated with dance, motion and rhythm. Decades later, I was privileged to see Gypsy again. She hosted a TV talk show from San Francisco, and I was her guest many times. She had mellowed: gone were the outrageous clothes, devil-may-care attitude and ravishing looks. She had grown into a rather prim and proper middle-aged loner, scarred by too many broken promises and failed dreams. A victim of revolutionary changing styles and social mores, Gypsy no longer shocked or titillated. She was the remnant of a vanished past, a curio from another time and place. She seemed wary of men, of adulation, yet she had survived, and for that I admired her wholeheartedly. But her influence on me had been so great that after the World's Fair show closed in 1939 and I returned to Los Angeles, I was determined to begin dancing myself. I sought out one of Hollywood's most talented choreographers and teachers.

Father and creator of contemporary dance, Lester Horton was a mass of contradictions. Although he personally resembled a chunky, round-faced, small-town pastor, his choreography sizzled, it was sensuous and avant-garde. Horton's work predated Bob Fosse's stylistic body movement by decades. In other words, Lester's vision of dance was a hell of a change from Ginger and Fred. All of us in his classes wanted to stand out. One member of the company was the soon-to-be-famous couturier Rudi Gernreich, who was shy and decidedly less than conspicuous. But dance he did, and did it well. Determined to make a name for myself, I worked harder than I ever had—on the floor and off. Soon I became Lester's unbilled "protégé," which put me in the enviable position of being hated by every other student—especially the tall, attractive, intimidating young woman who was his leading female dancer, the now legendary Bella Lewitsky. Bella refused to acknowledge I had any dancing ability—she was right—and caustically referred to me as "Lester's closest friend." Naturally, I was accused of having a relationship with him to get in his class.

"I never slept with Lester," I retorted defiantly. "I was wide awake."

Bella was not amused, she was infuriated. She fancied herself to be the number one prima donna of dance. Bella was strong, fiery and overly dominating. But she had certainly earned the respect of the dance world, so consequently we bowed, scraped and occasionally curtsied, while the entire dance company gossiped, twitched, twittered and giggled behind our backs. Round and round this merry-go-round of life went on.

What amused me especially was Lester's teaching technique; under the guise of modern dance, he had all of us doing the most bizarre free-form twists, rolls and snakelike motions, spread-eagled on the studio floor. Truly a voyeuristic fantasy—considering that most of us wore next to nothing. Lester liked seeing skin and sweat. In Hollywood, sexual thrills were often camouflaged by artistic pretense, but with Lester, I didn't care. He was a master teacher and his belief in me gave me the support I needed. He sensed that need and encouraged my efforts, regardless of the unfortunate fact that I wasn't cut out to be the new dancing sensation, by any stretch of the imagination—even mine. Lester nurtured my courage, and told me more than once that I did have talent. I wanted to believe him, but my career was fading into the valley of has-beens…that final resting place for Hollywood's overlooked and unlucky. I sweated, slunk and stretched in Horton's studio to forget the truth about my life— but reality always surfaced walking home to Selma Avenue, bringing a sea of questions and a drought of answers.

I knew I had to do something to give my lackluster career a shot in the arm. I had become a member of an army of wanna-bes, and this sad, ugly truth about my professional life was hardly amusing.

After arguing for weeks, I finally convinced Mother that if I wanted a future, eliminating Richard Selzer from my life was the best alternative I had. After all the years of emotional abuse I had suffered under Henry, I was sure that renaming myself would erase my familial history with a sudden, irreversible power, that I would create a whole new life for myself—as Dick Ellis.

Enter Dick Ellis

Along with my new name came a new image. Dick Ellis—well dressed and (hopefully) well connected—would be a very different person from the Brooklyn roughneck I had played before. He came complete with a new nose, ears surgically pinned back and a hairline raised to duplicate that incredibly beautiful widow's peak of Robert Taylor's. Looking back now on my life, I would give my unabashed soul to retrieve only a tenth of the hair I removed. But as I became more outgoing during the next several years under my new name and persona, I met a new breed of people who helped mold my personality, my career and my sexual habits in myriad ways. I went from casting couches to auditions, and I went to a thousand of them. They were all the same—except for the infamous "fishbowl" audition at Paramount Studios. The Fishbowl was a huge, one-way glass bowl surrounded by rows of seats, jammed with producers, writers and directors, who peered like gods on Mount Olympus into a sunken circle of actors. Since the glass provided one-way viewing, all-important eye contact was impossible. It is not a mystery to me how a goldfish must feel, endlessly whirling and twirling in his private domain.

Inevitably, the script would shake as I read the lines to the battery of strangers sitting in the blackness beyond the glass, while the lights blazed on us from distant corners of the room. These hideous performances were dubbed "cold readings," an appropriate description in more ways than one. As the first chill of sweat dripped down my back, I'd usually get to the second line of dialogue before the dreaded words wafted forth:

"Thank you. We'll call you."

For any actor, regardless of how many years they've survived in the Hollywood jungle, the sting of rejection is the most depressing feeling imaginable. Forgetting lines, missing cues, ruining scenes, even ending up on the cutting room floor, are all minor annoyances. Not getting the job in the first place is the biggest cross to bear. And then, of course, there's the obligatory agent—every actor's savior, and nemesis. In everyone's search for great roles—or any role, for that matter—the bridge between unknown status and stardom is built by an agent. Still, they can push you into a bomb as fast as they can push you into a smash. After their ten percent is paid, the resulting flop, or success, appears on your resume, not theirs. But they are an absolute necessity, and at the age of seventeen, I lacked any kind of representation. So after walking up and down "Agent's Row," I secured an agent on the Sunset Strip. In the past I had secured my roles on my own, and not for the right reasons. I decided that would definitely end with Dick Ellis. I was prepared to follow the rules, as long as the rules resulted in roles.

Once again, I was kidding myself. The only jobs I was able to get were a string of ten-second spots in a succession of forgettable films, and those were due less to my professional efforts than my personal contacts. Very personal. Sex sold in Hollywood, on and off the screen, and I soon discovered that whatever future I had there would depend on my talents off-screen and not on it. I became one of the most popular boy-toys in a town where all the big seducers had their choice of the best there was. I got to sit at the director's table in the commissary; I was invited to all the posh parties—but the invitation always included an interlude in the bedroom. Or more often, accomodating a casting director in the shuttered back room of an office guaranteed a meeting with the decision makers, and if I pleased them, the role was mine. My "performance" was usually as quick and impersonal as a memo, but when the paychecks arrived, I couldn't complain. To tell the truth, I loved it; I loved the fact that these famous and powerful people had a need for me. My social calendar was standing room only with some of the biggest names in the business.

You have shared so much of my life till now that I should take a moment to explain something about myself. It has always disturbed me when we blame past incidents in our lives for our current behavior patterns. Thinking back, perhaps the encounter at summer camp with Ray in my younger days did catalyze for me an alternative lifestyle, a choice of social behavior. Much of it I have done willingly, and some less so. But I was always living right on the edge of each alternative—neither at the moment being wrong. I found many experiences emotionally rewarding and satisfying, and at other times my actions generated a defensive anger that I was compelled to lock up inside myself. But as I reach this point in my story, you have to know that I have not only accepted the different alternatives but in reality invited them, without any conscience or guilt.

It was in 1940 that I met Cesar Romero, who was already a big star. Born in New York, of Latin heritage, he had enjoyed great stage success in the early thirties before coming to Los Angeles. Tall, dark, suave and charming, Cesar enjoyed an elegant private life. I had located his address, went to his house, asked for an autograph and, incredibly enough, we became great friends over the following months. Through his influence I began working at 20th Century Fox, and doors that once were closed, magically began to open. In Hollywood it's not a necessity to have talent, but it sure as hell helps to know someone who does.

One morning at the Fox commissary, I was introduced to Tyrone Power, the studio's most sought-after romantic star—the man dubbed "The New Valentino." To be honest, I had been infatuated with Tyrone. He was preparing to film *The Mark of Zorro* when we first met—and the attraction between us was instantaneous, electric, unforgettable. Of all the men I knew in my Hollywood years, Power was the one I remember with the greatest fondness and regret, because inevitably it had to end. Tyrone's face was liquid; it moved and changed at the slightest touch. I was spellbound by the cameo-like profile, the curve of his mouth, the chiseled nose, the raw strength of his body. We met and parted much too quickly. But when we were together I felt secure, proud. I imagined time standing still.

We met for romantic moments in his dressing-room apartment in the Star Building on the lot after work. We took long rides, speeding down Sunset to Malibu, we shared dinners at the nondescript seaside diners that bordered the dark shimmer of the Pacific Ocean. Tyrone loved giving gifts: gold jewelry nestled in burgundy velvet boxes, white cashmere sweaters, leather-bound books—everything but the stability and commitment I needed most.

I sought out other men during my years at the studio—men who offered kindness, affection and career guidance. I've forgotten many of those sometimes happy moments, but there are many I still recall vividly—including the months I spent with two other fascinating people in their white mansion by the ocean—Cary Grant and Randolph Scott.

Cary Grant epitomized screen elegance, movie-star panache and British gentility. He was also the quintessential example of the Hollywood publicity machine working overtime. With his unmistakable voice, impeccable timing, romantic good looks and patently debonair aura, Cary zoomed to stardom in Mae West's 1933 comedy *She Done Him Wrong*, fulfilling the promise he displayed in 1931's *Hot Saturday*. Career-wise, *Hot Saturday* was a milestone for Cary, professionally and personally. It brought him to the attention of the Hollywood power circuit, and it gave Grant the chance to meet Randolph Scott, a young Southern actor who would quickly become a close friend and roommate. Grant and Scott were opposites. Cary was exuberant, easygoing, almost always happy. Scott was far more subdued, serious, stable—but they were deeply, madly in love, and their devotion was complete. On and off, for the next decade, they lived together in Westwood, the Hollywood Hills and finally, when I met them, in Santa Monica, in Norma Talmadge's house on the beach.

The two-story, twelve-room mansion was breathtakingly beautiful, ablaze with sea colors, endless vistas stretching from stone terraces and French doors, and blue and gold rooms that seemed to go on forever. With a black baby-grand piano, stacks of vintage jazz records, and radios blasting out the latest hits, the house was often the site of beautiful, intimate parties. Cary and Randolph lived like dukes in a dazzling, forbidden dominion.

Behind closed doors, in the privacy of their own world, they were warm, kind, loving and caring, and unembarrassed about showing it. I envied what they felt for one another. But they knew as well as I did that this sort of relationship between two men was considered absolutely unspeakable, and whenever they were in public, they couldn't even touch, and could hardly walk together or even speak to each other without being watched for the slightest sign of their feelings. Only when public exposure threatened—and the studios put down their hypocritical feet— did they finally get married. To women of means, of course. Even then they continued to see one another very discreetly on the sly, but for the rest of their lives, they had to live that lie. It must have been terribly lonely for them. Fortunately for all of us, times have changed since then. It would have suffocated me to live my whole life like that, and thank God I haven't had to. But in those days, I had to be as secretive as they were.

We were open only with each other. Neither man was possessive, and I had wonderful relationships with both of them. Randolph was the one I admired most. His elegant blond persona, sensitive personality and natural kindness appealed to me far more than Cary's less sincere outlook on life. Randy was a wonderful, loving man, and I felt with him the same closeness I had known with Tyrone. Cary's interests were temporary at best, but with Randy, alone in his cool, dark bedroom that faced the ocean, the darkness seemed to reach into eternity. We talked of everything—moonlight and sunbeams, kings and cabbages. I felt fulfilled. Perhaps more than anything else, he taught me the value of true affection and commitment, which he displayed with Cary whenever they were together. Even in a crowded room, they saw no one else. The fact that I shared their affections didn't harm their relationship in the least. In fact, I think my visits strengthened their realization that outsiders could never shatter the bond of love they felt for one another.

Throughout town, Cary and Randy were treated with respect—so unlike today, when the paparazzi, in search of the priceless giveaway shot, most certainly would have hidden behind the great trees that lined their lawn. In the forties, the studios protected their stars, but that protection came at a very high price. Today it's up to the stars to protect themselves. The golden era of cinema is definitely over.

I auditioned for MGM's *Cross of Lorraine*—the largest cattle call I'd ever attended. Since the roles being cast were that of prisoners, the line of actors resembled a mass of refugees waiting for unseen horrors. The effect was startling—and so was the story, an all-male drama starring Gene Kelly, Hume Cronyn and Jean-Pierre Aumont. The plot, revolving around a group of French POWs who escape their German jailers and take up arms in unoccupied territory against their Nazi enemies, was a rousing, emotional plea for human decency and respect. *Cross of Lorraine* touched me deeply. My role as a young French Jewish soldier, sitting in the work yard, singing a haunting "Kol-Nidra" with hundreds of others before being executed by the Nazis, was a fleeting moment that created an unforgettable impact when the movie premiered. For the first time, I felt I had accomplished something memorable. *Cross of Lorraine* turned into one of 1943's biggest success stories, and I felt very proud to have been a part of it.

Following *Cross of Lorraine* came a small role in *The Bridge of San Luis Rey*, starring the great Czech leading man, Francis Lederer, who came to Hollywood in the thirties, after establishing a distinguished reputation throughout the European theater and film world. Francis was brilliant, and my amusing claim to fame was playing his double. However, the movie went down the proverbial tubes along with "the bridge" itself. Based on Thornton Wilder's fatalistic twenties novel, which traced the doomed lives of five people trapped on a falling bridge, *San Luis Rey* was a footnote in Lederer's career—and in mine, too—but brought about a friendship that has lasted to this very moment. Francis was considerate and kind, and a man with great class.

Song of Russia, my next assignment—if landing on the

cutting room floor counts—starred Robert Taylor. We became good friends. He was an elegant actor and a caring man who wore his mantle of stardom with surprising humility and ease—as did the two stars of my next minor hello/goodbye appearance with Alice Faye and John Payne in *Hello, Frisco, Hello.* In the sea of Hollywood egos, Alice and John were rare exceptions, always polite to the cast and crew, thoroughly professional on the set and ever aware of the fact that moviemaking is a purely collaborative effort. In the production number I participated in, which required lavish costumes, intricate camera work, split-second timing and difficult choreography, there was no room for temperament. We had an exhaustingly wonderful time working together.

In those days, when I lived as a human comet, flying from one twilight universe to another, I never stopped to think about what I'd already accomplished...the people I'd befriended...the personal recognition...the praise...the love. In a world torn apart by war, persecution, bigotry and hate, my family had survived—and somehow, miraculously, even flourished. Although I didn't realize it yet, I had been kissed by luck, and more than once.

It was then that my old friend Lester Horton was personally responsible for getting me a small role that could have been missed by a sneeze in Arthur Lubin's remake of Lon Chaney's 1925 masterpiece, *The Phantom of the Opera.* Shot at Universal, working on the movie felt like a homecoming of sorts, although I must admit no one at the studio remembered who I was. But Lubin and Horton provided friendship, reassurance and warmth during the shoot—something I really needed. Every actor who ever worked with Arthur will say the same: Throughout his career, he was sensitive to the plight of the stock-player and often created bits of impromptu dialogue to broaden an actor's part—and paycheck. Lubin's *Phantom* was given a different twist from Chaney's melodramatic original. Arthur's treatment, more restrained and polished than the original, featured superb performances by Claude Rains as The Phantom, Susanna Foster as his musical protégé and Nelson Eddy as her lover.

On the set everyone watched Claude Rains as he stalked the ornate splendor of the recreated Paris Opera House in his dramatic cape and mask, stunning even the other actors with the power of his performance. While I stared in awe, Susanna Foster and Nelson Eddy sang Edward Ward's romantic arrangements of Chopin and Tchaikovsky. The lights and cameras evaporated and I felt the fantasy of Hollywood seduce me all over again, drawing me in until I fell in love with the movie business for a second time. I even felt a bit spoiled—until Humphrey Bogart crossed my path.

Passage to Marseilles, a Warner Brothers war drama starring Bogart, was clearly a prestige property. After the success of *Casablanca*, Bogart was America's favorite male star—and he aimed to keep it that way. On screen, he exuded rugged charisma and a tough but tender magnetism that has never really been duplicated. But off-screen, especially as he grew older, I thought he was just a man who lusted after booze, bucks and Bacall—though not necessarily in that order. Nevertheless, Bogart's clout caused some serious problems for me.

The controversy started when *Passage*'s cinematographer, the legendary James Wong Howe, designed a close-up of my face reacting to a plane crash in war-torn Marseilles, a scene without dialogue created to mirror the horrors of war through a set of tormented eyes. Howe felt I had the ability to make the scene effective, and before we shot it, he explained why.

"Your eyes tell the whole story of death in war," he remarked.

"Why?" I asked.

"Because," he continued matter-of-factly, "your eyes are deep wells of emotion."

His comment struck a deep chord. I guess he didn't have to know too much about my background to see that my life had been a test of endurance.

Unfortunately, Humphrey Bogart disagreed. After he viewed the rushes of my one great moment in the celluloid sun, Howe was told to cut the footage. No explanations were forthcoming to a bit player like me—but Howe implied that Bogart thought the scene was too compelling. He was the Star—and he decided what stayed in and what wound up on the cutting-room floor. Like countless other actors who suffered career disappointments because of egomaniacal stars, my tour de force was reduced to a lukewarm twenty-second flash, in what was fittingly a Bogart star turn. Hooray for Hollywood.

After the "generosity" of Bogart, I doubted circumstances could get much worse, but of course they could—and did. Since I'd recently turned 21, I was informed by the lawyers who had handled my studio-earnings fund for the past five years that the time had come for me to collect my "trust." I had always assumed the Jackie Coogan Law—passed to protect child actors from losing their rightful money, because of family mismanagement, or simple greed—would protect me. But the sinister snake in that den of legal bureaucracy was found slithering around an "emergency" clause. Funds could be removed legally, and without delay, if such expenses were deemed a necessity. Well, apparently Benson's college fees and our household bills, plus Aunt Bertha's untimely hospital and funeral costs, had consumed much more of the money than I imagined, because when I discovered what was left, I felt raped.

The day of reckoning began innocently enough. Mother and I drove to the courthouse to receive my check. Both of us could barely contain our excitement as we arrived. But the court, somber and gray, dampened my enthusiasm considerably.

"Richard Selzer?" said the judge, peering down at me from his imposing perch.

At least he knew my name, I thought. Let's get this over with. Where's the money?

"Please approach the bench."

"Yes sir," I responded with as much servility as possible. Walking down the green tile floor towards his massive mahogany desk, I felt like the Cowardly Lion facing the Great Oz.

"Bailiff," the judge said with disinterest, handing me an envelope.

My hands trembled as I took the long yellow envelope and met Mother at the courtroom door. It took me exactly five seconds to rip it open, slicing two fingers in the process. But I didn't even feel the pain when I saw the amount of the check: $65.28! Mother stared in disbelief. I was stunned to the point of utter speechlessness—a quality for which I have never been famous. $65.28! Where did all the money go? What on God's earth was I going to do now?

Here I was—21 and a total has-been. And for a never-was, that's saying a lot. I was filled with self-hate, self-pity, self-doubt—you name it. Everything I'd struggled and sweated for—and yes, slept for—was gone. For what? A string of bit parts? Putting a brother who didn't give a damn about me through four years of college? Paying the rent on an apartment I never really stayed at? The frustration poured out at my mother in a biting speech I didn't really mean. Here I was, on my supposed day of financial freedom: a washout and a washup before most people get their first steady job.

And then something snapped. No more self-pity—I wasn't cut out for that sort of maudlin emotion. Of course, I had lost a lot. But I had also learned a hell of a lot in the same pitiless process. Life was filled with ugly surprises and bitter truths, but to be honest, I had known that since I was old enough to walk. I drew in my breath and turned to Mother, who sat nearly comatose in the car beside me.

Squeezing her hand, I said, "So what?"

Life for me was just beginning. I reached out to her and laughed. "Here we go again," I said. And we did.

The people who had helped me most in the past were now nowhere to be found. Cesar had joined the Coast Guard in 1942. A year later, Tyrone entered the Air Force. Cary and Randy had drifted away—and apart—for the moment, since Cary was now with the beautiful and rich Barbara Hutton. A slew of others left to join the service. It was a lonely time, but I held on to the hope that something great was right around the bend.

I was right.

Miss Mae West

By now I had more than enough experience in my brief Hollywood interlude to pen a hundred "How to Get into Show Business" books or to draw from memory a thousand maps to the star's homes. After all, in one way or another, I had been to most of them.

My hopes hit pay dirt when Mike Todd, who'd hired me for Gypsy Rose Lee's 1939 World's Fair stint, announced he was producing a Broadway show called *Catherine Was Great*, loosely based on the Catherine of Russia legend, starring that 20th-century legend herself, Miss Mae West.

Mae West was one of those incredible creatures who conjured up the wildest thoughts and emotions imaginable. Glamour, guts and glitter—that was Mae. Reams of hype had been printed about her, yet she revealed very little to anyone about her personal life. Few, if any, ever caught a glimpse of the Brooklyn woman behind the Hollywood myth, and La West liked to keep it that way. At the time, people spoke of Garbo, Dietrich and Swanson as the most enigmatic sirens of the silver screen, but to me, Mae West was always its most priceless puzzle.

People whispered she was a woman driven mad by lust, or that she was totally frigid, or that she was really a man in drag, and the biggest joke was on her adoring, gullible public. Gossip clung to every curve. I couldn't wait to meet her. I remembered the moments I'd spent fantasizing about her figure during my days at Columbia, when she used to swagger by in her long fitted skirts, smiling that Mona Lisa smile. And I remembered the rumors I'd heard about her even then: whether or not she really did have piano legs and huge bunions. After I arranged an audition for *Catherine* through Mike Todd's office, my thoughts were tinged with a sense of déjà vu. Maybe this time I'd find out exactly who the real Mae West was.

The 20th Century Fox rehearsal hall was filled with the most outrageous assortment of Hollywood humanity I'd ever seen. And that's saying an awful lot. Included in the mix were, first and foremost, the Mae West impersonators, who most likely did Mae better than Mae. Every eyelash, padded bust and blond-finger-wave was in place as they wisecracked to Mae's old lines, wiggled Mae's walk and smirked that smirk. Mae's smirk was like watching a camp version of *Invasion of the Body Snatchers*—in beads, no less. Amazing. Not to be outdone, every "Shakespearean" actor who ever recited "To be or not to be" in a bathroom mirror was on hand for the festivities…along with a gym's worth of Muscle Beach hunks attired in sequined posing trunks. And then there was me: positively hopeless, but willing to try anything. Little did I know.

For my audition as one of Mae's "ushers," I was given a mini-bathing suit and white terry robe to wear. Mini was a grand overstatement; it was nearly nonexistent. After putting it on, I was handed a number and a category card and instructed to wait in the corner. Covering up as best I could, I was more than happy to head for the shadows. As the young beauties gossiped, the Hamlets recited and the body builders posed, I wondered what I had gotten myself into. But the chance to be in a Mae West production wasn't something I took lightly. I needed the job.

The waiting was the worst, hour after interminable hour in a state of undress. If one more actor confessed he'd been in *Gone with the Wind*, I knew I'd scream. Everyone lies at auditions—but not as badly as these lousy amateurs. Finally my name was called by the studio casting secretary, and I knew it was now or never. Mae West herself would be the judge.

I walked into what appeared to be yet another gigantic waiting room. The room was nearly dark except for a circular string of white spots that shone down from the center of the ceiling. In

the corner, in front of blood red velvet curtains, stood six faceless men who resembled high executioners from a Boris Karloff
film. They hovered around a surprisingly tiny woman sitting in
the shadows: Mae West. The pinlights only managed to empha-
size my pale skin. Compared to the bevy of bronzed gods waiting outside, I wondered why she bothered to see me at all. But
since she hadn't already thrown me out, I could only pray that
the vast difference in skin tone—and muscle tone, for that matter—would make me stand out. I was the only man auditioning
for the "usher" role who wasn't 200 pounds of gristle. Maybe Mae
liked to diversify a bit, I reasoned. Before entering Mae's inner
sanctum, I had been warned not to glance her way unless I
wanted to risk immediate dismissal. She liked to watch, but
hated to be seen. She seemed to be the classic voyeur, who had
an almost sadistic need to dominate and control, which she did
through her power and fame. I felt like the sacrificial lamb
before the aging cartoon's altar.

As I stood frozen under the spots, I was instructed to remove
my robe. Did they want a striptease? Or just do the boyish, naive
bit? I slowly opened my robe and it slipped down my shoulders
and chest and fell to the floor. My skin, covered in goose bumps,
felt icy, coated in a sheen of nervous sweat. I closed my eyes and
began performing. I felt Mae's eyes scan my body, sliding down
my thighs. She was wondering, I imagined, if she could control
me like she controlled all the others who surrounded her with
insincere yet slavish devotion.

Beside the seated queen, the men stood and stared. The only
sound I heard was a heavy, almost harsh breathing. It began to be
perversely exciting for me. To heighten the feeling, I imagined I
was alone, looking into a mirror. Suddenly, a voice from the darkness called out, shattering the surreal moment of self-adulation I
had created for myself.

"Your name, please," she commanded brusquely.

"Ellis," I answered.

"First name."

"Oh, sorry...Dick. Dick Ellis."

Her voice murmured in the patently seductive, lusty tone she affected for the movies. I masked my fascination with tight-lipped indifference.

"Tell me, Dick, does this embarrass you?"

"No. Not at all, Miss West." God knows I'd grown accustomed to selling myself by now.

"Turn," she directed.

I did, slowly.

Around and around. Again. Pose. Head up. Around again. Turn. Faster now.

I was getting dizzy. Feeling faint from the lights. I turned, and turned, and turned, each time glimpsing her face, a mask of paint and powder. A slight smile played across her scarlet lips. I wondered who was seducing whom. I felt her interest intensify. Like a spoiled spider slowly spinning her web, she drew me into her own private fantasy, breath by breath.

"Get his name," Mae demanded in a husky-throated whisper.

"What's your name?" asked one of the executioners. He sounded like a trained parrot.

"I told you...Dick Ellis." They were testing my ability to be bullied. I peered out from my spotlight and smiled. But then I added: "My name is anything you want it to be."

I was ready to be anyone and anything Mae West desired. Erase the past—again. Become someone new—again. I decided I'd no longer spurn the affections of women. They could take me far—all the way to Broadway.

I dropped slowly to my knees and picked up the robe. Then, with all the confidence I could muster, I spoke the one line of dialogue I knew she was waiting to hear. "This has been a great moment for me. Thank you for this opportunity, Miss West."

Leaving her lacquered lair was a blessed relief. Especially since I knew I'd gotten the job.

Mae's next victim wasn't as fortunate. Upon entering, a loud crash was heard, followed by a chorus of disapproving voices. Much to his eternal shame, Mr. Muscle had tripped and fallen in a wall-shaking, floor-quaking display of utter klutziness. He stammered pathetically, "I'm so sorry," before flying past the open-mouthed auditioners in near hysterics. If it hadn't been so tragic, the pratfall would have been perfect for a Marx Brothers movie. I doubt that the Great Mae was amused. Nobody, but nobody, stole the spotlight from her and got away with it.

The circus of remaining wanna-bes descended on me en masse as I walked into the dressing area.

"What's she like?"

"Did you see her?"

"What was she wearing?"

"Did she touch you?"

"Did you get the part?" I looked at them and smiled.

"Sure did," I beamed.

And for the first time in years, I knew I was right.

Mike Todd's office called the next morning with the good news—although they were quick to stress that my role was small. Twelve lines, to be precise. Of course, I didn't tell them it was my largest speaking part since *Cross of Lorraine* and that I was thrilled to simply have a chance to get back on the stage. Always the careerist, I fantasized that *Catherine* would be the big breakthrough I'd been searching for. Mother wasn't so sure.

As I started to pack for New York, my plans seemed to be mere abstract dreams until I pulled out the battered suitcase and began stuffing it full of the clothes I had piled in stacks on our living-room floor. I watched out of the corner of my eye as Mother sat on the sofa knitting, her shoulders hunched up like a child being punished. Who would look after her now? Would she continue to live on Selma Street without me? Benson had already moved to live in New York with Dad after graduating from UCLA, so there was no one left. Cautiously, I looked her way, hoping to avoid any teary-eyed dramatics. I snapped the suitcase shut, but she just continued her handiwork, never once glancing in my direction.

Hours later, I stood by the window and stared out into the streets below. The boys of Selma Avenue still wandered in and out of the YMCA, smiling blank-eyed promises under the dusty streetlights. Nothing had changed for these sad young men who sold themselves to survive. I wondered if things would change for me.

In the morning, as I put my luggage into the waiting taxi, Mother stood in the doorway of the building, watching. She looked frail and sad in the entrance. Her eyes were puffy and red. She hadn't slept much the night before; neither had I. I ran over and kissed her goodbye.

She whispered, "Please take care of yourself."

I smiled and told her I'd try.

> I kept my eyes on her slowly dissolving face
> as we drove away and turned the corner,
> freezing her image in my memory.

As the plane rose into the clouds toward New York, the palm trees became tiny green dots that hugged the blistered pavement. A series of red-tiled roofs, blue teardrop pools, gray ribboned highways and brown, windswept fields merged with rivers, mountains and valleys as we crossed the West. Checkerboard cities sprang up, their black-and-white streets huge man-made grids from the sky. Looking down on the land below, I felt removed from the people who lived there—and oddly able to draw strength from the mistakes I'd made in the past seven years of my life.

Catherine Was Great

I never really resented the years I wasted as window dressing for the best parties in town, nothing more than a body on a dance floor, or in a bedroom with a stranger. I was the "Who is he?" kid, the other half of a good time, conveniently forgotten in the morning. I had counted the cracks in those high-priced Hollywood ceilings. I knew how many two-way mirrors had stared down on all of us. I was last year's model, ready for a trade-in, used up, burnt out, thrown aside. I was the other side of the dream—the side no one talks about.

New York offered a way out. But typically, I'd forgotten to arrange for any kind of lodging, even a hotel room. Faced with the grim knowledge that if I didn't think of something quick, I'd be back on the streets, I thought of Henry Selzer. He lived near Eighth Street and Fifth Avenue—a perfect location. I debated whether or not I should call him. What if he said no? What if he slammed down the phone? Damn it! He owed it to me, didn't he? So I took a very deep breath and dialed his number.

A voice said, "Hello." I barely recognized it.

"Dad, I'm here in New York. I'm at the airport."

"Take a cab, I'll meet you downstairs. If you don't have a place to stay, you can stay here with me."

He actually sounded happy to hear from me. I nearly fell over in shock. He really wanted me back, after everything that had happened. Maybe it was time for me to give a little, to love him for what he was, not what I wanted him to be.

A rare, nearly euphoric happiness flooded me. I ran to the

baggage counter, grabbed my luggage and hailed a cab. Gray Manhattan buildings, lining the noisy streets like mute soldiers, grew denser, taller as the cab veered onto Fifth Avenue. Minutes from a reunion I never thought would happen, the faceless web of New York didn't threaten me anymore. I had a place I could call home—with a man I never imagined would accept me, perhaps even love me. I kept telling myself this isn't a dream. For once, this is real. Could this be the "happily ever after"? No, my luck hadn't changed that much. I had too much to accomplish, too many risks to take, too many decisions ahead of me. Reconciling with Dad was a good start, and I had to admit I had harbored a secret desire to do so.

The car stopped in front of a respectable four-story Georgian walk-up. Henry Selzer, looking much older, stood at the base of the stone steps. I couldn't smile, I couldn't breathe. As I got out of the taxi, I had no idea what to say to the stranger who began walking in my direction. Just be yourself, I thought. Don't fight this feeling. I really wanted a father. I wanted to call him Dad, and mean it. From that evening on, I hoped I would.

At first, I was dazed by our reunion, his kindness and concern. I accepted his advice and protection gratefully. I can't begin to tell you what it meant to me. There were many moments I cherished during those first days in New York—listening to him reminisce about our old neighborhood, still wrapped up in its ancient dogmas and traditions, a simple "good night" before going to bed, a cheery "good morning" over coffee. Those are moments I will always remember. But I soon discovered I was far too independent to live by anyone else's rules and regulations. Henry's newfound paternal concern grew dense and confining. Since I was dependent on Dad for most of my necessities until *Catherine* started rehearsals, I felt trapped. So as usual, I'd take off for a few hours on my own, usually ending up in Washington Square.

Washington Square attracted an artistic hodgepodge of unknown actors, poets, artists and musicians. Who could have known that the good-looking young violinist playing on the corner for the villagers would turn out to be Marlon Brando? The bohemian set epitomized Greenwich Village, a section of the city near Dad's that was, quite unlike today, very unfashionable. I didn't care. I felt connected to these so-called misfits. I was one of them. Despite its social stigma, it was also the home of Eleanor Roosevelt. I remember standing there for hours just to see the great lady for a fleeting moment. And then it happened—she stepped out of a car, looked straight at me and said hello in that incredible voice. I will always cherish the thrill I felt. The Village was brimming with the kind of self-expressive freedom I loved— the kind of freedom Hollywood took great pleasure in destroying.

Once rehearsals began and I was on the Mike Todd payroll, I moved uptown near Broadway. It was nothing much—just a bed, closet and a toilet. Six weeks of grueling work loomed on the horizon if *Catherine Was Great* was going to be ready for its August 1944 opening at the Shubert Theatre. Hour after hour crept by as we sat in the corner of the theater, waiting for Mae, who had sequestered herself in a dressing room, working on rewrites. When she did appear, tension was thick. And when we made mistakes, she nearly levitated. Mae wanted perfection. As I stood with a broom as my makeshift spear, West's tantrums were, in their own grotesque way, fascinating to behold. At least when she screamed we felt safe. It was the muffled whispers between Mike Todd and director Roy Hargrave in the dark corners of the stage that we found terrifying. We never knew who would get the ax next when they retreated into those Shubert alcoves.

Mae's random firings merely mirrored her massive insecurity. To have the ability to hire and fire at will must have pleased a woman as frightened as Miss West. We were merely token cardboard cutouts for her amusement, victims of a spoiled star's power-mad ego. But for all the power she wielded over us, West had no control over her own future. I knew from my own Hollywood education how impossible it was for a star like Mae to constantly top herself. Like so many other great talents from Theda Bara to Marilyn Monroe, she was afraid of realizing that age-old Tinsel Town prophecy: The gimmick that makes you a star could be the very thing that destroys you in the end.

During rehearsals, I noticed she hardly resembled the tempestuous screen siren America had embraced. But even when she dressed in simple suits and short skirts, I could hardly believe my eyes: Mae's legs weren't piano-shaped at all. In fact, they were incredible—beautifully toned and elegantly slim. For a woman well into middle age, she was remarkably well preserved—but in an almost matronly way. Was this really Mae West? Outrageous rumors continued to fly around her like smoke from a bonfire. None of us knew what to believe.

My confusion deepened when I went to visit her one evening after rehearsals ended. I had been granted this audience only after inundating her secretary with so many daily requests that she eventually gave up and gave in. Mae and I met for just a moment—but it's a moment I'll never forget.

When I entered her chandelier-lit dressing room, I nearly gasped. The room had been decorated in a style that could only be called "Nightmare in White." Heavy white damask drapes, tufted satin chairs, chaise lounges, tasseled bellpulls and ornate lacquered furniture were strewn around the room like spilled cream. In the midst of this colorless environment sat Mae at her makeup mirror, her back to the white-paneled door. She seemed absorbed in her reflection. Dressed in an elaborate marabou and lace lounging gown embroidered with silver sequins, she glittered like a star in her room of white. It was just the effect she wanted to achieve.

Mae's secretary, a generic schoolmarm in a high-necked dress, accented with the obligatory Wedgwood cameo, motioned for me to come in. Mae did not acknowledge my presence.

"Miss West," her assistant began, "someone in the cast would like a moment of your time."

Mae turned from the mirror and glared.

"Miss West," I stammered, "I just wanted to know if you received the flowers I sent. The white roses…?"

Her finely tuned hands fiddled with an elaborate blond wig. Slowly, she turned away and resumed staring at her reflection. "Yes, she did," she answered.

"Thank you," I managed to reply before being ushered out of her inner sanctum. As quickly as it began, the private audience was over.

Walking home that night, Mae's baffling response, "Yes, she did," echoed over and over in my mind.

Was it just a slip of the tongue? Did she, in fact, see herself as two separate people? Or was the woman I had just visited an impostor? My head reeled. The thin legs, short skirts, youthful appearance, third-person reply—yet another Mae West mystery I'd never unravel.

What was far more obvious was the threadbare state of the production. Not in terms of costumes or sets—those were dazzling—but in terms of the script, which was mindless at best. The basic plot, described by Mae in a telegram to Sam Zolotow of the *New York Times*, was summarized in this frothy fashion:

TELEGRAM

LOS ANGELES CALIF 221P JULY 12—SAM ZOLOTOW NY TIMES

PRELIMINARY ARRANGEMENTS HAVE BEEN MADE AND UNLESS UNFORESEEN DEVELOPMENTS OCCUR I WILL APPEAR FOR MICHAEL TODD IN MY PLAY, "CATHERINE WAS GREAT" AS SOON AS I AM FINISHED WITH THE PICTURE "TROPICANA".

THE PLAY BRINGS OUT THE INTERESTING HIGHLIGHTS OF THE LIFE AND LOVES OF CATHERINE THE GREAT WHO RULED AS EMPRESS OF ALL THE RUSSIAS FROM 1762 TILL 1796. IT WAS SHE WHO ALMOST 200 YEARS AGO PREDICTED A GREAT FUTURE FOR RUSSIA AND PLANTED THE SEEDS OF GREATNESS THAT ARE COMING TO FLOWER IN THE SOIL OF RUSSIA TODAY.

THE MEN AROUND CATHERINE, WHOM SHE PLAYS ONE AGAINST THE OTHER, ARE THOSE WHO LOVED AND SERVED HER AND RUSSIA FAITHFULLY AND WELL. SHE RULED RUSSIA WITH ONE HAND AND HER MEN WITH THE OTHER.

IMPERIALLY YOURS, CATHERINE THE GREAT

SINCERELY YOURS, MAE WEST

Mae's tongue-in-cheek salutation, "Imperially yours," was a lot more accurate than Mr. Zolotow would ever know. And despite her cheery insistence that the show was hit-bound, everyone else smelled doom and disaster.

Working with Bogart was a walk in the spring rain compared to the havoc that reigned during this production, and the Matterhorn of Mayhem herself—La West—was the biggest problem of all. Director Roy Hargrave suffered the brunt of her dictatorial demeanor, her persistent line and scene alterations and her random disregard for everyone but herself throughout every hellish rehearsal. Her outrageous behavior and rude, often cruel manner created a nightmare of hostility. And the show hadn't even opened! I could only imagine what would happen once the opening-night reviews started pouring in.

Rewrites, new staging, more rewrites—Mae's original script was reduced to a jumble of deleted lines, added jokes and scrapped sketches. Utterly hopeless. But all of the underlings plodded along. We had to: We were on a perpetual two-week notice just to keep us in line. In case the terror of unemployment didn't work, she also had a habit of changing dialogue in mid-scene just to watch us stammer and stew. Mae was a master of stealing scenes, and since Catherine was totally tailored to her own special brand of bedroom bravado, she resorted to every trick in her dog-eared book: rolling her eyes, shaking her hips, fondling a statue and—the ultimate power blow—cutting our lines if they got a laugh. The rules were simple: The laughs were for Mae, the applause for Mae. We were just a string of faceless boys posing and primping around this legendary Hollywood illusion.

Mike Todd plastered Manhattan with gigantic billboards heralding Mae West's August Broadway comeback. A barrage of newspaper articles, radio interviews and an ever-mounting box-office line seemed to bolster our chances. But when the curtain rose on opening night, all our fears were confirmed. No elaborate Todd PR campaign could disguise the fact that Catherine was a bona fide bomb. Our critical doom was sealed when the *New York Times* cat-called: "*Catherine Was Great* ought to be good. It isn't."

If the critics carped, at least the audiences at first were ecstatic. Everyone except Mike Todd had underestimated Mae's power over a room filled with devoted fans. And no one basked in the limelight like she did. Mae West seemed to transform herself every night, blossoming into the gilded icon of sex she knew they expected to see. But not even her coterie of admirers could keep the show running forever. Rumors were already afloat that an early closing was imminent.

Preparing for the worst, I secretly auditioned for a small role in *Ten Little Indians*, playing at the Ethel Barrymore Theatre adjacent to the Shubert. The Agatha Christie mystery, starring the fabulous Estelle Winwood, had opened to rave reviews and sellout crowds since June. The difference between Estelle and Mae was like heaven and hell. Even though my messenger part was hardly a star turn, Winwood always treated me as if I really mattered. Her low-pitched "Good evening, Mr. Ellis," a greeting she never failed to deliver upon my arrival, was a welcome relief from West's "Who are you?" attitude.

Since my appearance in *Ten Little Indians* was limited to a brief bit in the first act, I had enough time to run over to the Shubert, change clothes and arrive on stage with seconds to spare. No one ever noticed my mad dashing to and fro. *Catherine*'s dwindling crowds and Mae's constant complaints kept everyone oblivious to the charades of a bit player like me.

One evening several weeks into *Catherine*'s run, I noticed a tall, very elegant gentleman, about 50, staring at me. He stood outside the stage door, directly under the backstage entrance sign in the alley. Dressed in a dark blue suit, with black wavy hair and piercing brown eyes, he looked familiar. Our eyes met and I felt a shock of déjà vu. I wanted to go over and introduce myself, for I was almost certain we had met. But as I started to walk toward him, he disappeared into the shadows. I froze, without breathing.

Many years later, when Mother was ill, she told me of a letter she had received that was one of her most treasured memories. How I wish I had known about it that night. What magical and wonderful things could have happened that might have changed the entire course of my life. She repeated the words of that letter as if they were etched in her memory with a golden pen:

> *Dear Eva,*
>   *I saw our son in* Catherine Was Great *last night, but*
> *I couldn't bring myself to speak…he looked so like me.…*

I read the lines over and over again. Until I read that letter, I never realized the man I'd glimpsed that evening was my real father—wanting to reach out to me.

I never saw him again.

With the end of *Catherine Was Great,* I had a lot of time on my hands to take a look at the world around me. The more I thought about what was happening beyond the privileged streets of Broadway, the more determined I became to set my priorities straight.

World War II had been raging for two years, and I had been so self-absorbed that I'd hardly taken conscious note of it. I was ashamed, and however belatedly, I wanted to do something to help the war effort. I remedied the situation by joining UTWAO, the United Theatrical War Activities Organization.

Soldiers Without Guns

We were soldiers without guns, but our ammunition—vaudeville shows, hospital visits, writing letters and phoning families—was extraordinarily powerful. When I first joined, I was told to concentrate on entertaining, that I was better suited for clowning for the troops than visiting the grim hospitals where hundreds of broken and battered men and women suffered in silent agony. I soon made it clear to the UTWAO officials that visiting the hospitals was my top priority. There, among the rows of bedridden, often forgotten victims of war, I could be useful. I wanted to make a positive difference in their lives, and to some small extent I think I succeeded. I had always found it difficult to reach out to anyone emotionally, but during those hospital visits I felt connected to the injured, lonely patients. By helping them, I helped myself. I confronted the harsh reality of war, and a real bond developed between the soldiers and myself.

Most of the time we sat in silence, punctuated by random, often chilling cries from unseen rooms down faraway halls. The air was thick with the smell of death, a heavy, oppressive, medicinal odor that permeated the tragic atmosphere. Visiting the men and women was an emotional merry-go-round for me, riding a dark horse. Some would smile and take my hand, but others would simply turn away in anger—reminded, perhaps, of a time when trusting in someone had brought them to this hellish place. I understood all too well their refusal to communicate, for in a very real sense, their will to live was gone.

One of the saddest aspects of visiting the Army camps was

eating in the commissary, not because of the food—although definitely not a culinary delight—but because of the young waiters who served us. They were prisoners of war, most as young as me; and just as frightened as our own POWs thousands of miles away. These men had been brought to the States to serve time; thousands were shipped to Colorado, Texas and New Jersey to build roads, clear fields and collect garbage. Watching them wait tables was painful; one could feel their anguish and humiliation. We were forbidden to speak to them, or, for that matter, even look their way. I tried to sneak a smile, but harsh reprimands from my superiors curbed my sympathetic manner.

Mercifully, the war finally ended, yet the need for volunteer work was greater than ever. And though the confetti-strewn parades ended and our war heroes tried to slip back into their civilian lifestyles, the hospitals with their long, dark, seemingly endless corridors remained packed with the wounded and wasted bodies of World War II.

> I continued my efforts on their behalf
> until I realized my bank account
> was rapidly dwindling...

It all started when, on a sudden impulse, I contacted "The Agency," one of New York's hot-shot booking houses. I was broke, and my rent was long overdue, so I applied for "representation." Strictly legit, of course— at first. So began my "Agency Days"—beginning as a model and ending up as a well-paid escort.

The Agency Days

"The Agency" specialized in print work, especially layouts for magazines like *True Detective* and other assorted pulp publications. These slicks used a wide variety of models to illustrate their sordid stories of forbidden love triangles, passionate murder plots and South American espionage adventures. Compared to Mae, I reasoned, the work would be easy and lucrative. I was hired in the spring of '45 and soon began appearing in a multitude of roles—as a mad scientist, a crazed rapist, a killer priest and a blind fortune teller, among countless other grade "C" incarnations. I loved it. After Hollywood and Broadway, I felt like I was on an extended vacation.

After proving that I was a valuable commodity, I was informed in veiled whispers that "The Agency" also provided "escort" services for wealthy women. I wasn't surprised. In one way or another, New York literally brimmed with good-looking gigolos. I might as well get paid for it. The benefactresses of The Agency, some married, some widowed, drifted through the penthouses of Manhattan like jeweled ghosts. These washed-out dowagers needed men for many reasons, from rounding out a table of eight to warming a solitary bed after the party ended.

The Agency's rules were written in stone: We were to show up at the proper time, dressed for the occasion per specific instructions from our employer's private secretary, act slightly awed over the luxurious atmosphere, and accept with utmost discretion the hundred-dollar bill pressed into our palm. These lonely socialites reveled in the idea of exposing us to what they thought were the finer things in life, possibly meaning themselves.

Each desperate evening promised an identical performance with identical props: silk-draped grande dames in sleek limousines stocked with Dom Perignon, dinners at the Stork Club, the Maisonette, the Plaza, the St. Regis and the Copa. The nights blended into a mindless whirl of slow dances under glittering chandeliers, moving a little too close, smiling a bit too much, bodies touching bodies, heads thrown back in forced gaiety, long manicured fingernails that ran possessively through my hair, brushing against my cheeks. I tried to avoid direct eye contact, but I could still sense the hunger within. I avoided the judgmental stares of Madame's friends with an icy, well-rehearsed air. Later, a Broadway show, followed by a late-night aperitif in their candlelit lairs—and then, improvisation.

Up until midnight, my escort fees were split with The Agency's business office. At 12:01, I was open season for these sad-eyed shells who collected people like objets d'art for their transitory amusement. Most of us lingered far beyond the witching hour, later accepting our frivolous parting gifts—robes, ties and wallets were de rigueur—with as much grace under pressure as possible. Driving home at dawn, my Oscar-worthy performances sickened me; the atmosphere of sexual desperation was depressing. Only the most jaded models lasted beyond the saturation point of six months. I became a human vacuum, as empty as the women I slept with. At times I caught myself wondering where I was going, but I already knew the answer. I was going nowhere—fast.

Late one afternoon The Agency called as usual. "Is eight P.M. okay?"

"No! No! Damn it, no!" I cried, slamming the phone back onto the receiver.

I held my head in my hands, grabbing fistfuls of hair. Slowly, I shook my head, rocking gently back and forth. I had lost part of my soul.

In that single moment, I knew my escort days were over. None of us had the right to turn down a client's request, for I was nothing more than a windup court jester—a well-dressed, perfectly polite, unabashed fool. But I didn't care. I wanted out.

The telephone, a coiled snake ready to strike, waited in silence. Then a ring, and another—no doubt The Agency calling back. I imagined threats, anger, blackmail. A thick, sour taste churned in my throat. Again, the phone rang—or had it ever stopped? I closed my eyes and visions of crazed clowns rushed toward me, arms outstretched, laughing sadistically, reaching, grabbing. I spun round and round looking for an escape, endlessly turning, turning, darkness overcoming me.

I heard that The Agency tried to track me down—but I had long since disappeared, changing my address and keeping a low profile. I knew too much. I had been playing a high-priced game and The Agency was worried: Would I talk? Would I whisper their secrets to some sleazy reporter hungry for the scandalous scoop of the season? Marriages could be desecrated, closets thrown open. The tired, ancient women of pseudo-society who clung to their pathetic fantasies, who fooled themselves into believing they were desirable, would be irreparably humiliated if their sordid behavior was made public. I could have destroyed them all, forced society to its knees, crumbled its very foundation. But why? I was too tired, too disgusted. I had already sunk too low.

Hats in the Attic

I walked along the wind-whipped Manhattan streets. I watched families, friends and lovers glide by. I wanted to be like them. Farther down the street, more smiling crowds veered into view. I seemed to be the only loner in sight. And then I saw him—a cameo-like face in a sea of faceless passersby. I was drawn to him. Six feet tall, slim, he had soft brown hair that fell away from his face, revealing gentle brown eyes. He walked more like a panther on the prowl as he approached me—and I knew. I knew I would no longer be alone.

His name was Stan Harris. We met, we spoke and he brought me to my new home—the Van Courtland Hotel. Located on the crumbling corner of 49th Street and Broadway, the hotel was a certifiable flea trap, a hellish haven for hundreds of out-of-work actors. I fit right in.

The Van Courtland's seven stories consisted of drafty, dark corridors and dim cubbyhole rooms connected by steep stairways and a creaking elevator. No one complained about climbing the mountain of steps after hearing the groans and moans of that ancient iron cage. Death by elevator was not my idea of a suitable finale for a life already brimming with failure. This questionable emporium was a hymn to horror, but what happy, hopeful, often hilarious characters lived there—a wild mix of has-beens, would-bes, never-wases. And on the upper floors, sitting in the shadows of their red-lit lamps, ladies of the evening, often stuffed seven or more to a room. Even they had to compromise.

From the moment I moved into Room 309, a fraternity-like camaraderie wafted through the Van Courtland corridors and made these hard times some of the most joyous I'd ever known. My new family was incredible. First, there was Stan and his sister, Betty. What a pair! They would sing, dance and clown for anyone who'd listen. We were quick to become friends. Betty became deeply involved in our lives, nurturing and caring, but she was also just like "one of the boys." She was bawdy and broady—literally—laughing that she had the only inverted nipples in all of Broadway! There was also the delightful singer Fran Warren; the talented composer Sherman Edwards; the Skylarks, a musical group that would soon skyrocket to international fame; and a ragtag assortment of down-and-outers and future up-and-comers. Through it all there was a great feeling of togetherness I had never known before. And I must not forget to mention Doris Day, known to everyone as "Doe-Doe," who, while in New York singing at Billy Reed's Little Club, visited the Van Courtland nearly every day. Doris had so many friends living at the hotel that we thought of her as an honorary tenant. To this day, she remains one of the kindest and most talented women I've ever known—but in those days she still hadn't become the star we knew she was destined to be. If she hadn't made it, how the hell were we going to?

It wouldn't be too long before Doris fulfilled our predictions: She was "discovered" at one of her performances by a talent scout from Warner Brothers and the rest, as they say, was history. She soon had a million-selling single, "It's Magic," a contract with Warner Brothers, and her first of many musicals, *Romance on the High Seas.* I followed her career closely and received a vicarious thrill when she soared up the Hollywood ladder with breathtaking speed. She went on to star in such diverse films as *Love Me or Leave Me, The Man Who Knew Too Much, Pillow Talk, Lover Come Back* and *Midnight Lace.* Doris was a positive lesson in painstaking perseverance; she inspired me, for her life hadn't been a bed of begonias, either. Unfortunately, her monumental talent as an actress and a singer wasn't a quality we shared.

Since I hadn't made it past the first rung of that infamous ladder, I had to find other ways to pay the rent, so I began making hats, an unmistakable influence from Aunt Bertha. Almost by instinct, I knew exactly where to place a pin; if that failed, I covered up my mistakes with a silk flower. Needless to say, my hats were bogged down with more silky blossoms than the Hanging Gardens of Babylon.

What later was dubbed my "Hats in the Attic" period started innocently enough with Betty Harris, who had been given a gorgeous, emerald green Chanel suit studded with big gold buttons and banded in navy silk braid. I surprised her by designing a tam to accompany the suit. She loved it. Made of shantung straw with a band of green satin, Betty's hat looked just like the Parisian-flavored designs Aunt Bertha had concocted in Hollywood. Betty promptly told everyone about her marvelous new milliner and, in our cramped third floor quarters, my designing career began. Granted, the beginning was humble, but as usual I had big dreams.

Stan and Betty assured me that I could make a living selling my creations to their friends in the business. Soon Stan wanted in on the action, so we rented an 8 x 12 broom closet in the attic and started yet another cottage industry from the Van Courtland Hotel. The prostitutes upstairs loved the idea and I often used them as models during the day, since their evenings were booked.

I usually started out with an inexpensive straw-brimmed hat, which I bought by the dozen from a wholesaler in the garment district. (He swore they were imported directly from Rome, but the outskirts of New Jersey was more likely.) From there, I gathered tulle—pink, red, pale blue, black and ivory—mixed silk flowers and jeweled brooches, then whipped everything together in a series of Theda Bara headdresses, dainty schoolgirl bonnets and outrageously avant-garde "wearable gardens." The hats—as mismatched as they were—proved to be a smash. Naturally, I had little time to enjoy it. Like the Mad Hatter himself, I remained locked away 24 hours a day in my attic fantasyland, covered head to toe in straw, satin and silk. The battle scars of a thousand ornery pins covered my hands as I worked my fingers to the bone. So did Stan, Betty, Fran, Sherman and anyone else I could corral into helping out. Even Murphy, the less than brilliant elevator attendant, got into the act. Smiling broadly, he took great pride in shutting down the elevator so we could use the creaking catastrophe as a loading dock. He even began modeling my hats, much to the delight of the ladies upstairs, who teased him mercilessly. From Murphy's elevator, the merchandise would be lowered to the lobby and later delivered to my hopefully satisfied customers. The "309" clan, as Murphy called us, celebrated with grand parties featuring chili prepared on a rusted hot plate accompanied with a case of beer. Since every penny mattered, we kept the bottles and sold them to bottle collectors down the street.

As the orders grew larger, so did my prices. I must admit they were neither cheap nor reasonable, usually ranging from $20 and up—and most of them were up, up and away. Everyone around me was sworn to secrecy over the identity of the mysterious milliner. The wealthy socialites who bought my hats were told, I'm sure, that the extravagant chapeaux were Parisian haute couture. What they didn't know only helped me and the rest of my new family, who had given so much time and talent helping me get started. And a family is what we were. We thought nothing of going anywhere or doing anything for each other. We were just comfortable, close and content.

It was ironic, considering my childhood, that poverty created an environment of love and caring at the Van Courtland, where usually such circumstances would suggest exactly the opposite. But whether it was the weekly scavenger hunts we participated in, the games of bridge that lasted for hours or the weekly excursions to the garment district in search of supplies, we shared an uncorrupted love and trust in our young world.

Throughout the years we lived together, Betty and Stan had performed in nearly every conceivable situation. Their cruise-ship excursions, they raved, were fabulous—two weeks of complimentary lodging and food in return for nightly entertainment in a lounge invariably named after Neptune or Captain Nemo. The audiences, often too old to hear, were wildly enthusiastic. For a few shining moments, Stan and Betty were treated like stars. They were paid like stewards, but the tips were good, the food free and the job secure. When you're in the middle of the Atlantic Ocean, the poor passengers haven't a choice. You're it in the entertainment field. Cruise-ship devotees, a bemused Stan used to say, define the term "captive audience."

Taking their advice, I sent my application to Eastern Steamship Cruises, embroidered with a flurry of half-truths, and, incredibly, I was hired—voice unheard—as the lounge act.

Stan didn't think I'd have a problem at all. "Just be yourself," he advised.

"They'll love you," Betty reiterated.

Famous last words.

The nightmare began on a windy April morning after I boarded the ship, sleek and shiny in New York Harbor. Appearances can be deceiving; when I saw my "living" quarters, I knew I was in trouble. I had visualized a lovely, sunny suite with portholes, aquatic accouterments—perhaps a conch-shell sink or a sand-dollar lamp. No such luck. My room—more accurately, closet—was located below sea level, and take it from me, there wasn't a conch shell in sight. The Van Courtland was the Ritz compared to this 2 x 4 disaster, but I held on to my composure until I spied my bathroom. I really shouldn't say "my"—"our" is more suitable under the circumstances. Twenty other employees shared the single sink, shower and toilet cubicle. Little did I know, as I burst into shrieks, that I would have little need for bathroom privacy, since constipation was the chronic consequence of the frightening food prepared by the ship's chef.

But I took my revenge: I had no singing talent. Posed under a "DIRECT FROM BROADWAY" banner in the lobby stood a huge cardboard cutout of my face, the remaining remnant of my Mae West days. It made an impressive, if misleading, image statement. The tottering shuffleboard teams scurried in on opening night expecting Sinatra. The performance they were treated to suffered by comparison to anyone except perhaps their husbands in the shower.

I'd sent the band Stan's musical charts after memorizing every note with surgical precision. Since my vocal style was nothing more than talk/singing at the very best, staying on pitch and in key was imperative. I refused to admit I had no idea how to accomplish this task. Waiting backstage to go on, I suddenly wished I'd been a lot less stubborn. An image of Daniel facing the lions loomed in my head as a brigade of butterflies went berserk in my belly. My mouth momentarily turned into the Mojave. Then, showtime.

My opening number, a frisky version of "Happy Days Are Here Again," bombed bigtime. My throat closed. Was I dead? My eyes frantically scanned the crowd. Were they dead? They certainly looked like suntanned zombies. Either my pathetic attempts at singing had lulled them into a coma or their hearing aids had shorted out. They stared open-mouthed from their tropical fish-festooned tables, barely blinking as I ran through my sparkling repertoire. And when I belted out my final note—silence. Except for fitful clapping from some inebriated bozo in the back who must have assumed I was a comedian. He might have been right.

Rushing offstage, thoughts of suicide flashed before my eyes. But I needn't have worried about self-inflicted injury. The entertainment director was waiting in the wings with a murderous glare etched across his flushed face. "Mr. Ellis," he began sternly, pointing a pudgy finger in my direction. "It seems you have misrepresented yourself."

"I have not," I shot back with theatrical conviction. "I'm just having a few minor problems with my voice."

"That's pretty obvious, judging by the reaction from the audience." His eyes, turtle-like, began to recede into his head as he sneered in disgust.

"What do you want me to do?" At this point I was desperate.

"Cut your act—if you can call it an act—by at least five songs. And try to follow the piano. Stay in tune! You're all we've got," he barked.

"I'll try," I managed to answer with as much conviction as possible. "I really will try."

"You've got one more chance, kid. After that, you're gone."

Did he plan to throw me overboard? Petrified, I ran to my

room and began a crash practice session: deep-breathing exercises, attempting scales, straight-ahead singing—until I was rudely interrupted by two stewards barreling through my door with shocked expressions. They thought I was being tortured. At that humiliating point, I gave up.

My second show was even worse. I opened with "Can't Get Started," and God knows I couldn't. Even the band, mostly mediocre New Jersey bar musicians, were either so stunned or offended that they stopped playing in the middle of my second number, a teeth-aching rendition of "Over the Rainbow." I should have walked the plank instead of trying to hit the final ear-splitting note—a cappella yet. The band leader personally escorted me offstage.

Fearing for my life, I didn't dare appear in the lounge again. The prune juice set made do with two accordion players from Florida recruited from the passenger list, and the entertainment director's sixteen-year-old daughter, who was as off-key as me. But she had connections. As usual, I didn't have even the option of fleeing the crime scene. For the next six days I was a captive at sea—forced to wander about the ship, meekly avoiding eye contact and counting the hours till I could abandon forever the underwater coffin my brochure called a "cabin." Misrepresentation works both ways.

When the glorious, long-awaited morn arrived, I shoved my way toward freedom as five full decks of sunstroke victims made their mass exodus down the runway. I was almost ashore when, appearing like a vision from hell, the cruise captain handed me a bill for my cabin and food.

"You're lucky we're not gonna sue you."

I guess I won't be getting a future recommendation from him, I thought, nearly laughing in his tight-lipped, squinty-eyed face.

I politely accepted the bill, stepped onto dry land with a grateful sigh, quickly hailed a cab and threw the budget buster in the backseat—where, judging from most New York taxis, it still remains today, untouched and, I hasten to add, unpaid.

I never heard a word from Eastern Steamship Cruises again. I suppose they thought I might retaliate by threatening to sing

"Nobody Loves You When You're Down and Out" in the courtroom.

If a bill collector had come to the Van Courtland looking for me, he would have found nothing but an empty room and a few unsold hats scattered about, because by then, past threats about never returning to Hollywood forgotten, I went home to California for good.

I hated admitting to myself that New York hadn't been the problem solver, career-wise, that I had fantasized it would be. Mother's constant offers for me to come back home sounded more tempting with each letter, and the way my future was going, I had no room for negotiation. Swallowing my abandoned pride, Stan and I flew to Los Angeles.

Everything had changed. Mother had moved to a new home on Cloverdale Avenue, far from the steamy environs of Selma Avenue. The tree-shaded street that led to her brick and stone apartment building welcomed me with a serenity unknown in New York. Our reunion, after years of separation, was wordless, emotional. For the first time in months, I felt at peace with myself. No phones, no hassles, no lies.

Mother and Stan gave me the support I craved. As I took the next several months to search for an agent who believed in me, Stan became Mother's most devoted friend and confidant. She loved him as a son and he treated her with great love and respect. He took the overwhelming feeling of responsibility off my shoulders and allowed me to pursue my own career with diligence.

What I didn't know at the time was that my relationship with Stan was soon to end. He was there—and then he was gone. His departure was to leave a large void in our lives. I've often wondered if he felt he had lost me to the "bright lights of Hollywood" or if it was his own sense of futility that drove him away. I really missed him.

Vendetta:
Howard Hughes

After tireless days and endless phone calls—and maybe because my resume had been slightly padded—I was finally accepted by the Paul Kohner Agency, one of the most respected theatrical agents around. Stanley Bergermen was assigned to secure movie roles for me, certainly one of the best representatives to ever drive a Mercedes down Sunset.

Stanley was the perfect agent; his face was an elegant blank, revealing nothing. Tall and commanding, with his buttoned-down, middle-aged Wall Street broker look, he had only one eccentricity: He never rose to greet anyone entering his office. I could have cared less. At least he was sitting up—a rarity for me. Several morale-boosting meetings later, my addiction to acting returned full time. Stanley assured me I'd make it—and I wanted to believe every soothing sentence he tossed my way. Maybe this time, I thought. Maybe this time...

In 1946, Howard Hughes' California Pictures, in association with the great producer-director Preston Sturges, announced they were making *Vendetta*, a film for Howard's latest discovery, Faith Domergue. Based on Proper Merimee's classic French romantic drama, *Columba*, the project was clearly a prestigious undertaking, laced with many of Hollywood's most powerful and talented artists, producers Hughes and Sturges and director Max Ophuls, for starters. Stanley sent me to audition, knowing I had a good chance of landing a role since Hughes had instructed his casting office to hire dark "unknowns." He wanted Faith to shine, unencumbered by any kind of star-power competition. How a Jewish kid from Bensonhurst could wind up in a story about betrayal between two rival Corsican families was beyond me—but I took Stanley's advice and drove over to California Pictures.

Auditioning for *Vendetta* was a comic nightmare. In order to get to the elusive Mr. Hughes, I had to impress Sturges, who oversaw the cattle calls at the Hughes-owned RKO Studios. With his haggard, jowly face, thin mustache and prominent bags bulging under perpetually bloodshot eyes, Sturges looked like an alcoholic basset hound. A frightening sight—even if he was the boy-wonder genius of Hollywood at the time. Hundreds of dark-complected kids filled the sweltering room, each one swearing they were Corsican even as Max Factor Egyptian base dripped down their cheeks in the heat while Preston sipped whiskey and smoked cigarettes, mercilessly crossing off the names he found unsuitable. Perched on a director's chair—the same one he had used for such legendary films as *The Lady Eve, Sullivan's Travels* and *The Palm Beach Story*—Sturges asked me to read several lines of dialogue he had written for a character named Esteban. Out of sheer fear, my voice shook—but I plowed on, determined to impress him. I didn't try to "act"—visionaries like Preston had no fondness for actors with preconceived ideas on line delivery. To people like Hughes and Sturges, I was unformed clay, and that element of rawness helped get me a callback—the first of many.

After days of silence from California Pictures on whether I'd gotten the role, Stanley called with the news that Howard Hughes would see me personally. No promises, Bergermen stressed, but since I'd made it this far, I had every right to be optimistic. And terrified. Howard Hughes intimidated me. I wondered if he really was as odd as everyone said. Of course, the eccentricities Howard exhibited in 1946 were minor affectations compared to his schizoid behavior in later years, but resident gossip queens Louella Parsons and Hedda "The Mad Hatter" Hopper wrote about his escapades with dutiful regularity. Whether he was landing his airplane on a house near the Los Angeles Country Club in Beverly Hills, or riding around Hollywood in a beat-up station wagon, or wearing mud-caked tennis shoes to Chasen's, Louella and holier-than-thou Hedda printed anything they could about this fascinating, complex and mysterious tycoon. Like the rest of Hollywood, I read every word.

Stanley warned me not to dress well; Hughes mistrusted anyone whose appearance was too immaculate. After seeing his office I knew why: shoddy carpets, rundown furniture, smudged walls—hardly the type of surroundings anyone would expect. Obviously, conventional luxury meant nothing to him. I wandered down a maze of halls to his disheveled two-room suite, strewn with mismatched chairs, crumpled scripts, empty coffee cups, dusty photographs and, in the center of the wreckage, a huge carved desk. Behind its scratched sides sat Howard Hughes, leaning back in a black leather wing chair, smoking. The smoke filtered up around him, wrapping his face in eerie blue shadow.

Even through the cigar fog, he was surprisingly dashing in a lanky, sleepy-eyed, Jimmy Stewart-like way.

"Hello," he mumbled, lapsing back into silence.

After a full five minutes, which felt more like 50, I blurted out, "Mr. Hughes, would you like me to read?"

No answer. More silence. The stillness grew suffocating. He finally put his feet up on the desk, picked up a brass hourglass—probably to time meetings with people like me—and stared at the ceiling, his face frozen into a mask of supreme indifference. The soles of his shoes looked like Swiss cheese, with more holes than I could count. No wonder Ava Gardner refused to marry him. You can always tell about a person by looking at his shoes, and Howard's were the worst.

He seemed to be acting, creating his own cryptic image. I stared back and saw a very lonely man obsessed with power. Let him play games, I thought. This is what he enjoys—dangling lives from his moneyed fingers like puppets on a string. Futures hanging in the balance, with Howard holding the scissors. Well, if he wanted to mold and control his employees, I was ready, willing and able to accept the sacrifice.

I repeated the question, "Should I read now?"

Hughes' eyes drifted down and darted in my direction. He seemed a bit startled that I dared to interrupt his reverie.

I was born Richard Sylvan Selzer to Eva and Henry Selzer. At least that's what I thought until Henry and I found out several years later that he wasn't my real father. It was a traumatic moment neither of us would ever forget.

Even at three, there was no love lost between me and my brother Benson, whom I often wished I could have been friends with. However, one act of Henry's years later emotionally breached us forever.

My mother (far left) was there for me from the day I was born to the day she died. She was the strongest woman I ever knew.

When Aunt Bertha (left) opened a hat shop in Hollywood (below), our family joined her there in 1937.

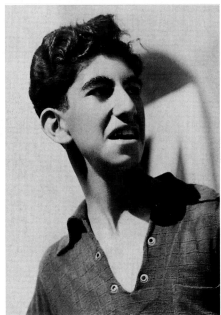

As Richard Seltzer, it wasn't hard for me to play a Dead End Kid. I was one. Typecast, I played "Ears" in Universal's 1937 release, "Little Tough Guy." It was a start.

I was serious about a movie career as "Dick Ellis" (above), until Howard Hughes suggested I change my name to Richard Blackwell.

One part I played very well was that of Hollwood's most prolific boy-toy (right). I was on a downward spiral until I met the man who turned my life around: Robert Spencer (above right).

Wanda Curtis (above right) was a plain Jane when she posed for this publicity shot with Fifi D'Orsay, Mack Sennett, Hilo Hattie and Spencer. As her manager, I transformed her into a glamorous nightclub star (below left). I designed all her gowns.

After Wanda's performance at the Flamingo Club in Buenos Aires (above), I was jailed by the Argentine police in a rat-infested prison from which no one had returned alive. But Peter (above left), one of the boys in the chorus, risked his life to rescue me—and soon paid the price for it.

From the beginning, my fashion shows were glittering extravaganzas with music and glamour (above). This one was at Ciro's night club in Hollywood, for store buyers.

Two of my favorite early models were Barbara Blakeley (left and top center), later to be Mrs. Zeppo Marx and now Mrs. Frank Sinatra and Geraldine Saunders (above) who went on to write the "Love Boat" book.

It was easy for me to
play the character of
the outrageous Mr.
Blackwell. It would be
my most unforgettable
creation, and it would
launch my career—with
Spencer at my side—to
heights that neither of
us would ever have
dreamed was possible.

"An artist in the design of subtle witchery..."

R. L. SPENCER, INC., LOS ANGELES, CALIFORNIA

APPEARING IN HARPER'S BAZAAR AND VOGUE MAGAZINES—FEBRUARY 1960

My first fashion ad—a full-page portrait of me—outraged the fashion establishment. Designers just didn't do that. It put me on the map and in the headlines, as an enigma in the fashion world.

"No, that won't be necessary. You seem to be right. We'll let you know."

My heart plunged: that "We'll let you know" line was usually the kiss of casting death. But Hughes, as it turned out, was quite sincere. As I turned to leave, one of his assistants scampered from a cobwebbed corner and told me to report directly to Max Ophuls, the great German director. After meeting with Ophuls for an equally brief, one-sided audition, Mr. Hughes' office instructed me to read for a variety of "associates," including—I kid you not—the elderly RKO janitor. I thought it had to be some kind of bizarre joke, and I was right: But the joke was on me. I can't imagine what would have happened if I hadn't impressed him, but since I was asked to return the next day for a screen test, I assumed I'd made a decent, if not dazzling, impression.

As I stood facing Preston Sturges, Max Ophuls, Howard Hughes and his gray-suited minions, words were shouted in my direction: "Smile," "frown," "anger," "peace," "memory," "love," "jealousy," etc., etc. I contorted my face into the spectrum of looks they wanted, just as I had done many times before. Humiliation still weighed heavily in the casting process as unknowns barked, begged and rolled over like performing dogs for the Hollywood power brokers.

When I'd finished going through my paces, I was told Sturges wanted me to audition again before a final decision was made. Another delay, another anxiety attack, another late-night phone call to Stanley. Bergermen assured me if I weathered the next meeting, I had a 99% chance of being signed. He was right. Within a week, a final meeting was arranged between Hughes and me.

I sat in his bare-bones anteroom and waited. And waited. His secretary, after being buzzed ominously from an inner office, disappeared down a corridor—only to return moments later with a sheepish, guilt-ridden look. Mr. Hughes was unavailable, she clucked sympathetically, and had decided to phone Bergermen with his decision when he could find the time. I left in a blind fury.

I sped down Sunset Boulevard toward Stanley's office, unable to go home and sit by a silent phone. But when I arrived and saw the look on Stanley's face, my foul humor evaporated in a flash.

"Congratulations," he beamed. "You've been signed."

In a rare break from Bergermen tradition, he actually rose from his chair, crossed the Oriental rug and gave me an affectionate hug. I felt like I had entered a hazy, surreal dream—but when the contracts arrived, I woke up fast. All the waiting and worrying and wondering vanished. *Vendetta* was really, absolutely going to happen, and I was going to be in it.

Still, there were a few minor details to attend to—like my name. Dick Ellis sounded too pedestrian. Hughes said it reminded him of an insurance salesman. So by direct edict from Hughes himself, I was given a new name—a name Hughes felt was theatrical, polished, memorable. So, like a chameleon changing colors, I left Dick Ellis behind forever and became Richard Blackwell. As I signed the California Pictures contract, I christened a new man to go with the new name. A man who would evolve into an outrageous personality far removed from who I really am—and who I want to be.

From the first day of shooting, chaos reigned. My dressing room—a sweltering cubicle in the dark recesses of the studio— was assigned and reassigned dozens of times. Schedules were lost, filming was constantly delayed and, to make matters worse, Max Ophuls was unintelligible. Faith Domergue's dailies were viewed by Hughes with ever-increasing horror: The cinematographer, shooting in arty half-tones, had given her a mustache— hardly the romantic effect Howard was searching for. As for me, I remained in the acting position I knew best—on the sidelines, at the bottom of the totem pole. We were shown no courtesy on the set—or off it, for that matter. I especially enjoyed the 4:00 A.M. wake-up calls, only to discover after arriving bleary-eyed on the set that I wasn't needed till noon. The utter lack of organization drove me mad—but we were under contract, obligated to obey even the most mundane request.

On a multitude of occasions, the supporting cast members were told to appear at a godforsaken desert location, a location Max Ophuls never seemed to be able to find. We sat like burnt toadstools in the broiling heat, hoping in vain that the pampered principals would appear. We didn't dare leave. We would have been suspended or, more likely, just plain fired. I sweated and cursed and fumed under the hot August sun. It didn't do any good. *Vendetta* was now completely out of control.

Unable to keep the production on schedule, Ophuls incurred the wrath of Hughes—and was removed from the project two months into filming. Gossip columns brimmed with unflattering on-the-set exposés, and unfortunately, most of them were true. The power of the press, especially hacks like Louella and Hedda, was omnipotent.

Confined to a hospital bed after a serious plane crash, Hughes dictated his frenzied demands via the phone; Preston Sturges would take over directing chores immediately. Ever the dreamer, I imagined the situation would improve. Hardly.

Sturges worked feverishly at first, often shooting 30 takes before yelling "Print!"

We waited, watched and worried. Even I could see that his doomed attempts to achieve perfection were hopeless. Each take just grew worse. As the cast grew more morose by the minute, we banded together like rats on a sinking ship. Misery loves company, and I never had so many newfound friends. Time continued to crawl by in a blur of horrendous boredom. By lunch we were ready to drop, but at least eight more hours of slavery remained. After one too many whiskey-sodden nights at his restaurant on the Sunset Strip, The Players, Sturges seemed to be sleepwalking, as out of control as the film itself. Naturally, Hughes hit the roof. He hated wasting money, especially on a project as cursed as this one. As the days progressed and Hughes' complaints grew more and more serious, Sturges tried to speed up the beleaguered schedule—but by then it was too late. *Vendetta* had self-destructed—and Preston was left holding the carcass.

Exactly why Sturges became so ambivalent about *Vendetta* is still a mystery to me. I doubt Howard's tantrums were the sole cause, for Sturges had endured tight-fisted producers dozens of times before. I personally feel his unprofessional behavior revolved around his then-recent divorce from his wife Louise. The bitter settlement reportedly included 50% of Preston's interest in California Pictures. In my opinion, smarting from Hughes' reprimands, Sturges decided to sabotage the film as a personal "vendetta" against not only Howard but Louise as well. Bad move.

There's little doubt that *Vendetta*'s failure at the box office would seriously jeopardize Louise's future income—but as usual, Sturges had completely underestimated Hughes. Instead of simply removing Preston from the film and allowing him to remain a controlling partner in California Pictures, Hughes played his trump card. On October 30, 1946, Preston Sturges was not only fired from *Vendetta* but removed from California Pictures. Sturges also removed himself from Hollywood, fleeing to Europe a short time later to escape the entire debacle. In the end everyone lost. *Vendetta* proved a fatal blow to the genius' once brilliant career—and in Hollywood, no one ever forgives an egomaniac with a flop.

Torn between completely scrapping *Vendetta*, hiring a third director to finish the Ophuls/Sturges version or simply starting over again from scratch, Hughes assembled a rough cut and screened it for a group of well-paid Hollywood troubleshooters. As the lights went down, he hoped for a miracle. When they came up, Armageddon was at hand. *Vendetta*, Howard was duly informed, was worse than anyone could possibly imagine. Equally devastating from a business and image standpoint, was the news that Hedda Hopper, through one of her minions, had the sordid scoop on this celluloid *Titanic*. Even worse, she had uncovered a few details about me as well.

Hedda Hopper—the Goddess of Millinery—had more hats than sense. Forever in the shadow of Louella Parsons, Hedda was forced to try harder. Unfortunately, in her desire to uncover the dirt, she helped destroy more careers than a dozen *Vendettas* combined. And I was one of them.

La Hopper retorted that one of Hughes' big finds—Richard Blackwell—was really Richard Selzer hiding behind a new nose-job, hairline-lift and Hurrell-like lighting. And since no one knew who the hell Richard Selzer was, Hedda reminded them: He was the washed-up Dead End Kid whose acting career had been deservedly damned. At first, Hughes paid no heed; he was in the Herculean process of bringing *Vendetta* back from the dead with a new director, new set and new script. But the big question was: Would he recast the movie, too? I got my answer soon enough.

As fate—and Hedda—would have it, none of us were destined for the remake except Faith and a few well-respected featured players—including Hillary Brooke and George Dolenz, who would later see his son Mickey shoot to superstardom as one of The Monkees. The rest of us weren't so lucky. We were handed pink slips as we entered the soundstage the next morning. Our dressing room doors had been locked and we were told to make a list of the valuables inside, for which Hughes would reimburse us.

Hughes was welcome to whatever I'd left behind. It was nothing compared to the hopes and dreams he'd taken from me. My contract had been dropped. This part would have been my first big break—a meaningful role in a major film—and I'd made the mistake of believing it was really going to happen. I couldn't kid myself anymore. I'd wasted years chasing rainbows, looking for that pot of gold, but it kept slipping through my fingers every time. Well, it all was over now. I couldn't do it again.

I'd always believed I was going somewhere, that someday I was going to make it. But I'd tried so hard—and lost—so many times that I wasn't even angry about it. I just felt numb. Driving back to the apartment in shock, I don't even remember how I got there. But when I arrived, Mother was away at work, and looking around at all the pathetic mementos of my so-called Hollywood career, a fury came over me. I started tearing up photos of myself, I emptied drawers and threw them out, I pulled all my clothes out of the closet and ripped them to pieces. Raging and weeping, I wanted to destroy everything that reminded me of Dick Ellis, the actor.

As Errol Flynn once said, "They've great respect for the dead in Hollywood—but none for the living."

The year was 1949—the end of a hope-dashed decade. But I didn't want to die. I just wanted to stop hurting. So I hid away, retreating to a tiny, one-room seaside hovel in Santa Monica, several miles from Malibu's Millionaire Row. Sun battered, a pale gray, with a rickety front porch that creaked louder than the Van Courtland elevator, my new beachfront dive was only a slight improvement over my cruise-ship cell. At least, I reasoned, I was above water— and just 40 feet from the sun-baked beach. I stayed there for a few weeks, drinking and gazing at the Pacific view— all white-capped waves, aqua skies and bronzed surfers. It was enough to make me forget that my future was a bewildering blank.

Like so many of the stars who occupied the privileged coastal canyons, I was determined to be somebody. I just didn't know who. Movies were out, I was too old to model, Las Vegas wouldn't have me and Broadway had turned its back. I entertained thoughts of reprising my gigolo days or becoming Hollywood's hottest milliner. But nothing really interested me. And then, as fate would have it, I met the man who was to quickly become my closest friend and business partner: Robert L. Spencer.

Starting Over— Again

I first met Spencer—I've never called him Robert—at the dazzling Club Gala in the fall of '49. Seated at the art deco bar, he seemed intelligent, charming and—on a far rarer level in the land of vipers—honest. Tall, slim, good-looking and gregarious, Spencer intrigued me. His background, so opposite from my own, stretched back hundreds of years—beginning in England, where the Spencer family was and still is one of the most prominent lineages in Britain. If you don't believe me, just ask Princess Diana.

The son of a building contractor, Spencer was born in Indianapolis in the early twenties. Although he enjoyed an upper-middle-class life, the Midwest offered little in terms of creative self-expression. He read every glamour magazine that flew off the press, went to the movies and dreamed of being part of a glittering social circuit. An article he read profiling the Duchess of Windsor and her entourage—including a personal hairdresser—inspired him to apply for a job at William H. Block, Indianapolis' finest hair salon. He was a quick study and soon outgrew his hometown, both personally and professionally.

Moving to Beverly Hills in 1944, he joined the staff of Saks Fifth Avenue and in less than a year had established himself as one of the hottest stylists in town—the new sensation of Wilshire Boulevard. Marlene Dietrich, Lady Elsie Mendel and Cobina Wright, Sr. were among his most opulent weekly clients—and his claim to fame in a name-dropping town. A familiar figure at the smartest soirees, he was a favorite escort for two other clients, the internationally famous society leaders Gloria Vanderbilt and her twin sister, Lady Thelma Furness, "the Morgan Sisters." Within five years he was financially secure and built a redwood cottage on Yoakum Drive in Benedict Canyon, a wild, wooded area in Beverly Hills famous for such former dwellers as Rudolf Valentino and Jean Harlow. His life was serene—until he met me.

The second time our paths crossed—at a Hollywood Hills party—I knew Spencer was going to be an important part of my life. Still broke and living on the beach, I accepted his invitation to share his home. After living in a single room, Spencer's home seemed as huge as the majestic Beverly Hills Hotel, rising in pink splendor a few minutes away. I felt safe and happy, and those early days on Yoakum Drive were the beginning of a 40-plus-year relationship that changed our lives forever. Somehow, I knew through Spencer that my destiny would change, and that, like other guideposts in my life, he represented the next step forward.

Life among the bougainvillea vines took a little getting used to. Our neighbors included Jayne Mansfield, Mamie Van Doren and other peroxided, cleavage-baring blondes. Up-and-coming UPI correspondent Vernon Scott lived directly across the serpentine road; he often stopped by for an impromptu dinner. Scott felt safe with us because Spencer was not only the best informed but the tightest-lipped hairdresser in Hollywood.

Another neighbor, Steve Cochran, was an actor I remember all too well. Star of such films as *Copacabana*, *White Heat* and *Love and Desire*, he epitomized the age-old Hollywood swinger. Muscular, intense and erotically handsome, he possessed a John Garfield-like magnetism that a bevy of stars, starlets and harlots found irresistible. His huge retreat on the hill witnessed a never-ending stream of female guests. So many cars flew up the street toward his lascivious lair that I assumed he was either throwing parties we weren't invited to or holding a wake for some unfortunate family member. I was wrong on both counts.

The Casanova of the Canyon, Cochran had a sex drive that knew no limit. Since sound carried quite clearly in the hills, my evenings were spent listening to the shrieks and moans that erupted with alarming frequency from his bedroom window. I felt like an unwilling participant in an audio orgy.

Of course, Steve did have a few mishaps in the scheduling department. I distinctly recall a frustrated Diana Barrymore, swathed in satin, pounding demonically on his door in the middle of the night—only to be turned away by Cochran, who was already busy in the bedroom. How do I know it was Diana Barrymore? The police arrived and recorded the incident.

Tragically, Steve's jazzy joyride of a life came to a melodramatic and mysterious end. After going on a short cruise in a private yacht with two of Hollywood's most desirable beauties, the boat disappeared, finally turning up later with Steve's body on board—dead. His guests claimed he had just died, but the coroner discovered he had been dead for some time. As for the cause of his demise, discrepancies still abound, and the mystery remains unsolved.

As we entered the fifties, Spencer and I began our personal management business. The Club Gala, we decided, would be the perfect launching pad for our future acts. The elegant nightclub, now the site of Spago, held a sentimental affection for us— romantic, glamorous, brimming with café society and lacquered luxury. Club Gala played host to Johnny Walsh, America's version of Noel Coward. I loved watching a tuxedoed Walsh perform in his scintillatingly chic way. Like me, he had a lousy voice; unlike me, he knew how to use it. Impeccable phrasing, superb arrangements and a fabulous sense of humor made Walsh legendary in the L.A. nightclub world. Years later, when I began appearing on television, I gratefully "borrowed" everything I could from Johnny's act. Bobby Short played the Club Gala, too—and I managed to pick up a few tips from him as well. If you're gonna steal, steal from the best.

Inspired, Spencer and I vowed to create what we jokingly called "Blackwell's House of Divas." We both loved female singers ranging from Piaf to Garland to Ethel Merman, so we decided to take frustrated unknowns and turn them into musical stars. I figured with Spencer's ability to beautify and my showbiz experience and manic energy, we could be a formidable team.

After a year of false starts with a bevy of doe-eyed wanna-bes who just couldn't cut the musical mustard, I discovered a 25-year-old chanteuse named Wanda Curtis at Bob Keith's Vocal Studio on La Cienega Boulevard.

Wanda wasn't conventionally beautiful—but she had the voice, drive and guts to make it in a bloodthirsty business. Before I signed her, I made it clear that if she really wanted to become a star, she would have to turn her life entirely over to me. Wanda would become my own creation...no outside opinions allowed. Bob Keith balked; he thought Wanda's short-cropped coiffure, scrubbed face and conventional interpretations of musical material were positively perfect. I thought the style was as passé as Keith himself, so with great opposition and daily temper tantrums, I set out, brush stroke by brush stroke, to turn Wanda into the success I knew she could be.

How Wanda survived what appeared to be sadistically endless training to which I subjected her still stupefies me. But the metamorphosis was awesome and breathtaking: A butterfly emerged from the cocoon. Both of us worked 'round the clock for weeks. I wanted to create through Wanda the kind of star I longed to be myself—every move a concerto, every glance a seduction, every note a magical memory.

As the weeks turned into months, Wanda still struggled, but still learned under my Svengali-like thumb, still believed in the glorious future I envisioned for her. Her once short, unfashionably drab hair had grown since I'd signed her, and we decided to dye it red—Lucille Ball bright. Wanda absolutely hated it; I didn't care. Audiences would react and remember. In the wardrobe department, I felt Wanda's clothes should mix high glamour and sexual magnetism. Since we were far from rich, I designed them myself, using any scrap of fabric I could find—mostly the drapes and bedspreads from the hotel rooms where we stayed on the road. Starting with netted hosiery and a bathing suit, I would wrap the material around Wanda, attaching it to the bodice or the waist, gathering it up in the back and allowing it to fall in soft folds all around her. Since we had to return the borrowed items without damage, the excess yardage was left to follow behind in an elegant train. As a master of illusion, I used flowers and bows to hide bulky clumps of fabric and possible errors of design. Occasionally caught up with a clip at the waist or a broach at the hip, the gowns were redraped and reused nightly at each performance.

The sensuous results worked so well that Wanda's gowns often received better reviews than her singing. With my new-found success I even crafted a daring, jeweled Merry Widow bra—four decades ahead of its time—for her to wear onstage during the finale.

Wanda screamed, "No!" but I pretended to be temporarily deaf.

As for the actual performance, I wanted her musical personality to constantly surprise, tease—and arouse. She was bold and brassy and sexy, so we reworked songs like "I'm Through with Love" into powerhouse passion plays; the overall effect was spellbindingly sensuous. For a closer, I thought "Swanee" would jolt the audience back to reality—and I turned out to be right.

Next, photographs—which had to be the height of old-fashioned Hollywood. The more shadows and airbrushing the better. I found Wally Seawell, who had studied with the great John Engstead. Wally was a genius. Like Engstead and Hollywood's other master, George Hurrell, Seawell's lighting was an art form unto itself. His portraits were ravishing, and Wanda needed one incredible, indelible, irreplaceable photograph. After a photo session was booked, I scraped together enough money for several beautiful gowns. The maneuvering was more than worth it: her photographs were guaranteed head-turners.

Wanda's career really began at a small San Diego club named Tops, an old drive-in converted into a showroom for performers breaking in Vegas-bound acts. I wrote her opening, which began with Wanda, dressed in a negligee, wandering onstage and answering the phone. Sitting down in a chaise lounge, she picked up the receiver and cooed as a maid appeared from stage left, carrying clothes for the performance.

"Marie, Marie," Wanda said with a smile. "My gown, my fur, my jewelry," and pointing to a tray holding two large bust pads, she winked and added, "Oh, yes, those, too." Then she hurried behind a screen and, as the overture played, began dressing for her grand entrance.

And grand it was—draped in blue velvet, blue fox, navy high heels and sapphires, she was an image of grace and glamour as she began to sing into the microphone, which I had garnished with one red rose.

As she tore into "Getting to Know You," I laughed to myself. How appropriate for both of us. "Getting to know you...getting to know all about you."

I wondered if Wanda ever really understood why I devoured her entire life with my demands, scoldings and tantrums. I treated her the way I would have treated myself: It takes enormous drive to reinvent talent and make it work for you. Wanda was learning that often exhausting lesson from someone who craved the spotlight and knew how to attract it. I couldn't make it happen for myself yet, so I found someone who could project what I thought was wonderful and magical about live performance. Wanda became my mirror into the inner me.

Before booking her into Club Gala, I threw a lavish press reception at the Hollywood Roosevelt Hotel—replete with vegetable-dyed, rainbow-hued poodles, rented jewelry, furs and, waiting to whisk her away after the poolside chat with reporters, a borrowed Rolls. The press fell hook, line and sequined sinker. My star was born.

In six months, Wanda nearly owned the L.A. nightclub circuit. With her trademark fresh flowers adorning the microphone, her lips shaded only the palest pink, her eyes sequin-sprayed, Wanda became someone else on-stage. The fans adored her, the critics raved.

Much to my pleasant surprise, our plans were progressing smoothly, the dominoes placed in perfect order, ready to fall on cue. But in a world ruled by Murphy's Law, a reversal of fortune loomed—in, of all godforsaken places, Argentina.

Argentina— Hello

What began as a simple, polite invitation for Wanda to play Argentina's famous Flamingo nightclub in Buenos Aires ended up being an absolute nightmare for everyone concerned. Of course, I had little knowledge of Argentine politics, although I had heard of its enigmatic ruler Juan Peron and his icon of a wife, Evita.

Juan Peron represented to me a rather mysterious symbol of hope to a people I quite frankly had little interest in. I had no idea he virtually controlled the entire country with militaristic zeal and a strange sense of psychological domination. He coerced the huge, ungovernable Argentine middle class into believing they were entitled by their birthright to wealth, luxury and power. Unfortunately, when the economy finally began to crumble and the Argentine people realized Peron's promises were impossible to achieve, chaos reigned. But during my unfortunate stay in Peron's fascist country, Argentina lived in a blissful state of ignorance, and of intolerance for anyone who dared question government policy.

Before Wanda flew to South America to begin her Flamingo engagement, the Argentines proved to be remarkably cooperative in every contractual request we made. A large advance was deposited to our bank; a guaranteed weekly salary, with escalating perks, was agreed upon; free lodging, maid service, transportation and food were also included in Wanda's textbook-thick contract. It looked too good to be true—and as the saying goes, it was.

Since very few Americans had ever played Argentina, due to its checkered political past, Wanda's arrival in 1954 made headlines throughout the country. An American artist playing an Argentine club was a real coup. I remained in the States, exultant over her biggest break so far, and Wanda's initial series of letters were filled with praise for the Argentine people. And her act was a smash. I was happy she was being taken care of. What she didn't know was that the agreed-upon deposits from the Flamingo Club owners had suddenly stopped. Weeks passed, and still no money.

I had a gut feeling Wanda was overpowered with the opulence and glamour. It was a world she had never known. She didn't even think about the fact that I wasn't receiving my percentage of her salary. For the first time in months, she was free of my Henry Higgins act and, like a prisoner leaving jail, was intoxicated with her sudden independence. I hated thinking she was being used for Peronist propaganda: "American Star Adores Argentina," that sort of thing. When Wanda's letters stopped arriving, I began to worry, and when my phone calls, letters and cables didn't go through, I panicked. Even Wanda's mother, who I barely knew, began inundating me with dozens of phone calls begging me to do something. I finally decided to visit the Argentine consulate, but that turned out to be useless. There seemed to be a communication problem whenever the phrase "Wanda's wages" was spoken. In a last-ditch effort to solve the mystery of Wanda's sudden lack of communication, and why our contract had been broken, I told Wanda's mother I'd fly to Argentina—if she'd pay for the ticket. She agreed. I contacted the Consulate and informed them of my plans, and then, like a fool, I flew right into the mouth of hell.

The flight was endless. Hours spent worrying whether Wanda was dead or alive left me as tautly wound as a caged cobra as I stepped off the plane. Obtaining my police pass to enter Buenos Aires made me shiver. A mere slip of paper separated me from the thousands of Argentine citizens who were rigidly controlled and manipulated by a government on the verge of disaster. Inflation was mind-boggling. Peron, desperate, began policing the country relentlessly, looking for any sign of upheaval. He knew the end was coming. And everywhere I turned—like a bad joke—the benevolent face of Evita smiled down from a thousand life-size posters.

With armed guards watching my every move, entering customs was terrifying. I clutched my luggage and peered through a steel mesh screen into the greeting area beyond, searching for Wanda in the vast throng of expressionless faces. But who knew if the consulate had even informed her of my impromptu plans to pay her a visit? I scanned faces over and over, looking for her familiar smile. Then, suddenly, a flash of scarlet hair, followed by a shout: "Blackwell!"

There stood Wanda, followed by four absolutely magnificent examples of South American masculinity. Looking like a queen, she was breathtakingly beautiful, tanned, relaxed, seemingly oblivious to her problems. Everything I had ever hoped for and dreamed for her was standing in front of me. Her smile, though, was tight-lipped and guarded. I felt reluctance as she embraced me; something was wrong. Was she angry at me for bursting her idyllic bubble? Or was she putting on a brave front for her escorts—most likely government employees? I'd have to wait until we were alone to find out.

We drove to her apartment in an elegant black limousine. She spoke nonstop about the show, the great reviews, the "bravas" that punctuated each song. Avoiding my stare, she rattled on about everything but the real reason I was there. By this time I realized we were being watched, and her "escorts" listened in insufferable silence.

Her apartment, located in a chic high-rise hotel, was an ode to opulence: hand-carved furniture, gold fixtures, elaborate molding, lots of fine art. Silent servants stood stiffly in her marble-floored living room, which boasted a sweeping view of Buenos Aires below. Obviously, Wanda wasn't as destitute as I'd imagined. After walking through the palatial home she so grandly inhabited, jealousy was welling up inside me, and I could barely hold my temper. But one glance at the bronzed bodyguards who still surrounded her quickly convinced me otherwise. When we had a chance to be alone, I reasoned, I'd discover what was really going on in all this oasis-like splendor.

Hours later, Wanda arrived at my suite—a sparsely furnished two-room apartment located directly above her own luxurious quarters. One look at her frightened face and I understood why she had been so maddeningly cavalier at the airport. Wanda was petrified. As tears streamed down her face, she admitted that none of the entertainers had received any wages—but due to the precarious political situation, no one dared to complain. If she did, her police pass would be confiscated. God knows what would happen then—most likely jail. Her lavish apartment, she admitted between sobs, was owned by the government—nothing more than an ornate cage. As she paced the room like a caged tiger, I dramatically informed her that I'd take care of everything.

I hoped Wanda's evening performance would prove to be a welcome relief from a disaster of a day. The Flamingo, considered the premier talent showcase in all of South America, was a triple-tiered cabaret magnificently appointed in deep reds and burnished gold. As I waited for Wanda to appear, I noticed huge crystal chandeliers hanging from a hand-painted, Botticelli-like ceiling. Elegant sconces, shaped like crystal flower bouquets, studded the silk-slung walls, and directly ahead, I saw a sheer chiffon curtain sprayed with a thousand sequined stars slowly begin to open.

A line of dancers emerged, incredibly costumed in glittering, color-drenched outfits that rivaled the Folies Bergère in sheer extravagance of material and design. Next, the showgirls appeared in diaphanous mesh. Statuesque and stunning, they were the most beautiful group of women I'd ever seen. Nothing on Broadway compared, but at this point I didn't care. America had other, more important advantages—like democratic freedom, for starters. As cymbals crashed for startling effect, Wanda, in a flash of scarlet silk, stepped onstage to wildly enthusiastic applause. As she launched into "Getting to Know You," I felt a curious cross of pride and envy. I wished it were me up there under the lights.

I didn't mourn too long over my own lackluster performing career; my thoughts were occupied in concocting a surprise attack on the owners of the Flamingo Club. After the show ended, I decided to call a group meeting and suggest that everyone in the show strike for their back wages—something unheard of in a dictatorship. When only a few sad souls were left in the dark corners of the bar, floating in their gin and tonics, Wanda and the other entertainers crowded around me in a quiet back room. Having changed to their street clothes, makeup removed, there was no mistaking the fear that clung around them like a wet garment. As we stood under the flickering light, I watched their faces drain of color as I explained my plan. As they slowly realized the enormity of what I was saying, I heard gasps and frightened whispers questioning my sanity. I tried to make clear that such a strike would receive a great deal of publicity—but they didn't buy it. Finally, in desperation, I vowed to be the spokesman, stand in front and make the demands. Only after they realized I was willing to go the dangerous distance did they agree. Holding a strike was truly a revolutionary act in a country like Argentina. None of us knew what the consequences would be—but we all finally agreed to make our stand at the first show the following night.

The next evening, the Flamingo was filled to capacity. We waited backstage, frozen; the deafening sound of our wildly beating hearts was overpowering. The first bars of the overture began, the curtain parted, the house lights dimmed and the audience waited in hushed anticipation. No one moved in the wings as a giant spotlight hit the empty stage. Murmurs from the crowd grew louder. The entertainers looked grim, sweat beginning to bead on their foreheads. As everyone's eyes darted furtively around the room, we silently nodded to one other, offering encouragement as our stomachs churned in protest, waiting for the first weak-willed member to run onstage. Miraculously, no one moved. Their courage astounded me.

The stage remained empty. The audience started stamping their feet in protest. I knew as sharp "boos" began to erupt from the crowd that we were enraging a very prestigious group; only the most prominent citizens and politicians had the money to attend the Flamingo's nightly galas—a group, no doubt, that included former Nazis who had fled to Argentina after the war. The repercussions seemed horrific.

I motioned for everyone backstage to keep calm as the curtain finally dropped and the house lights were turned up. As the glittering black-tie crowd exited, the Flamingo owners, surrounded by three beady-eyed security guards, raced backstage, demanding to know who was responsible for this outrageous and illegal act. Sweat poured down my body. Stepping forward, I managed to stammer that I was—and furthermore, we were prepared to strike for nonpayment of wages. Visualizing a sudden and swift death, I grabbed a disbelieving Wanda and ran to the dressing rooms.

Mass pandemonium followed. Screams. Crashing props. Shouts for the police. And then, as Wanda and I hid behind the mirrored walls of a rehearsal room, the door flew open—and the Flamingo manager, with two thugs, bolted toward us. I couldn't believe it. In a sudden, irrational rage, I picked up a chair and started swinging wildly as North and South American curses blended into one ear-shattering frenzy. After Wanda smashed a lamp over a startled goon's head, we made a beeline for the auditorium, where a veritable riot was taking place.

On our way out, we saw that the entire backstage area had been destroyed. Shattered glass, trampled costumes and broken props lay in ravaged heaps on the littered floor. The arriving police at first were no match for the outraged strikers. Pushing Wanda in front of me for protection—yes, my courage had evaporated—we escaped through a side door, fled down crooked back streets and found ourselves laughing so hard we literally cried. Watching Wanda cream that thug had been pure classic comedy. Unfortunately, this was no movie, and tomorrow promised to be a black day indeed.

Wanda's apartment seemed quiet and safe, but both of us hesitated uneasily as we slowly opened the door, revealing shadowy stillness beyond. I whispered that the police could be waiting. She slowly reached up to the light switch and flipped it on, prepared to scream. Both of us imagined the place had been ransacked, or worse, we would be placed under arrest. But no one was there—yet.

Running on borrowed time, I dashed to the International Wire Service near the hotel. There, in a stroke of profound luck, I presented my hastily scribbled story to an inebriated operator.

Thank God he's drunk, I thought. Outgoing cables were usually censored; one as inflammatory as mine, under any other circumstances, would have been destroyed. But this guy was too smashed to care—or even read—so he sent my cable to the States. Now all I could do was wait, hope and pray.

I managed to sneak back into my hotel room without being seen. The bedside clock read 4:30 A.M. Darkness still shrouded the streets of Buenos Aires. Too keyed up to sleep, I sat and stared into the bleak blackness beyond my window, regretting the whole ugly, ridiculous incident. What the hell had I started? I began to realize—far too late—that democratic principles meant nothing under Peron's iron-fisted regime.

I began to doze off until a sharp rapping sound startled me. Someone was pounding at my door—and it sounded like thunder. With a sickening crack, the door burst open—and the Argentine police swept in, shouting, cursing and pointing at me with fiery hatred.

"Mr. Blackwell? Richard Blackwell?" a depressingly dark-suited officer barked. His voice sliced like a knife.

"Yes, I'm Richard Blackwell." No sense in lying. They knew who I was and what I'd done.

"You are under arrest."

The words flattened me like a hammer through my skull. "For what?"

"Illegal narcotics, inciting a riot. Shall I continue?" He smiled, satisfied.

"But that's ridiculous!" I shouted.

Still grinning, the officer held up a packet of white powder and waved it in my face.

"This is yours, no?"

"No! No! No!" I yelled. "You've put this here! It isn't mine!" I felt like I was strangling.

I was handcuffed, led out of the room and down the hotel's main flight of stairs into a waiting car. Oh, God, I was scared. Scared and alone.

Back in Beverly Hills, Spencer, as was his usual custom, walked into Milton Kreiss' drugstore in the Beverly Wilshire Hotel to have his morning coffee. Picking up the *L.A. Daily News* on the counter, bold headlines screamed: SINGER SOCKS MANAGER IN ARGENTINE NIGHTCLUB!

Confused over the way the accompanying story was written, Spencer thought Wanda had attacked me—since he was accustomed to our usual fighting. After calling the Argentine Consulate in Washington, the situation, to his horror, was clarified. He listened incredulously, unable to fathom what I'd done. Inciting a strike and drug possession weren't qualities that he was accustomed to in my day-to-day behavior back home. Frightened, he asked what could be done.

"We really can't interfere," was the reply. "Our families live there." After pressing them further, they added ominously, "Pray. Pray very hard."

Spencer found out what I had already discovered: In Argentina, Juan Peron had his own set of rules.

My hands fought in vain to break free from the handcuffs behind my doubled-over back. As the police held me down in the backseat of the car, we sped toward...I was afraid to ask where. My mouth was bone dry, my throat raw and my body ached. Brutal pain shot through my arm as a club slammed down on my wrist. A barrage of questions followed, then laughter, cruel and cutting. I managed to raise my head up toward the car window. Dawn had come. Shoeshine boys sat against mud-caked walls, staring at us as we drove by. My hands were numb, turning dark red, then purple, like a rotting tomato threatening to burst. The thick steel bands grew tighter as I struggled, slicing my skin, grinding. In the front seat, someone mumbled that my room had been sealed. Everything I had would be confiscated. I didn't care. I thought I was about to die.

Faces filled the streets as we turned onto a busy boulevard. Men and women walked by the row of small stores, children played happily along the sidewalk, a frisky terrier chased a passing car—all oblivious to my pain. I wanted to smash the window and cry out for help, but it was useless. Only the sounds of taunting police filled the car as we drove toward doom.

We made a sharp right into an alley. On my left, a huge granite building loomed, dark and officious. The car crept through a covered arcade past military officers marching in pairs. Black iron gates opened and we made our way toward a side entrance and stopped. My body was shaking.

I was hustled into what appeared to be a huge empty room. The handcuffs were unlocked. A chair, kicked in my direction, enabled me to sit—no doubt for an interrogation. My wrists were bloody, bruised; my back knotted in burning bursts of excruciating pain. I knew they were watching me, so I tried to cover my face, now swollen and scratched from their beatings. I hated thinking how pleased they must be seeing me like this, reduced to nothing more than a trapped animal, squirming in fear.

I waited for what seemed like hours before my interrogator entered the room: an oily, black-eyed beast—the devil himself, I thought. Four young assistants surrounded him, holding various folders stuffed with government forms and documents. A thousand questions followed: who I was, why I was here, what I had done, why I had to be punished. I finally stopped trying to defend myself. My fate had already been decided.

"You have no right to come here and interfere with our people," the official spat. "No right whatsoever. Striking is no way to collect salaries—salaries which have been paid. And then there's this matter of narcotic possession."

The trumped-up accusations droned on and on. I gave up caring—or even listening. Instead, I wondered if this hellish place was Casa Rosada, Peron's palace. Even through my daze, I realized no police station looked like this—so huge and ornate, judging from what I had seen when we arrived. My mind clicked. Perhaps my interrogator was Peron himself. I'll never know. But I believe it was.

His orders were given with venom: "Take him to the caves."

The caves were often spoken of as hell on earth, the

Argentine Devil's Island. No one has been known to return from there. Leaving Buenos Aires, the land became flatter as the truck rumbled past the thick pampas grass that grew beside the road. We stopped nearly an hour later in a rocky, barren compound. Crude stone cells had been carved from tall granite boulders, jutting out of the parched earth like rotting tusks. A row of iron-grated doors revealed only darkness within.

A guard led me from the truck toward my cell. I struggled to glimpse a face, even a pair of eyes, within the gray crypts ahead—but I saw nothing. I seemed to be alone. He pushed me into a black pit and padlocked the door. My eyes squinted, and slowly I began to see what lay on the floor: the shadowy outline of a grass mat and something moving along the side of the wall. I wanted to scream. Rats. More than one, scampering about, squealing in spine-chilling shrieks. Their teeth looked yellow, the skin dark, scabbed and infested. And the stench was unbearable. Obscene. I finally broke down and cried. The hole carved out of the mountain grew darker and darker, closing in around me as I crouched in a corner.

I never saw a soul except the guard—a giant of a man, bearded, perpetually coated in grimy sweat. His hands, arms and bear-like neck were covered with wiry black hair. Ape-like, sub-human, he was a monster with the perverted power to keep me here forever.

Meals were nothing more than a pan of water and slices of moldy bread. My toilet was the packed dirt I slept on. I imagined myself growing old in this rat-infested hole—just another stupid American with a cause.

Now that I was accustomed to the darkness, I could see the moonlight streaming through my barred door. Outside, the wind whistled around the rocks and sent gusts of cool air into my cell. The dirt smelled rancid—moist, dank, putrid. I was so thirsty my throat swallowed involuntarily, like a machine. My split lips felt sticky. They burned when I ran my tongue over their crusted surface. My head pounded, muscles knotted, vision blurred. But through the iron bars, in the eerie glow of a pale moon, I could see all the way into the flat yard beyond.

To my left, the guard stood like a stone statue watching the cells. He was not alone. I heard him speaking to someone I couldn't see. Whispers, a short chuckle, the metallic rattle of keys—and then silence. Minutes later, the guard suddenly appeared in the moonlight again, followed by someone whose face still remained cloaked in shadow. When I saw who it was, I gasped. Peter, Wanda's dancer, was moving across the yard with the guard.

Oh, no! What have I done?

It was one thing to be brought here myself. I was the one who had incited the strike. It was my fault that a riot had taken place. But to be responsible for the imprisonment of others! How could I live with myself? How naive could I have been? How many more would be brought here?

I envisioned the small stone cells occupied by Wanda and the other Flamingo entertainers. Despair welled inside me—and then I heard my cell door creak open.

What was going on? They couldn't possibly think two of us could fit in here! A hand reached in to help me up. I felt lightheaded. Were they going to let me go? And then a ball formed in the pit of my stomach. Were they going to execute me?

Filled with apprehension, I followed the guard outside. My head hung low. I was defeated. He led me to a small table. I looked up and saw Peter standing stiffly beside it, clutching a folder of papers. He and the guard said little as they handed me several official-looking documents and motioned for me to sign them, which I tried to do as fast as possible. I could barely hold the pen. I thought at first that I was hallucinating—but somehow Peter had gotten me out. I searched his face for a clue, but his stern look warned me not to ask why or how.

I never knew the price he paid—but watching his sadly etched face, I knew. He had no reason to help me. In fact, I had created a deadly situation that threatened his very future. But he was young, kind and impressionable. He must have realized I was trying to help, as misguided as that had turned out to be.

Through his contacts, I was allowed to return to the United States that same evening—on a cramped cargo plane that seemed to me the most wonderful place on earth. Before I boarded, I thanked him again and again for saving my life. But words would never be enough. How could I ever thank him for what he did for me? But how I wished I could do something, anything, in return. When I stepped on board, I literally felt as if I'd been given a second chance to make something of my life. Of course, I was told I'd never be allowed to return to Buenos Aires—as if I'd try—nor would I be allowed to contact Wanda. I agreed to everything. As the hatch finally closed, an indescribable feeling of peace overcame me. I was leaving Argentina, alive and on two feet.

I spent the long flight back to Los Angeles in shock. I clung to my dog-eared passport as if it were a life preserver with no land in sight. I sat huddled between two large dusty crates, rocking gently to the rhythm of the plane's engines. Sitting wide-eyed, I could vividly hear the guard's gruff voice and the clang of my cell door slamming shut over and over again.

When we landed, I stretched my stiff limbs and climbed out of the small plane, greedily gulping down deep breaths of air. I was exhilarated to be back home, never happier to be an American, understanding for the first time what it really meant to be free.

The pilot handed me some change to get home. He had known the horrors I had been through. Little was said on that long journey, but as I left, he wished me good luck. The money was enough to get me most of the way home by bus, and I walked the remaining few blocks to the house. Spencer, who'd spent weeks on the phone, desperately trying to discover my whereabouts, couldn't believe it when I walked in and shouted out his name. He thought he would never see me again, dead or alive.

We talked deep into the night. Sitting by the crackling fire, sipping warm brandy, the whole episode felt more and more like a bad dream slowly slipping away with the early morning light. But I knew I would be haunted by nightmares for years to come. Sometimes, even now, when I least expect it, the jangling of keys, the creaking of hinges, the sound of a gate slamming shut brings it all back with startling clarity.

It would be days before I could even think beyond what had happened. Spencer and I needed time to rediscover each other, to appreciate life and be thankful for every minute of it. It was a time for soul searching, for getting our priorities straight, for realizing what was truly important in our lives—and in ourselves.

After some time, we came to the conclusion that life was way too short to exist vicariously through others. Personal management was another venture best left in the past.

> If I was going to spend time, energy
> and imagination on someone's life,
> it was going to be mine.

I soon found out I had become a kind of hero to the various unions across the country. The American Federation of Labor wanted to present me with a citation for courageous and heroic behavior for my exploits in Argentina. I refused. I was terrified Peron would punish the Flamingo entertainers if I allowed the media to shower me with publicity.

I received a smuggled letter from Wanda—who stayed in Argentina for many years after my escape. She wrote that Peter had been killed, mowed down by a battery of gunfire while fighting Peronist police. Wanda wrote he died almost instantly, without any suffering, for which I thank God.

After months of self-reflection, I decided to actively take part in my future again. So I began the toughest transition of my life...

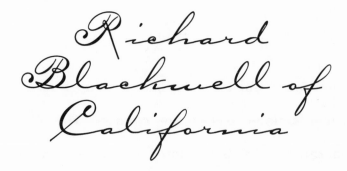

Richard Blackwell of California

I tried waiting tables for a day, but I was too vocal, and certainly not subservient. I sold used cars—that lasted a week. Too humiliating. Then came five hours in counter sales at a department store—but I couldn't be a soldier in the army of a controlled society. With Spencer's encouragement, I finally decided to try my hand at design. After all, it was the only thing they couldn't prove I couldn't do.

Recalling the remarkable reviews Wanda had received for the elegantly flowing gowns I had creatively wrapped around her, I gathered up all the photographs and press clippings I could find and assembled a wafer thin, but promising, portfolio. Armed with this little scrapbook, as well as an endless supply of stories, I hit the streets of the fashion jungle. High-rise buildings towered above, separated by one-story businesses catering to the needs of the industry around me—buttons, zippers, trimmings, anything and everything the "young and the restless" fashion business needed. For weeks I walked up and down the bustling streets of L.A.'s garment district, knocking on virtually every door.

I was turned away countless times.

"I'm sorry, we're not hiring at this time."

"Oh, the person you need to see isn't in today. Come back next week."

And then when I did: "Oh, I'm sorry, he isn't in again today." Does he even work here?

"Leave your resume, we'll call." Where have I heard this before?

"Where else have you worked?"

I was just about to call it a day one scorching afternoon and go home when I noticed an unassuming sign: MAHLER BELTS.

Oh, why not, I thought. One more stop isn't going to kill me. Little did I know.

The owner was a pint-sized egomaniac with a severe Napoleonic complex who openly hated my portfolio and I suspect me as well.

"These dresses are terrible," he screamed, and then added along with a string of obscenities that I'd never make it as a designer.

"What else do you do?" he asked as an afterthought.

Not having any other ideas, I told him I could custom-design jeweled dog collars. The Doris Day classic *April in Paris* had recently hit the movie circuit and was reminiscent of my days with Wanda when I had dyed dozens of poodles in rainbow colors. Sensing that custom dog collars were soon to be the rage, I managed to get quite excited at the prospect.

"You'll be a millionaire in a month!" I raved.

Mahler wasn't impressed.

"Ridiculous!" he yelled, waving his arms like a monkey on Benzedrine.

"What do you mean ridiculous? This is the wave of the future," I enthused.

"That's the stupidest thing I've ever heard. But I'll go ahead and let you try designing belts, and if you're lucky, checkbook covers. That's it! Take it or leave it."

I reluctantly agreed—not knowing that we were to both rue the day.

Designing belts and checkbook covers—yes, I was "lucky" enough to graduate to that exalted designing peak—was a total bore, but I tried to inject as much style as I could into Mahler's mundane products. After he saw some of the work I'd done, I was "elevated" to designing toilet-seat covers. I was totally humiliated and had zero interest in pursuing this particular design area, but my goals were meaningless in Mahler's autocratic kingdom. I did as I was told—or yelled at, in his case. Just to prove I could create art out of anything, I poured my soul into designing the most gorgeous toilet-seat covers known to man. If I wowed him with these ridiculous accessories, I figured he'd be forced to take me seriously.

To make these toilet-seat sensations, I took ruffled, colored net and stitched the fabric onto a heavy, commode-contoured cotton base. The effect was not unlike a rainbow as I laid them side by side in the cavernous workroom of Mahler's tomb of terror. For the finishing touch, a sprinkling of rhinestones were sewn into the filmy net. I thought my toilet-seat covers were absolutely beautiful, but Mahler, as usual, disagreed.

He had to eat his arrogant words when a buyer from a major lower-priced department store chain saw my bathroom bonanzas and flipped—ordering them by the thousands. My jaw dropped in amazement as Mahler, dollar signs swimming in his greedy eyes, asked me to design another line. Unfortunately, my brief success was doomed. After a month of sellout business, customers began returning the covers in droves, saying the sharp stones that decorated the net cut into areas of the anatomy seldom seen by the sun. In other words, their asses looked like the Marquis de Sade had made a sudden return. And speaking of returns, nearly 10,000 of my ravishing, razor-sharp butt busters flooded back into Mahler's shipping department. He was stuck with the bill and the professional embarrassment.

"You're gonna pay for every single one of these damn mistakes! You hear me? Every single one," he bellowed. "I don't know why the hell I ever hired you in the first place!"

To save my job, I racked my brain for solutions and finally decided to use the rejected merchandise as headgear—an idea spawned at a drive-in in Santa Monica where the waitresses wore huge curlers in their hair, pitifully covered with skimpy scarves. What they needed was a stylish curler cap—and boy, did I have just the thing. One size fits all. All you have to do is pull the string.

My "Bird of Paradise" curler caps were a hit with every waitress at every drive-in this side of Azusa, and trust me, I should know. I personally went to every one, peddling my wares in a presentation Howard Hughes would have been proud of. God knows I wasn't. I convinced the ladies who lunch—make that the ladies who brought lunch—that my fabulous designs would make them all look like Ziegfeld Girls.

The beachside drive-ins of Southern California exploded in color. I sold nearly every one, with lots of additional orders arriving from women who saw the headdresses and just had to have a personal toilet-seat cover to wrap around their noggin. We all know how crazy fashion fads can be. Let it never be said I was above perpetrating outlandish schlock on the American woman. The only difference was that I felt horribly guilt-stricken about doing it. But the Mahlers of the world could have cared less as long as the ledgers were written in black ink—not red.

Materialistic Mahler was so impressed with my business savvy that he actually smiled—once. I thought the world might end. I assumed that after proving myself with the "Bird of Paradise" bonanza, he'd finally allow me to design actual garments. I must have been dreaming.

"Hell, no!" was the deafening reply. "Stick with what you do best."

I didn't want to ask what that was.

Screw Irving Mahler, I thought. I'll create my own dress collection without his holy approval. After dropping hints that several other manufacturers had fallen in love with my work and were literally begging me to join their firms, I ran up to the Sunset Strip, bought eighteen yards of black wool jersey, located a wonderful woman who was a maestro on the sewing machine and started designing my first "collection." To be honest, it really wasn't a collection at all. It was more like six dresses whipped up in a tiny alteration room above a discount beauty shop.

I racked my brain thinking about the style of the dresses. In a fashion scene of chemises that were beyond boring, I wanted my line to be simple, sexy and elegant. I created what I thought was a dynamite dress that curved over the body beautifully, while the jersey material enabled me to have a product that basically fit all sizes. Satisfied, I packed the dresses in bags, hauled them into Mahler's workshop and hung them conspicuously on a rack in his office. I waited, and waited, and waited. No comment. His technique of intimidation still worked overtime.

Flat broke—all my savings had gone to pay for the material and the seamstress—I left work and took a long walk. While I was out, Mahler phoned a nearby fashion buyer and showed her my work. Obviously, her verdict was great, because by the time I returned Mr. Monster had suddenly turned into Mr. Congeniality.

"Enjoy your walk?" he drawled as I slipped through the door, hoping to avoid one of his "You've been gone for two damn hours" diatribes.

"What?" I could scarcely believe my ears. I looked around to see if he was actually speaking to me. He was.

"I said," he slowly repeated, "did you enjoy your walk?" His voice positively dripped with fatherly concern.

"Well, as far as walks in the garment district go, I guess I did."

"Good! Because now you've got a lot of work to do."

"Look, Mr. Mahler—"

"I've decided to give you a big break," he interrupted. Then, pausing for effect, he boomed, "Those dresses of yours are just what America needs."

"They are?"

"Hell, yes! But you've gotta get busy…I want 'em ready for the fall season."

He smiled one of his precedent-setting half-cocked grins and waited for me to respond. I made the bastard wait. After working for Mahler for over a year, I was finally in the driver's seat, and it felt great. I decided to go for broke.

"I don't think I can do that, Mr. Mahler."

"Why the hell not?" he rasped, the grin quickly sliding off his pigface.

"Because I've gotten another offer. I've decided to take it."

"What offer are you talking about?"

"Well," I replied haughtily, "they're planning to give me half of the business—and creative control."

"I don't give a damn what they're planning to give you. I'll match their offer, dime for dime."

"I suppose I do owe you—"

"You're damn right you do! Anyone else would have fired your ass after that toilet-seat fiasco."

"But does this mean," I asked in mock innocence, "that you want me to sign a contract?"

"Hell, yes! What do you think we've been talking about for the past ten minutes?"

After naming my price—and enduring another stream of obscenities—he drew up the papers and signed his infamous name on the dotted line. And, though it was a forced delivery, "Richard Blackwell of California" was born.

The details of design were a complete mystery to me. I simply made dresses in an assortment of sizes and prayed for the best. My prayers were partially answered. Although none of the garments fit properly, the feminine, high necked, body-hugging collection became so popular that the various stores that purchased the line altered the dresses themselves. No returns. Great reviews. Mahler, to my utter shock, dubbed my efforts a "smash." I was on a high that lasted for months—until the time came to whip up a new collection.

We had been besieged with phone calls requesting scoop necklines, which I thought would be relatively simple to accomplish; I cut out the necks of my previous line in a semicircle. After shipping the dresses to my buyers, I discovered, through a barrage of customer protests, that one doesn't just cut out a neck; the dress falls to pieces. I had no idea that dress patterns, to accommodate a different neckline, must be totally reshaped. The unlucky women who bought my scooped dresses found out the hard way. Along with the occasional bared shoulder, they exposed a few bare breasts as well. Needless to say, they were not amused, and neither was Mahler.

Seething with rage, he ranted, raved, threatened, screamed and cried for hours. Finally, after he had exhausted every four-letter word in a variety of languages, he demanded that I straighten out the whole horrendous mess.

"But I don't know how."

"You damn well better learn! Clean up this mess or else!"

Terrified yet angry over his venomous assault, I resorted to my own way of coping with failure: I simply became hysterical and had one of my first infamous Blackwell tantrums. Spotting the cage of over a hundred parakeets he kept for decorative effect, I unlatched the door and let them fly.

Chaos reigned as the flock of chirping birds left little white polka dots on their way throughout the showroom—ruining every black jersey dress in sight. Mahler, neck veins bulging, was apoplectic. I then grabbed my dress patterns, ripped them to shreds, turned on the water faucets in the adjacent bathroom, flooded the floor and—in a final act of vengeance—smashed the mirrors. I raced out of the godforsaken dump and never saw him again. As you might have already guessed, "Richard Blackwell of California" was finished. But Richard Blackwell, the person, was just getting started. Even though Mahler spread the most malicious gossip about me to every fashion industry member he knew, I continued to look for work. Promises from "friends" were made and broken. I visited dozens of manufacturers who, over dinner for two, offered me hypocritical smiles and, more often than not, their house keys pressed discreetly into the pocket of my pants.

"No dice," I informed them in a loud voice. I had given up decorating bedrooms ages ago.

Thank God for Spencer. He continued to help me financially, but for how long? I didn't know—and I wasn't about to ask. What I did know was that our savings were rapidly dwindling due to my jobless status, and to make matters even more complicated, he decided to buy another home, larger and more suited to our tastes, on Braeridge Drive in Beverly Hills.

Our new neighborhood wasn't your everyday casual cul-de-sac—not with Ann Miller, acting coach extraordinaire Michael Chekhov, and Tony Curtis, with his wife Janet Leigh, living nearby. I felt like a minnow in a sea of celebrated sharks. And then there was the day I took a stroll past Michael Chekhov's ranch-style house and spotted a rather plain-looking girl dressed in faded jeans and red kerchief, standing in the yard, obviously waiting for a tardy Chekhov to arrive back home. In those days, strangers actually spoke to one another, which is what I did in an off-handed way as I walked past.

She purred "Hi," asked if I knew where Michael was—I didn't—and proceeded to carry on a brief but delightful conversation.

After several minutes of innocuous small talk, I left, feeling a bit guilty about leaving her to wait all alone in Chekhov's yard. It wasn't until I got home that I realized the simple, sweet-voiced girl with the childlike eyes was none other than Marilyn Monroe.

In 1957 I interviewed for a job with Arthur Pines, owner of Pines of California. Originally founded as a petticoat manufacturer, Pines wanted to expand into outerwear—dresses, coats and matching hats. Although he offered me a position, I hated him on sight. He seemed to have studied etiquette at the Irving Mahler School of Sadists. Still, beggars can't be choosers, so I reluctantly accepted a minuscule salary—$125 a week—to start, hoping to pull myself out of the emotional mire I'd sunk into after working for Mahler.

Pines turned out to be a vicious, violent, mean-spirited oaf who kept a loaded gun in his desk. If possible, he was even more hostile and ill-tempered than my former employer. He knew he had me in a no-win situation and strung me along for nearly eleven months without paying me my full salary. Finally, after Spencer forced me to confront the tightfisted tyrant, I walked into Pines' office and demanded my back salary. If my final confrontation with Mahler was high drama, this one was positively epic in scope.

After screaming that designers were "too stupid" to be paid—and that he had donated my salary to his favorite charity—I quit on the spot. Infuriated, he lurched up from behind his desk, raced toward me, shoved me into the hallway and down the flight of steps toward the parking lot.

That's where all hell broke loose. As fists flew, my car keys fell out of my pocket and scattered across the cement. Now completely over the edge, Pines scooped them up and ran over to my car, which he proceeded to start and back into a low brick wall. In absolute amazement, I watched him ram the car into the ledge, shattering glass in a loud crunch of broken taillights and battered fenders. He jerked the vehicle in drive, veered in my direction and finally slammed on the brakes, stopping a few short feet from where I stood, shaking. To this day I still don't remember how I managed to drive my ravaged car all the way home to the Hills. I would never see Arthur Pines again. But I did visit the Los Angeles District Attorney the following day to prosecute. I wanted revenge in spades.

Unfortunately, it was his word against mine. And then there was the negative publicity factor—which Spencer pointed out was the last thing I needed. After much protest, I dropped the charges. As bitter as I was over this latest fiasco, I learned a lesson; I wasn't cut out for partnerships with repressed Godzillas. If I wanted to be successful, I'd have to do it on my own. With Spencer by my side, I said to hell with the Arthur Pines and Irving Mahlers who dominated my fashion world. We'd go it alone—and if I had anything to say about it, we'd have the last laugh. Or die trying.

And 1957 drew to a welcome close...

And so, again I was moving on to a new facet of my life. With $8,000, most of it begged, borrowed and practically stolen, Spencer and I were about to launch a new line of clothes—my own. We found an office in the heart of L.A.'s garment district and set up shop. I knew that if I was to become a fashion designer, I'd soon be labeled with all of the clichés: talented and temperamental, nervous and neurotic, elegant and effete. I wanted to be one step ahead of the critics, so I decided to create the ultimate fashion peacock.

I needed to "design" someone who would be an enigma to the sane and civilized, someone who would outrage, yet with equal vitality be sensitive and warm, someone who was sharp-tongued and controversial, someone who always went just a bit too far. I would create for the world exactly what they wanted—only more.

Shakespeare once said, "All the world's a stage, and all the men and women merely players." I was soon to be playing another part, and it would turn out to be the longest-running and most successful role in my checkered career: MR. BLACKWELL.

Introducing... Mr. Blackwell

In the clothing business, the practice of labeling goes far beyond sewing a simple swatch in the back of a dress. After all, those slips of fabric are usually just an ego boost for the doubtful designer. Most reasonable women admire the look of a dress long before they check to see who's autographed the neck. But those signatures in silk are labels I can live with. The labels attached to people are different—the ones acquired just because of how you look or what you do for a living. Whether it's driving a truck or designing clothes, there's a label just for you.

Since I knew I, too, would be stereotyped, I decided to perform the part crazier and campier, bigger and brighter, larger and louder than anyone else. God may have created man—but I created Mr. Blackwell. I wondered if I could ever accept the role I was destined to play, but I knew it was necessary to become a success.

I had a blank script to work with. Like a writer creating a character or a painter brushing life onto bare canvas, I began the transformation. I stood in my bedroom, surrounded by mirrors, and turned round and round, spinning with excitement. I loved the idea of changing into someone new, developing a facet of my personality to elaborate, outrageous proportions. Everything had to be larger than life. Overstated, overdone. If the fashion designer stereotype intrigued, then Mr. Blackwell would shock. One step further than anyone else. The concept, at least, was promising. But the set remained undressed, the lines unwritten, the costumes unmade. I had a lot of rehearsing to do.

I started with the clothes. Normal tweeds and subtle colors were out. Either all black or screaming colors would be worn. I wanted the shirts to be tight, unbuttoned to the waist, revealing smooth, satiny skin. But my hairy chest signaled truck-driver virility, so I compromised and decided that Mr. Blackwell would wear turtlenecks softened with gold chains and silk scarves in colors that blazed, that announced, that reflected from my mirror the illusion I wanted to create.

My eyes dropped to my pants. They should be taut, a tease. As for shoes, definitely nothing conservative. Give the press ammunition; every detail matters. The image began to gel. I could almost hear the whisper: "Only he could get away with wearing that." Next, the coat, which I would sling over my shoulder seductively. No secret now what I have to offer. My cartoon costume covers the possibilities. Finally, I'll pitch my voice lower, soften the sentences, run them together like warm, melting caramels. I'll even lower my eyes, to discourage intimidation. Let the creation become their idea, not mine, as the props, the performance and the public persona loom to life.

I would create for the world someone to wonder about, to confuse and confound—a real attention grabber. And if this character did indeed outrage, then I would have succeeded.

I asked myself, with a sense of satisfaction, how could I fail? But I also wondered: Could I live with my creation? Would I grow to hate what I saw? Or would I eventually become the role I'd decided to play? And when the time came for my part to be over, would I be able to resume the personality of Richard Blackwell? Whoever that is.

I laughed—through the tears. Yes, through Mr. Blackwell, I thought, I will become a conversation piece. Something new, flashy, memorable. Someone to make people forget their gray lives. Someone to defy their intolerable prejudices, their preconceived notions about who and what a designer should be. I will become the luxurious label they want. I will become the name in the back of a thousand dresses. And I will become my most unforgettable creation: King of the Caustic Quote, Arbiter of

Good Taste and Bad, the ultimate mix of madness, marketing and media attention.

I will become Mr. Blackwell.

Our first garment district office wasn't much to look at. In fact, in those days we were located in an old ten-story thirties building on Los Angeles Street, strategically located three blocks from the Salvation Army Mission and mere steps away from a seedy adult bookstore. Far too glamorous for words. A few blocks away, the faded Alexandria Hotel, once host to legends like Garbo and Chaplin, still stood sentinel in the brutal L.A. light—a weathered, washed-out monument to Hollywood's golden days. Although I was only 35, I could definitely relate.

Breaking the Rules

Many of the most talented and successful California-based designers worked within a six-block radius of our showroom in downtown L.A.—Edith Small, Dorothy O'Hara, Helga, Georgia Bullock, William Pierson. These already famous fashion leaders churned out hundreds of dresses, suits, coats and accessories. I hoped some of their success would rub off on me because, to be honest, despite my new acid-etched image, I still felt wholly inadequate.

As with almost all new businesses, the money was tight and our expenses were high. We couldn't afford the help we needed and we were bound by the rule that there are only 24 hours in a day. Spencer and I were almost always in by seven A.M. or earlier, and we usually didn't leave until well past midnight. Dinners were on the run and breakfast was nonexistent. And, of course, even a fifteen-minute nap was virtually impossible. There just never seemed to be enough time to get it all done.

We wore many hats. From decision makers to errand boys to receptionists to janitors, we did it all. Spencer never complained, even though the most tiring work always seemed to land on his shoulders. While I flitted from poring over sketches, to looking over the seamstresses' shoulders, to dealing with the buyers, Spencer would take care of all the mundane details. He kept track of the finances and my appointments, swept the scraps from the floor, made the coffee and generally made sure the office continued running like a well-oiled machine. I would scream and rant, whipping like a whirlwind from one end of the workroom to another, demanding perfection from everyone and letting them know it. Spencer would follow close behind me, smoothing the ruffled feathers, making sure no one quit and that our suppliers would return. I often watched him from across the room in amazement at how calm and reassuring he was. I was so insecure, so afraid of failure—and yet he never wavered. I showed my insecurities with my temper tantrums, but Spencer always understood.

In spite of being practically broke and operating on nothing but pennies split in half, we decided we needed help. It was much too much for just the two of us, so we hired a flashy, red-haired assistant, Maggie Beaumont, whom I'd known from Irving Mahler's corporation, to alleviate some of the pressure. Maggie quickly became my lead model, salesgirl and all-around girl Friday. Without her, I doubt I could have continued the grueling pace.

My first collection totaled a skimpy fifteen dresses, all in eleven-ounce black wool jersey reversed for a French-knit effect. My seamstresses looked at me like I was crazy when I insisted that wool jersey was suitable for the upcoming summer line. I argued that the women I designed for wore dresses in rooms equipped with temperature controls. They did not toil at construction sites beneath the broiling sun. Why should women be forced to wear specific fabrics in specific seasons? I wanted to break the antiquated fashion rules; with my black wool jersey dresses, which clung seductively to the body, I definitely did.

Our early buyers, who appeared literally by the dozens, came to the showroom with a convince-me-or-else attitude. Most of them were impressed by the understated yet conspicuously fem-inine clothes. I'd already created a minor controversy by refus-ing to follow the boxy chemise look that added twenty pounds and twenty years to any woman unlucky enough to wear one. I knew the market was ripe for change; so, too, was the American woman. I was determined to make her proud of her gender. The chemise was bad enough—but those shoes! The flat-heel, big-buckle pilgrim look should have stayed on the *Mayflower!* I saved every pair of three-inch heels I could get my hands on. The long, lean look they created accentuated the sensuousness of the female figure.

I was so exhausted that I felt that the hours were simply dragging by. Yet the deadlines were hurtling toward us at light speed. I was duly informed by armchair physicians that I was using my fatigue as a way to escape pressure, a way to bail out guilt-free if the business bombed. I grew sullen, moody, angry, cursing them all for assuming I couldn't take the heat. Maybe the pace was too demanding. But still I felt a burning need to prove to all the doubting Thomases that I had the talent and the guts to last. But in my state of exhaustion, it wasn't an easy task, and what they didn't realize, as I sat motionless in my office, was that I felt terribly ill, plagued with severe headaches and occasional spells of total body numbness.

As the pain grew more intense, I retreated into a shroud of silence. Unable to deal with the buyers, Spencer blasted me for my refusal to protect our investment. He didn't know—no one knew—how I really felt. I didn't want to burden anyone with my problems. Spencer had enough to worry about. He had his own fears that, at the time, I didn't understand. All the money he had was tied up in this venture, and our accountant warned him that the investment was rapidly dwindling away. Debts were piling up—employee wages, rent, fabric costs. If the situation didn't improve, there was little hope of surviving the year.

As the final week of January loomed before me, I felt like I'd been in business for a lifetime. We were all overworked and underpaid, and I didn't want to be known as the whiner and complainer, especially when it was my name going on the label, my name that was going to get the recognition, my standards I wanted everyone to meet. When I finally realized I needed help, it was too late. On January 20, 1958, I suffered a devastating nervous breakdown and stroke.

What might surprise you, my friends, is that there are no signals—no thunder and lightning, no chimes, no bells and whistles, no warning whatsoever. In fact, I was actually feeling better that day. I was sitting in my office, going through my mail, when I felt my legs grow suddenly hot. I grabbed the chair and tried to stand, but found I couldn't. My legs were heavy, and invisible weights seemed to be strapped to my feet. I was dizzy and light-headed, cold and clammy but hot and sweaty all at once. I started to call out but then toppled over, chair and all, everything clattering around me like an earthquake. As I rolled on the floor, a deafening roar of crashing waves filled my mind, as if a demonic seashell was pressed tightly against my ear. Darkness clouded my vision as I screamed, and screamed, and screamed.

Startled, Spencer and Maggie rushed in. They stopped for a moment, staring, frozen with horror, then sprang into action. Shutting the door, they knelt beside me, shoving papers, patterns and books away that had fallen on top of me. They tried to talk to me, gently patting my face and asking me questions, attempting to find out what had happened. I was confused, disoriented. I couldn't answer. I was too weak, and even if I'd had the strength, I wouldn't have known what to say.

Maggie and Spencer knew they needed to get me out of there fast. News like this would spread like wildfire, and could only spell disaster for a new designer. Somehow, they managed to drag me down the back stairs and pour me into the backseat of the car. Limp, unable to move on my own, I was almost unaware of my surroundings except for the overwhelming feeling of urgency to get home. A deep numbness spread over my body, from my ankles to my arms. My legs, bent in a sitting position, began to freeze up. I tried to move but couldn't. By the time we arrived home, I felt completely paralyzed. With the help of two neighbors, Spencer lifted me out of the car and carried me inside. For the first time, I saw fear in his eyes—a fear borne out of caring for me. That moment haunts me to this very day.

Thank God Maggie had the foresight to call a doctor, who arrived minutes after I'd been carried to my bed. I have never known pain, before or since, that equaled the torturous burning and icy numbness that flashed through my legs, arms and chest. I thought about how easy it would be to just let go and end this life of constant struggle. But death is the final absolute. I didn't know whether it would be the final disappointment or the ulti-mate triumph—and I wasn't ready to find out.

With Spencer keeping vigil by my bedside, I slowly began to rally—with the help of morphine shots that muffled the pain and sent me into a blissful state of momentary peace. One of Spencer's friends volunteered to be my nurse. Unfortunately, no one, including herself, knew that she was a hopeless alcoholic. During her first day on duty, in a Scotch-saturated stupor, she overdosed me with all kinds of pills. While I lay in bed frightened, I noticed my legs were blowing up like balloons. I'd been accused of having an inflated opinion of myself, but this was ridiculous! Soon my eyes were swollen shut. When Spencer saw me, he gasped and called the doctor, who said there was little he could do. The morphine had already entered my bloodstream. Suddenly, the whole Marx Brothers scenario turned deadly serious. Spencer was told I probably wouldn't survive the night.

Miraculously, I pulled through. I promised myself I'd make it. While recuperating at home, I would call Spencer several times a day. He didn't want to upset me, so I was unaware of the bedlam that was ensuing downtown. Rumors flew from every street corner that something was dreadfully wrong in the House of Blackwell. Spencer finally told me that the gossipmongers, knives in hand, were merrily slicing me to shreds; my sudden seclusion was attributed to every malady from mononucleosis to a complete nervous breakdown. We had to think fast. If word of my stroke leaked to the industry, my career would be over before it started. Few buyers would trust someone with such a precarious health problem to design—much less complete—a collection. Unbankability was yet another label I'd be strapped with—the kiss of death in the designing world.

The fashion business has always reveled in someone else's failure; there's less competition that way. But I refused to give them the pleasure. Spencer and Maggie told everyone I'd been in a serious accident and was at home. That should keep the vultures from hovering over us for at least another month.

Unable to oversee the day-to-day activities downtown, I left the pricing, selling and shipping of the collection in Maggie's hands. Through no fault of her own, she unfortunately underpriced the dresses to near disastrous levels, giving the rumormongers a field day in the process. We sold hundreds of dresses, only to realize, after material, labor and shipping costs, that we were taking a loss on every item we delivered. The vultures again buzzed joyously: Blackwell was broke.

Maggie, Spencer and I held a bedside summit and decided to give it one final shot. We discussed idea after idea, throwing them all out one by one. Spencer draped and redraped fabric over Maggie, trying to follow my directions while I pointed, waved and flailed my hands in frustration.

"This way!" I cried. "No, that way!"

"Pin it here! No, there!"

We finally decided on a silk wrap-skirt, square-necked, short-sleeved dress. We would make it in every color and size, and most definitely price it right. I blocked the idea of failure from my mind, personally and professionally. With an exercise routine that would have exhausted Charles Atlas, I slowly began to regain the use of my legs. I soon found myself hobbling around the house on a cane. The doctor pronounced it a medical miracle; I pronounced it a financial necessity.

I returned to work, elated that I'd proven the doomsayers wrong. But the rush of regeneration soon gave way to the harsh realities of our plight. The office was in a shambles. Summer was right around the corner, and the silk-wrap dresses still weren't finished. Within ten minutes, I became the bastard of the garment district, lighting a fashion fire under everyone. If the factory could finish the line in time, we still had a fighting chance. I saw to it that they did—in a 24-hour-a-day nightmare of a schedule that nearly put me back in bed for good. But the effort was more than worth the trouble: The simple, feminine, relatively inexpensive wraps turned into the fashion smash of the summer. Business blossomed, and my hopes soared. We were on our way to grossing $275,000 by the end of the year—and in the process, I was getting a million-dollar education.

I began preparing designs for my fall collection with one important goal in mind: pricing my dresses realistically. To accomplish this, I often designed several styles in one fabric, thereby eliminating extravagant material costs as well as having "fashion insurance." In other words, if one style failed, I still had another that succeeded without having to change the chosen fabric. I also learned how to whip up "stock-on-the-rack" clothes—the same design in a wide variety of colors, fabrics and prints, giving us an almost original flavor with each dress. I created patterns, and by using minor adjustments, turned them into different dresses at one cutting time—thereby holding production costs to a minimum. We were not the House of Chanel; every penny mattered.

At that time, all my dresses were designed in the same manner: I started out with a basic, long-sleeved, high-necked garment, adorned with some sort of scarf. From there, to create a second style from the original design, I merely reduced the sleeve length, altered the neck and, on occasion, gathered the back of the gown with sewing notches to create a pleated effect. The tricks of the trade were endless—as was the work involved in creating them.

I still had a lot to learn, but in fashion, ignorance can be bliss. One of my first major successes happened entirely by accident: my plunging V-necked dress. Originally designed as a nearly backless gown, one of my models, who was as flat-chested as me, put it on backwards—and the buyers went berserk. Caught totally off guard, I was forced to design, at the very last minute, a bra to accommodate my dramatic fluke. I chose the first bra manufacturer I could find. Negotiating with bra salesmen was a chore I had little interest in pursuing.

Much to my amusement—and the models' fury—this particular salesman was also a consummate voyeur who took a personal interest in "fitting" each of my female employees to an absolute T. During his lengthy showroom visit, one of Hollywood's most famous female impersonators arrived in need of a quick "push-up" look, so I sent him over to be fitted. Needless to say, the salesman flew out of the premises in a severe state of gender shock. Such was life in the never boring, always chaotic world of fashion.

As I look back on my roller-coaster life in the crazy fashion industry, I can now see a disturbing pattern of behavior that surfaced with some of the women for whom I designed clothes—and the more I tried to understand and control it, the worse it seemed to get.

For me, the fashion industry mirrored, in many ways, my earlier days toiling away in the horizontally inclined escort business. No doubt I was standing on my own two feet as far as fashion went, but the kind of one-sided attention—and at times, adoration—I received in both professions was exactly the same: They paid, I promised, and never the twain shall meet.

The world of fashion, like the dark, whispered promises of escorting, is built around marketing illusions, fulfilling fantasies and designing dreams. It is idealized perfection with a pretty price. I became a confidant to many beautiful, wealthy and desperately lonely women, and they invariably read much more into the personal attention I lavished on them than I intended. But my predicament was nothing new. Many fashion designers, hair stylists and interior decorators become the object of their clients' affections. We provide intimate, creative and image-enhancing work, and glamour can be an addiction on a multitude of levels.

For me, my passing remarks and impersonal affection were surface chatter, but I knew deep down that many wanted to, and in fact did, misunderstand my motives. Whether dressed in the showroom or undressed for a fitting, women confided secrets to me only a progressive priest should hear. To make it in business, I allowed them to pour out their feelings, problems and dreams within the hushed confines of my private dressing rooms. I was part designer, part beautician, part psychiatrist and part fantasy lover all rolled into one, and I was guilty of telling my clients exactly what they wanted to hear—how beautiful, chic and desirable they were as they slipped into one of my creations. My warm words and friendly touches were often nonexistent in their personal lives. Many husbands, too busy on the golf course or in the boardroom to pay attention to their wives, were hopelessly detached from their partners' needs and desires. I became, in an abstract way, a surrogate lover, a one-man wish list that offered instant self-esteem to the elegantly empty women wafting through my life.

Their need for constant approval disturbed me. I saw myself in them more than I wanted to admit. At night, after my daily charade had ended, I often worried and wondered whether my emotional dishonesty would somehow wreak further damage in their already uncertain and unfulfilled lives. Still, despite my late-night guilt trips, I continued stroking their egos and whispering bon mots whenever I felt it was necessary. In order to keep the business running smoothly, I accepted dinner invitations, theater tickets and gifts. They used me for companionship and I used them for financial and professional stability. Their husbands knew full well I had no sexual interest in their wives, and rarely objected. In fact, they often encouraged me to become a part of their glittering circle of candlelit dinner parties and lavish black-tie affairs because I took the burden of husbandly attention off them, if only for a moment. It was a charmed—and charmless—life.

Sadly, this mixed bag of emotions lasted throughout my career as a designer. For far too many insecure and neglected women, I became an escape route to a world of beauty, harmony and self-worth. In fashion, illusions are priceless. I paid the price of creating an atmosphere of sequined shadows and lustrous light—a world where a woman is made to feel eternally beautiful, eternally fulfilled. But the ever-increasing dependence many of my clients had on me was my Achilles heel. I could sense their underlying unhappiness and desperation, and I hated that I led them to believe that a mere dress could somehow alleviate their pain. I abhorred the fact that I toyed with their fragile emotions. But I also knew that if I wanted to become the kind of fashion success I envisioned, I would have to play the game. And so, I did.

Whether they saw me as court jester or crown prince, I really didn't care. I had created the setting, designed the staging and orchestrated a character to play. It was too late to turn back now.

One June morning I got a pleasant shock for a change: NBC phoned to ask if I was "interested" in designing the guest-star wardrobe for their bi-monthly "Eddie Fisher Show." Interested? Were they kidding? I was ecstatic! But I managed to maintain my composure, if only for the duration of the call. Being "the dress-maker to the stars" was a step up from toilet-seat sensation, but I didn't tell them that. I made them wait for an answer. At least five minutes.

"The Eddie Fisher Show" and Me

In the summer of '58, Eddie Fisher was at the peak of his Sinatra-like popularity. His one-hour variety show, which had premiered the year before, was a consistent ratings success and the network wanted to keep the 30-year-old golden boy happy at all costs. I fantasized that my lucrative job would last for at least a decade. But, unfortunately, thanks to a woman named Elizabeth Taylor, it went down in flames after a grand total of six months. But during that short-term association, I managed to create one or two scandals of my own—though certainly not on a par with the Debbie/Eddie/Liz fiasco that erupted into the cause célèbre of the decade. I was small potatoes in the controversy category, but on at least one occasion I was branded "the biggest bastard in the fashion business."

Doing television wardrobe, I discovered, is as much a technical talent as a creative one. You've got to know what fabrics look good on camera and what colors turn sickly green under the studio lights. If you don't, you're dead. Another prerequisite is pleasing the guest stars and the producer, who's paying the bills. My job also involved "capturing" the personality of each guest through the gowns I designed—not an easy task.

My first assignment was Kate Smith. To dress this gloriously larger than life "First Lady of American Song" would be a great honor, and to prepare, I flew to New York to discuss my ideas with her. Our meeting was wonderful; she was completely disarming, with a gentle, friendly manner that put me at ease. The fact that she and Aunt Bertha had been friends was another plus for me in the conversation department. After the obligatory small talk, I got down to business. When I told her I was doing her dress for Eddie's show, she seemed pleased, but I wasn't quite sure. Nonetheless, I left New York feeling I'd made a good impression.

When Smith arrived in Los Angeles, I was informed she would select her own wardrobe without me. Naturally, at first, I was devastated. All my old insecurities flooded back. Visions of being fired from "The Eddie Fisher Show" before designing even one gown hit me hard, but for once my fears of rejection were way off base. She had her own particular insecurities as well—and felt safer making wardrobe decisions alone. She had little interest in what the studio wanted her to wear. I called and told her I understood perfectly and wished her good luck on the show, then got on with the rest of my responsibilities. The following week she appeared on the program looking absolutely incredible—in a figure-flattering dress that was perfection. When a star knows her image as well as Kate Smith, there's little need for someone like me. Her great dignity was and is unforgettable.

Despite my short contact with her, many of the guest stars on Eddie's show were far less interesting personalities. Frankly, they're too boring to mention and designing for them was a chore too dull to detail. Almost anything out of the MGM costume department would have sufficed, but I was being paid to design, and design I did. Fittings were endless, schedules impossible to maintain. Work consumed me in a cloud of cigarette smoke and a river of stale coffee. Everything was back to normal and the pace rejuvenated me.

But nothing good lasts forever. My prickly penance was on its way—in the form of operatic diva Lily Pons, the most impossible woman I've ever had the horror of working with. And the feeling was mutual, I can assure you. Tiny, fragile, beautiful— and accustomed to complete subservience from her coterie of assistants, secretaries and whipping boys—she was incredibly gifted, incredibly demanding, and wreaked havoc on us all.

When I first began to dream up a design for Lily's gown, I imagined a latter-day Marie Antoinette look…something suitable for a garden party at La Petite Tranon, or an informal reception at Versailles. Since she told everyone within earshot that all her clothes were designed by the finest Parisian couturiers, I wanted her to feel at home. At this point, we hadn't even met, but after enduring endless phone calls from her staff telling me what I should and should not do, I felt like we were old enemies. NBC informed me that I'd be required to go to La Pons' home for the fitting. Between you and me, I was more than a bit intimidated. I felt far more comfortable in my own showroom, where my staff took care of all the technical details I never bothered to learn. I also had little interest in senseless socializing over dreary canapés and iced coffee. But more than that, I hated being sub-servient to anyone—and being surrounded by her haughty entourage would, I knew, unnerve me. I told them I wasn't about to grovel at Lily's feet. Besides, I argued, it made more sense for her to come to me. It was ridiculous to expect me to drop every-thing, pack up my showroom staff and spend all day catering to her prima-donna whims. Spencer argued, "You're just being impossible…again."

But I held my ground. She'd have to lower her heavenly stan-dards and pay me a visit if she wanted a dress.

Then the phone games began. Spencer, as my business man-ager, had the unlucky job of informing her secretary that all of my clients were expected to come downtown to the showroom. He was quickly told Miss Pons was not like any of my other accounts and I was expected at her home immediately. "Immediately" is a word I've banned from my vocabulary, and I informed Spencer to tell Miss Pons those exact words.

"Everyone comes to Miss Pons!" shouted Lily's exasperated assistant.

"Everyone but Mr. Blackwell," he replied, with as much con-viction as he could muster. He knew, as did I, that NBC would be burning up the phone lines in a matter of minutes.

Within a half hour, someone from NBC called and asked fran-tically what the problem was. Spencer, pale as death from being perpetually thrust in the middle of my daily mini-dramas, lis-tened. His eyes grew wider with each successive second. If I did not please Miss Pons, Spencer was told in the strongest manner possible, I might be in breach of my agreement and "The Eddie Fisher Show" would be a memory. I remained adamant. Spencer remained exasperated. And Lily Pons, tired of waiting, went to Saks Fifth Avenue to look for something suitable to wear.

I'd been in Saks and knew they wouldn't have anything fine enough for Pons. In this year of the chemise, a gorgeous dress off the rack would be next to impossible to find, especially one for a televised production number that cried out for a subtle yet dramatic theatrical flair.

Good luck, I thought. And good riddance.

It wasn't that easy. Within two days, Pons' office called again. Swallowing their overabundant pride, they politely asked if I'd reconsider—and would I also reconsider coming to her suite? The entire escapade was beginning to sound like a broken record:

"No! No! No!"

"Please! Please! Please!"

Finally, her side tottered and, to Spencer's relief, gave in. Miss Pons would—just this once—deign to come to me. Spencer joked that he felt like he was personally negotiating "The Pons Deal."

The following day, at the agreed-upon hour of one P.M., our entire office waited for the superstar's arrival. As the clock ticked toward 1:30, I lit a cigarette and shot Spencer an I-told-you-so glare. When it struck 2:00, I really began to stew. By 2:45, I escaped the entire scenario of ego madness and stormed out. If Lily Pons did show up, she could design her own damn dress.

At three P.M., Pons and her entourage arrived in a sea of smiles—and in an avalanche of anger. The in-between moments nearly caused poor Spencer to suffer permanent ear damage. When she realized I'd vacated the premises, she hit notes that threatened to shatter every three-way mirror in the place. Tempers flared, fingers pointed and feathers flew. So did Pons— back uptown, mad as Medea, shattering the sound barrier along the way.

After some very serious arguments with NBC, Spencer and everyone else in the general vicinity, I cried uncle. So bright and early the next morning, I set out on my godforsaken pilgrimage to the House of Pons, protected by my own entourage, a box of pins, a yardstick and my assistant, who knew how to sew. I was a nervous wreck. To compensate, I overdressed to the point of parody—lots of gold chains, rhinestone rings. I hoped my ostentatious outfit would set her back an aria or two.

After buzzing the door to her lavish quarters in Beverly Hills, a stone-faced gargoyle of a butler admitted me to her "waiting area"—all royal blue carpets, gilded mirrors and Queen Anne chairs. We waited and waited. Paying me back for yesterday, I suspected. Tit for tat—ego for ego. After half an hour the carved French doors that led to her private rooms slowly opened, giving me an expanding slice of the luxurious salon beyond. I didn't have the time to appreciate its beauty; pushing past my assistant, I marched in over the Aubusson, under the hand-painted ceiling, and asked for an aspirin.

"This episode," I grandly announced, "has given me a headache."

As startled attendants satisfied my request, Pons floated out of her dressing room. She was positively doll-like—a magnificent munchkin, to be exact. She said nothing—and neither did I. The room froze around us, ice cold with arrogance.

"Mr. Blackwell, be seated," she commanded finally in pearly tones designed for the La Scala stage.

I plopped onto a striped silk sofa that swallowed me in 100 pounds of goosedown stuffing.

"I hope you've brought the sketch," she announced. "I'll need to approve it."

I almost laughed. "I haven't done a sketch, Miss Pons. I thought we should meet first."

That lopsided justification went over like a lead balloon. Clearly, Lily was livid.

"Then you shouldn't have bothered to come," she said, her voice an icy waterfall.

I felt my headache pounding.

Before I could tell her what I had in mind, she went on in tones rapidly bordering on hysteria. "Real couturiers always have dozens of sketches and fabrics for my approval, Mr.

Blackwell. Why, in Paris this would be unheard of."

Then let her go to Paris, I thought.

After a ten-minute discourse on the superiority of European fashion, she relented and allowed me to take her measurements. With the speed of a striking rattlesnake, I did my designing duty, writing the numbers on my trusty pad. Within ten minutes we had exited her lair and were racing back to the office, mission accomplished. She did not ask us to return.

Knowing she wanted to make a grand entrance down a flight of white marble stairs, I returned to my original concept of Marie Antoinette at a garden party. That should please Miss Pons. As I rummaged through bolts of fabric, nothing seemed right. I needed a French import—something exclusive, preferably pastel-toned to flatter her new bottle-blonde hair. My eyes lit up when I saw, buried under a pile of black jersey, the fabric I'd tucked away for First Lady Mamie Eisenhower. I felt guilty when I realized Mrs. Eisenhower's pink-and-white dinner suit would just have to wait.

The silk fabric, off-white and sprinkled with dusty pink roses, was beautiful. The design came very quickly. I decided on a strapless bodice, tapering in sharply to show off Lily's tiny waist, with a very full skirt, ankle length, and a bustle effect for the back, underscored with dozens of ruffled petticoats in varying shades of vanilla to deep pink. When the dress was completed, even I was pleased. Of course, the acid test was perfectionist Pons.

On the day of the fitting, she actually arrived at my design showroom on time, unwilling to stir up yet another hornet's nest. As she entered the room, she still wondered why one fitting was enough—she was used to at least six—but I assured her everything would be perfect. And then, when she saw the finished dress, the tension melted away.

"This is glorious," she trilled. "Just glorious."

We all breathed a sigh of relief. I guess the end really does justify the means, especially in show business. Even Eddie Fisher—usually too busy to worry over wardrobe—stopped by after the successful taping to tell me he approved. Needless to say, wife Debbie Reynolds was nowhere in view. As it turned out, Eddie was busy with a lot of things, including the Widow Todd, old Violet Eyes herself, Elizabeth Taylor. Newspapers from L.A. to London blared the headlines, and NBC grew very nervous indeed. Practically overnight, Fisher flopped in the judgmental eyes of America—and with the powers that be in the Peacock Pen. On January 6, 1959, all of us got a fabulous New Year's surprise: "The Eddie Fisher Show" was canceled—and what was worse, I was out of a job.

> Reportedly, Elizabeth Taylor
> was extremely disappointed—
> and, with my income reduced,
> I wholeheartedly agreed.

Those first couple of years, despite our success, were lean. Everything we made went straight back into the company. Still, since most new designers—especially ones from California—lasted only a few years, I was pleased that the press began to give me lots of space. Sales were up. The "Mr. Blackwell" character was working. All I really needed was a dynamite model. I had grown weary of the flat-chested fashionoids who traipsed through the showroom. I wanted a girl with a figure—the more Rubenesque the better. Since the fashion industry was devoid of this dangerously curved kind of model, I called one of L.A.'s top modeling agencies and spoke to its owner, Mary Webb Davis. She volunteered to look. The girl she found was my dream model: tall, blonde, beautiful and hopelessly enamored with the world of fashion.

Barbara Blakely

Barbara Blakely was one of the most striking women I'd ever seen. Little did I realize that hidden beneath her soft smile and honeyed voice lurked a mind as cunning as Bette Davis' in *All About Eve*. I was merely a pawn in her elaborate and ambitious game of chess. Take it from me, she's come a long way from my humble showroom to the lavish Palm Springs compound she enjoys today. For Barbara, like her current husband, Frank Sinatra, did it her way.

The California-born beauty from Long Beach possessed a timeless quality that added pizzazz to my clothes like no other model I knew. Formerly a lead showgirl at the Riviera Hotel in Las Vegas, with a young son named Bobby from a failed first marriage, she rarely spoke of her past, although in time I discovered she had a sister named Patricia who, like Barbara, lived a less-than-opulent life. Barbara never discussed her days as a Vegas showgirl. But she was determined to give her son a better life than she had known up to that point and, believe me, she did.

Barbara was a fast learner and quickly drank up the meticulous details all major models are required to master: the proper way to turn, to coo, to seduce—and still remain aloof. Her brilliant smile, sexy saunter and golden-girl aura catapulted her into the latest flavor of the week. Many were dazzled, including Zeppo Marx, whom she met while working for me.

With Spencer, Maggie Beaumont, model Geraldine Sanders, who went on to write the *Love Boat* book, and Barbara at my side, I began planning my new collection for the summer of '59—lots of silk cocktail dresses embroidered in sunbursts of crystal beads and pearls. I needed a suitable presentation—something typically "Mr. Blackwell." Ciro's, the legendary Sunset Strip nightclub, would be the setting for a very different kind of fashion show. Instead of the traditional daytime affairs that had as much excitement as a migraine, I set out to rival Cecil B. DeMille—music, dancers and glittering sets decorated with glamorous models, all led by Barbara.

On the evening of May 7, Los Angeles witnessed what was unquestionably the fashion spectacle of the year. No one had ever seen anything like it. As 300 of the nation's top buyers, press representatives and celebrities packed the room to its triple-tiered rafters, I was finally the star of my own production.

The show opened with a brief musical intro, featuring Barbara and the rest of the models, that garnered, at best, polite applause. It wasn't until the opening bars of "I Wonder What the King Is Doing Tonight," as a coterie of dancers, singers and models pranced across the stage, that I heard audible gasps from the blue-haired social queens of the geriatric set. If that egomaniacal tribute to myself caused a stir, my actual entrance—to the tune of "A Pretty Girl Is Like a Melody"—wreaked havoc. Dressed in long black silk lounging pajamas, with a five-foot black satin train and a gold crown atop my head, I milked the outrageous image for all it was worth.

The closing number was my high-camp capper: an extravaganza of nearly nude men spinning around my models to the strains of "Indian War Dance." With a ten-minute standing ovation, it was my night to shine—although Barbara managed to weave her way into the klieg lights as well. Zeppo Marx, completely smitten with Barbara, sat in the audience like an adoring schoolboy with his first adolescent crush. She reveled in his rapt attention after the show, but was the legendary Marx brother willing to open his arms to Barbara, that was the question.

The morning newspapers carried the Ciro story in bold headlines. Some reviews were raves, but others panned me for turning the elegant, sanctimonious world of fashion into a tawdry circus show. My spirits plummeted until Spencer and I arrived at the showroom. The early morning vision of nearly 50 buyers lined up at our door soothed my hurt feelings. Controversy sells—not to mention clothes that celebrate women. By combining those two ingredients, I'd finally stumbled across the difference between winning and losing.

I was on a royal roll, in a royal role—and I wasn't about to rest on my newly minted laurels. After Ciro's, I said to hell with the lethal fashion press and began organizing my first New York showing, at the elegant Savoy Hilton Hotel. If I had managed to stick my neck out in L.A., it would surely be placed on a glittering guillotine in New York.

I finalized the first dreary details of the trip before turning my attention to Barbara. Her personal wardrobe was a total disaster, devoid of the most minuscule element of style. After all, her appearance reflected on me, and her Vegas-toned taste was entirely unsuitable for the staid New York Savoy. I borrowed furs, jewelry, elaborate hats and silk shoes, demanding that both of us arrive in style, despite the fact that our bankbooks were less impressive than one might suspect.

Since her affair with Zeppo had blossomed into something serious, I donated tons of gorgeous gowns for that cause as well. No one knew better than Barbara the power of illusion in catching and keeping a man, as she later proved so clearly. Still, her own wardrobe was too California for the silk and sable New York fashion set. Thanks to the generosity of my doddering dowager friends, who knew I wouldn't take no for an answer when it came to borrowing that $75,000 Russian sable coat or a $15,000 emerald brooch, the entire staff of the Savoy looked twice when we finally arrived in the Big Apple, ready to take the town by storm.

The Savoy, imperiously located on 58th and Fifth, was a ravishing refuge for many California designers, who rented suites for a week or two to preview their collections for the New York buyers. Tension at these showings was invariably thick, since New York openly hated California's fashion creativity, finding the clothes too glitzy, flashy and nouveau riche. I vehemently disagreed. As a New Yorker myself, I knew that some of the best clothes were being designed by L.A. couturiers, but the doyennes of the industry, stuck in their shuttered world of snobbery and bias, made California fashion suffer for years. I wanted to change all that. Unfortunately, I was never able to.

Nevertheless, we swept into the Savoy with our heads held high, armed with 42 samples of my collection, nerves of steel and barely enough cash to last a week. I immediately sought out the coffee shop, befriended an elderly waitress and conned her into reducing my breakfast tab to the price of a simple cup of coffee. In return, I gave her fashion advice which she committed to memory with the humorous frenzy of a desperate freshman the night before finals. I worked tirelessly to assure a nerve-racked Spencer that I wouldn't lose this week-long crap game. After all, with this jaded Seventh Avenue lot, you only got one shot, if that. If you failed to impress the dukes and duchesses in the purchasing kingdoms of Lord & Taylor, Bloomingdale's, Bergdorf's, Saks and Bonwit-Teller, best of luck to you in the fabric scrap business. A snub from New York was almost always deadly.

To economize, Barbara and I stayed in a large suite with a king-size bedsheet strung across the room, à la *It Happened One Night*. I slept on the couch—when I was able to sleep. The first night we were deluged with work, setting up racks filled with daytime and evening wear; labeling each accessory; numbering the hats, coats and dresses; and arranging the order forms placed discreetly on the entrance table. During this duller-than-dishwater routine, Barbara opened up for the first time since I'd hired her. It was no Pollyanna tale.

She had struggled every step of the way, from her "Miss Scarlet Queen" beauty pageant days in Long Beach to the showrooms of Vegas. Raising a son alone was no bed of roses—and she bluntly stated that she was absolutely determined to marry a man of means. Zeppo Marx was her target; she'd succeed in landing the comic—or die trying. Since she had no intention of dying, Zeppo, who enjoyed a comfortable life in Palm Springs when he wasn't working in L.A., didn't know what hit him. With visions of the exclusive Palm Springs Racquet Club dancing in her gorgeous head, I knew it was only a matter of months before I'd have to start looking for another lead model. Barbara Blakely moved fast.

Tacking up our makeshift divider in the wee hours of the morning, I walked over to the window, lit a cigarette and looked out over the jeweled landscape of a neon-lit Manhattan. Watching the smoking tip glow red-gold in the darkness, I thought about Spencer back in Los Angeles—the only person who'd ever really believed in me. I knew the next seven days would dictate our future in myriad ways, and I vowed not to let him down. Yes, I was scared—but few ever saw that insecure side of me. By tomorrow, I'd be a veritable force of nature: strong, self-confident, serene in my ability to sell the line I'd slaved over. As the first hint of sunshine drifted through the room, I realized I'd been standing by the window all night. The day I'd waited for was finally here.

Since buyers came to the designer's suite at all hours of the day and night, Barbara rose at seven A.M., since both of us had to look fabulous when the birdbrains arrived. It would take us at least an hour to pull ourselves together, pretend we knew all the answers and be impossibly sophisticated—to have seen and done it all. Thank God for coffee.

As I slurped down cups of java, the doorchime rang. I smiled: This was it. To have a buyer appear so early on the first day of showing was a great sign. As Barbara fluffed her immaculately curled hair, I retreated to the bathroom to orchestrate a grand entrance. What I heard next positively froze my blood.

"Who is it?" Barbara inquired in her best purr.

"Joan Crawford."

I heard Barbara chuckle, and I realized with a sudden sinking feeling that she had no idea there were two Joan Crawfords, and one of them was the head buyer at Lord & Taylor. I knew what was coming next.

"Honey, if you're Joan Crawford," Barbara laughed, "I'm Lana Turner."

With that, Miss Crawford, obviously insulted, spun on her Fabrizioed feet and stormed down the hotel hall.

Lord & Taylor was a make-or-break account, and my life flashed in front of me. It wasn't a terrifically thrilling slide show. I nearly grabbed my razor to commit hara-kiri, but I managed to regain some semblance of composure and ran down the hall to catch up with the fuming Crawford, who was standing beside the elevator. So much for my grand entrance.

Through hysterical kindness, I persuaded her to come back and at least look at the line. The fates smiled: She loved the entire collection! At precisely 8:23 in the suddenly sunny New York morning, I made my first sale—and a major one at that. Other accounts quickly followed: Saks, Bloomingdale's—which several months later awarded me with their "New Star of California Couture" Award—and nearly 20 other high-priced dress boutiques. After a week of perpetual parties, long lunches and a whirlwind of customers, success was a feeling I really relished; the perfect finale to a hectic, harried and nerve-wracking week.

Thanks to my tunnel vision, and Barbara's statuesque charisma, we flew back to Los Angeles in total triumph—even if I did have to return her furs and jewelry the next day. By the close of '59, the business had netted nearly $700,000 and Miss Blakely became Mrs. Marx. Not only did she gain immediate admittance to the Palm Springs Racquet Club, but she also joined the Tamarisk Country Club as well. I had a sneaky suspicion I would hear little from her after her marriage, and I was right. She certainly didn't need to borrow jewelry anymore. In 1973, she would move on from devastated Zeppo to even bigger game: Frank Sinatra.

For a time, life progressed more smoothly than I thought possible. I felt happy, secure and proud of what we had accomplished in the fashion business. And as for our personal relationship, Spencer and I were closer than ever before. It was a time that seemed too good to be true and, in retrospect, it was the calm before yet another storm.

It began quite suddenly one morning shortly after I awoke. A sharp pain shot through my left cheek, followed by a terrible burning sensation. I put the discomfort out of my mind.

But the days passed and the pain continued...

Lightning Strikes Twice

As usual, I refused to face whatever it was that was bothering me more and more each day. Another health problem—real or imagined—was not something we needed at this moment in our lives. Deep down, I desperately hoped for some answers, because the burning inside my cheek grew stronger as the hours ticked by.

I decided to ignore it as best I could, because I knew the business would suffer if anything else went wrong with me health-wise. Buyers of my collections had to feel secure in the fact that I could deliver the merchandise as promised. Even the shortest delay in seasonal shipments was unacceptable in the fashion industry. I had worked too hard to see the House of Blackwell fail now. Our network of buyers would most assuredly lose all confidence in me should any illness I might or might not have become public knowledge. I was doing my best to be rational, but I was very, very scared.

Finally, I said to hell with it. The pain was too much. I avoided the showroom with a litany of excuses and went to one doctor after another, filling out lengthy forms under assumed names for professional protection. No one ever asked for any kind of proof of identity, and since I hadn't become known yet, I managed to keep the ruse up. Every doctor I visited told me the exact same thing—it was just an irritation, nothing to worry about. But I knew they were wrong.

After more doctors and more bad advice, the burning began to affect my eyesight, and I was in too much pain for Spencer not to notice. Still whenever he asked what was wrong, I told him I was exhausted from work and left it at that. He knew, after living with me for so long, not to push it. Prying a secret out of me is impossible, and the more he asked, the more I shut him out. I was incapable of admitting to him that I had a serious problem that needed to be dealt with. The whole situation made me feel weak and useless. Maybe it was another self-induced detour to slow down the ride to success we had worked so hard to create.

I finally ended up in a clinic in Hollywood where I was told the news that a small growth had developed in my cheek that had to be excised immediately. I signed all the forms, had a biopsy taken and went home to break the news to Spencer. To my great relief, he supported me through the ordeal wholeheartedly. Days later, when I was told that it was possibly malignant, I finally realized I needed him more than ever. I couldn't face the dark days that lay ahead alone. The thought of cancer was just too brutal a possibility to face without Spencer by my side. I thank the gods he was there.

After searching and reaching out for help, the answer came to me in the form of The City of Hope, the famous medical establishment located about twenty miles outside of Los Angeles in a town called Duarte. After examining my cheek, the doctors there told me I'd made a terrible mistake because such an operation could actually aid the tumor in its growth. But they felt it wasn't too late for them to help me. "Not too late to help me"—that echoed in my head until it sounded like an epitaph. What on earth did that mean? It felt as if the sky had fallen and turned into a huge depressing black umbrella separating me from the real world. Was I facing a possible death sentence if they couldn't help me? Was I destined to fight for my life until the end? I began to hyperventilate, I felt beads of sweat across my brow. I was afraid to ask what they meant. Stunned and scared, I waited for answers, but none were forthcoming. All this took place in moments, but it felt like an eternity. Finally they admitted, to my dismay, that the treatment they would recommend was still in its earliest stage. If it didn't work, I was living on borrowed time. They said there would be little or no hope if I didn't give this treatment a try. And if there was hope, it would only be a miracle from the gods. "How much time?" I asked. "A month? Six months? A year?" I could see it in their eyes that I had realized the truth. They asked me to sit down, comforting me as much as possible. I was on the verge of hysteria, so afraid that I felt it would lead to madness. But finally I regained my emotional balance and asked them what it was they were talking about doing for me. They explained it was a new treatment using radiation therapy to burn out tumors that had recently been introduced right there at The City of Hope. Called the "Cobalt Bomb," it was a progressive, nearly experimental form of cancer therapy that was my last best chance. By this time, I was willing to try anything, so they began my treatments right away.

Dressed in a smock and seated in a tiny, cement-walled room, I nervously watched as this monstrous-looking apparatus was positioned against my cheek. The doctors and nurses were so afraid of it that they sat outside a locked door, as far away from me as possible before turning it on. Amazingly, the procedure itself was painless, but the side effects were serious.

Driving home after the treatment, I was overcome with nausea and was forced to stop more than once to throw up beside the road. Covered in a cold sweat, I feared rightly that this was only the beginning: I had to come back every day for a series of treatments that lasted fifteen to thirty days at a time. Needless to say, the police along the freeway got to know me and my car because I had to stop so often on the way home from The City of Hope. I couldn't sleep, couldn't eat, and began losing weight at an alarming rate.

In the midst of all the madness that had enveloped me during this period, I found a perfect sanctuary in the beautiful gardens that surrounded The City of Hope. The greenery resonated with peace and tranquility, and I often rested there after my treatments. Through the magnificently manicured lawns, I would walk down a path that wound between beds of pastel flowers beneath soaring palms that reached all the way to heaven, and calm myself on a bench situated under a graceful archway that had been donated by Al Jolson. It seemed to be a silent portal—a doorway to a secret place far away from the outside world. The petty objectives of the fashion scene seemed miles away.

Months passed, work continued and I struggled along with my treatments. I remember longing for rest, relief and a respite from the fear that weighed me down. There were times I didn't want to live, yet I didn't want to die, either. I had no right to expect a miracle, but eventually one occurred: The cobalt therapy was working!

Slowly but surely, I began to sleep without sedation and my dissipated energy returned. My overall appearance improved and the dizziness disappeared. The City of Hope had given me a new life and a whole new future as well. I remember their motto, carved in stone above the imposing doorway: We care, we love and we hope. Without these three extraordinary attibutes that exemplify The City of Hope and the lifesaving work that they accomplish, I would not be around to write these words today. I am eternally grateful for their steadfast devotion. And I always will be.

In the early sixties, the business exploded, thanks to such star clients as Ann Blyth, Gene Tierney, Mrs. J. Paul Getty V, Terry Moore, Kathryn Grayson, Eartha Kitt, Zsa Zsa Gabor, Dorothy Lamour and Jayne Mansfield, who really did have the greatest bustline in the solar system.

I also came up with a gimmick that would become my crown of thorns in the years ahead.

Causing a Commotion

A cultural revolution was brewing, and I wanted in on the action. After being relegated to the showbiz sidelines for most of my life, I decided to make up for lost time; my first step in that scandalous direction was an outrageous advertising campaign.

The state of fashion advertising at the time was as blandly boring as Sandra Dee: cutesy-boo, dull and dreary, posed to the point of perfection. Great fashion photographers were few and far between, and the ones I really admired—Richard Avedon, Irving Penn, Louise Dahl-Wolfe, Cecil Beaton and Victor Keppler—were light-years beyond my skimpy budget. Unwilling to settle for some tired photo, I designed—with that Tupperware Party panache—the first "Mr. Blackwell" layout on my own. Ever the egomaniac, I used a photograph of myself as the only visual. Even Spencer thought I'd lost my mind.

"No self-respecting fashion designer has ever exploited himself so crassly," he grumbled. I took it as a compliment.

To me, the ad was fabulous—just my face cloaked in shadow, announcing the new line. In bold, black script that would have made Mike Todd proud, "Mr. Blackwell" splashed across the page.

"Blatant self-promotion," Spencer carped.

But his reaction was mild compared to the rest of Seventh Avenue when the ad appeared in the February 1960 issues of *Harper's Bazaar* and *Vogue*.

"Outrageous!" they screamed.

"Incredibly arrogant!" they bellowed.

"More conspicuous than his collection," critics chirped.

I knew I had succeeded. After all, it's only the best fruit the birds pick at. Not since the days of Antoine de Paris had anyone defied fashion tradition in such a brazen way. I identified with notorious Antoine—one of France's most talented hairstylists, who was too ahead of his time for his own good. He slept in a coffin, dressed like a deranged dandy, dyed clients' hair shocking pink and peacock-blue—foreshadowing the punk look by 40 years—and was the ultimate Left Bank Bad Boy. He was a true original—and an inspiration to me.

The reaction to my ad was so horrific that even Spencer realized we had a hit. I was trying my best to make an absolute Venus out of any woman who would listen—and listen they did, which even further infuriated the fashion masters on their vacuous verandas in New York. People talked, trashed and threatened to throttle me—but little did they know they were buying my script, my show, my performance. Their hatred sounded like applause. Sales began to sizzle—and I began to celebrate—maybe a bit too much.

The glitter-drenched glamour of Hollywood was still working overtime. But for the first time, I felt like I belonged amid the perfumed salons of the L.A. social set. Every evening brought another party, another opening, another show. Invitations poured into our home from people who wouldn't have given me the time of day in 1959. In Hollywood, one's position is measured in party invitations, calendar commitments—and bulging bank accounts. We still didn't have money, but judging from the barrage of dates circled in my monthly datebook, I was as hot as my infamous temper.

Although most of the really wicked whispers revolved around me, my lifestyle and God knows what else, I had become the center of attention. Ruby-lipped millionairesses fawned over me, demanded my opinion, wanted my attention. I suddenly felt powerful and important. Deep down, I knew it was all a hypocritical sham—but it felt damn good just the same.

The sequined merry-go-round continued—Romanoff's for cocktails, the Bel Air Hotel for dinner, Ciro's and Mocambo for dancing. Arriving in sleek black limousines or a friend's shiny white Rolls Royce stocked with silver buckets of French champagne. Smiling for photographers as they clicked away, flashbulbs exploding in the dark night like bursting stars. Walking down red carpets into circus-like receptions where emerald-throated socialites dressed in Chanel and Givenchy swept over to whisper the latest gossip. I was privy to more secrets than the Pentagon.

Our sudden success enabled us to rent a desperately needed larger space on the third floor of 719 South Los Angeles Street. Equipped with 3,500 square feet, I felt like a true fashion king in my own dazzling domain. Our new offices had everything I'd ever desire to inject some much-needed excitement into a boring year in fashion; design space; a showroom; models' fitting and dressing rooms; sample, cutting and pattern areas; and the all-important shopping department. Everything was perfect—except for the hideous fluorescent lights Spencer insisted we install within the confines of my private office. To me, it was crazy to purchase yards of fabric, especially evening material, under the kind of eye-popping glare reserved for police searchlights. But despite my constant complaints, the fluorescent tubes remained, so I usually retreated to the bathroom where, under a 100-watt bulb—the equivalent of living-room lamplight—I chose the material for my collections. I wanted to be sure of what the customer saw in the privacy of her own home. Yet another eccentricity Spencer had to deal with.

One morning, right after we'd opened the showroom, my private line rang and I knew it could only be one person. I picked up the receiver to a symphony of shrieks—shrill, angry and damned mad. It was Mother. Through the flurry of less than stellar adjectives she tossed my way, a despondent tone began to surface. A martyred voice, a voice burdened with disappointment and confusion.

As the years passed, while I toiled away, trying to make a name for myself, Mother had quite happily minded her own business. She had never lived vicariously through me—she worked, traveled and scarcely made a nuisance of herself in the way many other matriarchs do. I'd heard that she'd resumed dating on occasion—which caused some wild rumblings about Mother slamming doors at night, shouting, "Not for a dinner, I won't!"

Well, that same sweetly melodic voice was now asking, "Just what in God's name are you trying to do?"

"Trying to do what? Succeed at something."

Hadn't she endured enough of my disappointments? Obviously not. She had read something bitchy I'd said about fashion and—to add insult to injury—had spotted my ad in *Harper's*.

"An embarrassment, flaunting yourself that way," she said.

I was growing madder by the minute.

"What way?" I asked, bristling.

"I think you know."

"No, I don't."

"I didn't raise my son to be a dressmaker."

I could scarcely believe what I was hearing. It didn't sound like Mother at all. And then I realized that she'd been listening to a lot of jealous chatter from the prim, proper, peroxided ex-princesses who gossiped at every bus stop near her apartment. These women knew nothing about me or my work—but they judged me just the same. And they had convinced Mother to judge me, too. I knew what was coming next.

"Everyone knows that you're living with Mr. Spencer," she continued in conspiratorial tones, as if she were ashamed to speak her thoughts. Although mother already knew, our being public knowledge embarrassed her.

Bringing up Spencer was the last straw; the emotional floodgates burst open.

"Spencer is living with me," I spat. "And yes, Mother—whatever you're thinking is true! Everything you've heard about me is true."

As our entire office listened in embarrassed silence, I slammed the phone down before Mother could reply. Grabbing my coat, I managed a frozen smile toward the astonished workers and flew out of the office. For a moment I felt incredibly relieved—and then the guilt set in. Why would I deliberately hurt her? She didn't mean any harm; she just couldn't comprehend what my life was really about. It's funny how most mothers never know the truth until the rest of the world finds out. Then again, if I'd told her, she would have rejected it as a "phase." But the situation was entirely different now—at my age, the lifestyle I led was no "phase." It was an inevitability.

By the time I reached the lobby, I knew I had to call her back. I found a payphone and dialed her number. I remember hearing my voice shake.

"Mother?"

"Yes?" she replied sternly, preparing for another battle.

"I'm sorry. I love you, I really do. Don't worry about me. I have to lead my own life. Please." My voice broke.

"I know," she sighed.

"We'll talk later, I promise," I said, wanting to end the conversation as quickly as possible.

"I'd like that, Richard," she whispered before saying goodbye.

I felt like I'd been through World War III.

A shadow crossed the lobby floor. I turned around and saw Spencer, looking helpless and sad.

"Are you all right?" he asked.

"I'm fine," I lied. "Just fine."

"Come back to the office then."

"No, I'm going to take a walk. I need to be alone."

I walked past him toward the street beyond, secretly hoping he'd follow me. I didn't turn back and he didn't follow, but I could feel him watching me as I wandered up the sidewalk and out of sight.

I walked for blocks and blocks, up and down the sun-shrouded streets, past shops, glass-windowed diners, throngs of preoccupied people. They seemed invisible. Lost in my own thoughts, the world at that moment didn't exist for me.

Several hours later I found myself climbing the steep steps to my office. They reminded me of other dark stairs I had climbed, only to face lonely hallways leading to unforgiving rooms. Why did I retreat to those cruel memories? Why did I continue to relive in the same old shadows? Why did my life, almost like an endless circle, seem to repeat itself? I sighed the sigh of a man who had no answers. No answers at all.

By the time I returned to the showroom, the crisis had passed, and I had begun to accept the fact that if I was going to dish it out, I'd have to learn how to take it, too—even from my own mother.

I enjoyed breaking the rules. If someone said no, I shouted yes. If someone said I couldn't, I would. I became known as difficult and demanding. But I knew all too well that if I wanted to last, I had to do things my way.

If Mother was upset about the ad in *Harper's*, she hadn't seen anything yet. The "Worst Dressed List" proved to be an ongoing controversy that would eclipse every other facet of my career. Looking back now, I realize the creation of my "Worst Dressed Women List" was one of the most positive/negative, fame-making/fame-crushing, self-promoting/self-defeating and instantly liberating/suddenly paralyzing decisions I've ever made. The mixed emotions I feel regarding the List revolve around the unfair image of my career success being completely based on my annual reporting on who wore what—and how bad they looked wearing it. After all, I was only saying out loud what had been whispered in powder rooms for years. But the sacred cows of fashion were not amused.

The Birth
of the List

The first Worst Dressed Women List was published on October 30, 1960, in *American Weekly*, a Sunday supplement magazine that appeared in newspapers throughout the country. Assigned to me as a one-time-only feature on what's hot and what's rot in Hollywood fashion, it was an article that included my nominations for the best- and worst-dressed women in town. There was no denying that Brigitte Bardot, Anna Magnani, Yvonne De Carlo, Lucille Ball, Anita Ekberg, Shelley Winters, Carolyn Jones, Kim Novak and Anne Baxter were all beautiful women, but that year they were all one huge collective nightmare in the wardrobe department, and I felt it was okay for someone to speak up about it.

Spencer liked it, and so did my mother, but apart from a few murmured compliments from close personal friends and a few lines of comment in showbiz columns here and there, I might as well have kept it to myself.

A year later, I got a call from someone in the media who asked, "Who's on your list this year?" I had forgotten all about it, but decided to make a list up to accommodate him. The third year, I decided to stage a press party at our house, and Spencer presented iced champagne and orange juice to greet the hordes. Well, no one—repeat, no one—showed up except for the same three or four friends, and they were as embarrassed as I was. But the day was rescued from complete disaster when a few calls started coming in—one of them from United Press—and a few newspapers picked up the item in places like Chillicothe and East Overshoe.

This wasn't exactly a mandate to continue the List, but in the fourth year, Spencer thought I should give it one last shot—and this time a few newspeople actually showed up at the press party, drank our champagne and were still sober enough to file stories when they got back to the office. A local television station even appeared, shooting enough footage to interest the network in picking up their feed, and all of a sudden I began to generate not only airplay but yards of newspaper linage around the country as well.

By the fifth year, we were knee-deep in clippings—too many to count—and the Worst Dressed List was in full bloom. From that time on, it was an international phenomenon. I had achieved with a few flippant quips issued once a year what years of struggle as a designer had never quite managed to accomplish. I had already established myself as a respected designer within the industry and among my clientele in Hollywood and New York, but it was the Worst Dressed List that made Mr. Blackwell a household name around the world.

All I was trying to say was that our most famous and emulated stars owed the public and themselves a beautiful look, wearing clothes that embellished rather than desecrated their hard-sought images, waltzing through a star-lit lifestyle that middle America only dreams about. That's why they're stars, whether in film, television, music, art or politics. They're unique, gifted, charismatic, special—and they should dress accordingly.

The fashion industry, unfortunately, took a dim view of what I was trying to do. The snobbish opinion makers were offended by my controversial public image, and they began not only to condemn me for it but to sneer at my reputation as a designer. They asked haughtily who the hell I thought I was for presuming to pass judgment on anyone else's clothes. They didn't seem to understand that it was all in fun. Even the people on my List knew that. And the public not only agreed with me, they ate it up, because I was simply saying aloud what they thought themselves, and they loved me for having the nerve to announce that the empress has no taste.

As the decades drifted by, the List became as loved and hated as many of the stars who appeared in its tongue-in-cheek text. One of the greatest misconceptions surrounding the List was that

I enjoyed biting the hand that fed me, that I used it to wield power over clients, press agents and the media. Not true. I never used the List to attract would-be clients, nor did I ever put anyone on my annual "execution" who couldn't stand the heat. I never felt that releasing a Worst Dressed List conflicted with my designing career—but in the closed-off, tight-knit fraternity of fashion designers, it was considered heresy. Many of the horrendous outfits I criticized were the wretched creations of my fellow "dressmakers." The public laughed, but the industry seethed.

For the past 30 years, the questions and accusations have remained the same.

"How dare he say that?"

"What gives him the right?"

"Who does he think he is?"

I always say it's merely an opinion—mine. I've made lots of enemies, lots of friends, lots of headlines and lots of money. I've also had second thoughts many, many times. I wondered, as early as 1960, if the public would understand the difference between campy humor and deliberate cruelty, the distinction between social satire and bad taste. Some didn't—but most did. I received from the List-makers themselves as many open arms and sly winks as cold shoulders and killer stares. Let's face it: They didn't mind the publicity, and neither did I.

One of the reasons the List has managed to last is its lack of pomposity. I have always hated those dry, self-inflated critical epistles on people in the spotlight. I liked to create images through snappy one-liners. Elizabeth Taylor: I never trashed her for gaining weight, I merely reported that there were too many yards of flesh poured into too few inches of fabric. Barbra Streisand: I never referred to her nose. I just called her a "boy Medusa" and left it at that. Bette Midler: basically "pot luck in a laundromat." The lines go on and on.

Over the years I've seen copycat lists come and go, but mine manages to remain, mostly because the American public finally understood how frivolous the whole thing was and took it in the spirit I intended: a truthful, humorous poke at the fashion flops of the year. Anything more—or less—was purely unintentional.

Bad news, they say, makes good copy, and from the very beginning of my notorious List, the press studiously ignored the fact that I always made a point of including a best-dressed list along with every list of worst-dressed ladies. But the stars I'd saluted were so stunned and flattered to be the target of a bouquet that they'd often send me one of their own in return. Some wrote gushy letters, others complimented me on my good taste and one sent me an invitation I'll never forget...

"I Am Joan Crawford"

I had always been a fan of Joan Crawford's dramatic personal flair—not only her distinctive fashion sense but her powerful charisma as a star—and it gave me real satisfaction to include her in my 1960 list of "Fabulous Fashion Independents." Imagine my amazement when she not only wrote to express her appreciation of my kind words, but to invite me for dinner the next time I was in New York.

Contriving a hasty pretext for a trip, I called to let her know when I'd be in town, and we set a date. That night at eight, I showed up at her posh East Side apartment and was shown to the living room by a maid. "Miss Crawford will be with you shortly," she said, leaving me on an overstuffed couch to admire the exquisite period furnishings.

I had counted the crystal droplets hanging from one chandelier and was starting on the second when the lady of the house, regal in black, appeared in a powder room down the hall. Oblivious to me, she was gazing intently at her reflection in a full-length mirror and saying slowly to herself, "I...am Joan Crawford." Then again and again, each time saying it with a different inflection: "I am Joan Crawford...I am Joan Crawford..." over and over again. And between each reading, she'd turn slightly to the left or right, thrusting one padded shoulder forward, then the other. Then finally, face straight to the mirror, head held high, she announced it one last time:

JOAN CRAWFORD

November 30, 1960

My dear Richard Blackwell,

I will treasure your letter of November 16th forever. I am so looking forward to having luncheon or dinner with you in January. Do please have your secretary drop me a note, giving me a little advance notice when you are coming on to New York, and where you will be staying here, and for how long.

Bless you for making my 1960 so happy.

Joan Crawford

"I...am...Joan Crawford."

Apparently satisfied, she turned dramatically and strode down the hall to meet me, extending her hand toward me from five feet away. What could I do? As those huge eyes locked with mine, I took the hand, gallantly I hoped, and told her how much I had looked forward to meeting her. But I couldn't get that scene I'd just witnessed out of my mind, and on our way out the door, I found myself saying, "I apologize for watching, Miss Crawford, but if you don't mind my asking, why were you doing whatever you were doing in front of the mirror? It was lovely, but what did it all mean?" She said, "Mr. Blackwell, I do that to psych myself up—so that when I go out to greet the world, I am Joan Crawford."

Well, we took a limo to the restaurant, and as she swept through the door, trailing black fur, it was an astonishing sight: The owner bowed, the maitre d' scraped, the waiters hovered, the diners gaped and gasped at her mere appearance among them. And I realized that whatever she had done in front of that mirror, it really worked. The rest of the evening was an anticlimax.

But the next morning in my hotel room, soon after I got up, I decided to try it myself and see if it would work for me. I was standing nude in front of the bathroom mirror when there came a knock at the door. I didn't answer right away, but the door immediately opened, and there was the maid, staring at me not six feet away as I stood stark naked in front of the mirror. But I didn't even bother to turn and look at her. Drawing myself up to my full height, I threw back my shoulders and said proudly to my reflection, "I...am...Joan Crawford." Without another word, she ran screaming out the door, slammed it behind her and called the hotel manager.

I felt compelled to build on the momentum I had consciously created as Mr. Blackwell. After experiencing "The Eddie Fisher Show," I knew television was the place to be seen and heard. I just hoped America was ready for what I had to say.

Since I'd already been accused of being a bad nightclub act, I decided to pull out all the stops with the launch of my spring collection in 1961. I proposed a live televised entertainment spectacular to showcase my clothes—something no one had ever done before.

When You Wish Upon a Star

I knew I could handle the pressures of television. The doomsayers around me vehemently disagreed, but I reminded myself that if I'd listened to them in the past, I would have bombed out before the business even began. The critics thought a televised fashion show was grounds for commitment, but remembering the triumph of Ciro's, I knew nothing was impossible. Ciro's reminded me of Barbara Marx, and I could picture her languishing poolside in Palm Springs. She'd be perfect to star in my show—and when I called her, she readily agreed. Being on television appealed to her, too.

My plan was simple—to produce the most elaborate fashion show ever seen and invite a Who's Who of buyers, celebrities, society figures and press members to the studio for the live show. As they watched from the audience, viewers at home could watch from their living rooms—multiplying not only the audience involved but the publicity this new kind of fashion show would generate. What audiences would eventually see, God willing, would be unforgettable: a collection of shimmering, flamboyant and luxurious gowns designed to make every woman watching covet the visions that floated across the screen. Much to everyone's astonishment, except my own, KTTV-Channel 11, an independent station that broadcast throughout Southern California, agreed to carry the show. We signed the contracts and started preparing for a May airdate.

I called the upcoming special "When You Wish Upon a Star." As corny as it sounds, it worked. The song spelled fantasy and storybook romance, escapist entertainment with a difference: interwoven within a singer/dancer format, a Blackwell fashion show spectacular.

In addition to the countless hours spent designing the garments to be televised, "When You Wish Upon a Star" was a technical and creative challenge of the highest order. Every detail, every camera angle, every word, every song had to weave effortlessly together. The show had to entertain, but more importantly, it had to sell the designs on-screen. The lighting, musical score, narration and pacing had to be perfection. My reputation was on the line. I began to wonder why I did this to myself—the pressure, the possibility of failure before a jury of my peers, the unforeseen production glitches and problems. Wasn't there an easier way to be noticed? Probably. But I had little interest in taking the easy way out. "When You Wish Upon a Star," in retrospect, was well worth the sleepless nights and anxiety-ridden days. It was, finally, a triumph. And a record-breaking one at that.

I imagined Barbara, bathed in rose light, wandering through a series of sequin-sprayed sets like Cinderella on her way to the ball, meeting different models wearing the collection along the way. The actual performance was as smooth as Steuben crystal. The songs, sketches, dancers and models were mistake-free. Barbara was, as always, gorgeous and thoroughly professional; I narrated with my usual touch of credible camp; and the buyers, after the show ended, made a beeline to the backstage area where Spencer and I had set up, with help from our sales manager, an appointment schedule. I was on Cloud Nine—or was it Ten? Whatever, I was, modesty be damned, the new fair-haired marketing genius of Los Angeles fashion, and the feeling was unforgettable. Setting precedents, breaking molds, changing traditional perceptions of what a fashion show should be. I never realized, until many years later, the depth of influence I had on the fashion-show format. Today, all major designers mount their annual showing with enough glitz and polish to rival the best MGM musicals. I did it first, with incredible results.

Except for one sole dissenter—that pompous, pious, petty and pretentious paean to John Fairchild's inflated ego: *Women's*

Wear Daily, the self-appointed arbiter of good taste and fabulous fashion.

Publisher Fairchild sent his "fashion editor" to review the show, and the article that appeared wasn't so much a critique as a crucifixion—my own. I was decimated by a white-hot stream of lava-like phrases. How dare I presume this was an actual collection opening? Who wanted to hear some Hollywood torch singer bleating away while leaning against a piano? And did Mr. Blackwell really feel it was necessary to close the "show" with his rendition of "For All We Know"? Not satisfied with merely condemning me personally, her diatribe savaged the entire show—cast, crew, performances. I'm surprised she didn't firebomb KTTV as a final assault against the senses.

I later heard from those who stood near my venomous critic during the show that from where she was sitting she couldn't even have seen the show. The viewing window from the sponsor's booth was covered with two huge spotlights, and a mouse with tunnel vision couldn't have seen the stage from her vantage point. And to make matters even more suspect, I also heard she had enjoyed more than a few drinks pre-showtime. Some said she wouldn't have recognized her own mother, much less a dress from 50 feet away. Regardless, the "review" appeared, my temper rose and my television special was the first of a series of run-ins with Women's Bore Daily. But as the saying goes, I cried all the way to the bank.

After the euphoria of making the Los Angeles fashion scene listen to what I had to say, grim reality had an unfortunate way of rearing its ugly head. It's called paying the bills. I had to get back to the daily grind, but I needed to try something different. There was an air of great change in the sixties, and I wanted to take advantage of that new freedom—without forgetting the glamour of the past.

Bewitched, Baubled and Bewildered

Feathers! Feathers everywhere! White marabou, rainbow-colored ostrich! My new look would be that classic Hollywood look updated. I flew to New York and visited a feather house famous for its Las Vegas boas and headpieces. Entering its showroom was like waking up in wonderland—great, glistening gold headdresses studded with faux pearls, strings of pink crystal beads, feather boas hanging from racks like confetti-colored snakes. I was amazed and inspired.

Back in L.A., Spencer was amazed, too. He wondered if our storeroom was ready for what appeared to be ten tons of pillow stuffing. It looked beautiful to me. The confections I concocted were as glamorous as the feathers I chose: a floor-length white marabou coat, short jacket and skirt—simple, flowing, yet wildly theatrical. The skirt and short jacket were merely an improvisation of the coat, which was cut off at the waist to make two separate garments: The top became a jacket, the bottom a bell-shaped skirt. The look was a tribute to the alabaster allure of Carole Lombard with a little Theda Bara thrown in for dramatic effect. And the line didn't end there. I designed an entire ostrich coat, dress and jacket line, too, all in vivid, nearly neon colors: parrot green, electric blue, ruby red and shocking-pink. This time the press dubbed me "costume maker for strip shows." I was elated. If I ever got a good review, my career most definitely would end. Like the press, the store buyers were leery of my feather fetish—but the ultimate judges—my clients—single-handedly made the fall collection a smash. As for the buyers, they were as unimaginative and unsupportive as ever. If I had to depend on their taste, I'd still be whipping up the safe black jersey slips from my first collection. But I knew that precious few of my buyers had a burning desire to wear marabou cloaks and ostrich capes, and since most buyers purchase only what they could or would wear themselves, I had a lot of delicate selling to do. Heaven help the average customer who wants to look sexy if the buyer from her favorite department store looks like Tobacco Road after a tornado or, even likelier, the prim-suited president of the local Librarians' Association. You know the type, but God knows I needed them. We were bound together irrevocably, each more than a bit wary of the other. I was, as usual, unwilling to compromise or alter any of the dresses they questioned and I told them so.

The buyers loved my lavishly trimmed evening gowns in silk and chiffon, with plunging necklines and bare backs. But the big news was marabou and ostrich, one of my favorite fashion fantasies. I had signaled I was ready to grow, take chances and create news through my clothes—not just my mouth.

By the end of 1961, we hit the magic million-dollar mark in sales, and skyrocketed into 1962 as the acclaim and attention fed on itself. Without even trying, we were deluged with requests for appearances, interviews and clothes, clothes, clothes.

Dressing the stars was fascinating and exciting to me. I understood their unique needs and created clothes that enhanced their image. I even performed an image make-over on a superstar from my own 1961 Worst Dressed List: Jayne Mansfield.

Dear Jayne

It all began with a phone call when Spencer told me the High Priestess of Cleavage was on the line. I was rather surprised. My clothes, though glamorous, were hardly the low-cut, bosom-baring, skintight ensembles Jayne had been threatening the public with for years. At first, I assumed she'd mixed me up with Frederick's of Hollywood, but Spencer was adamant. Miss Mansfield wanted to speak to me. She recognized and approved of another publicity-mad artist when she saw one. Jayne and I had a lot in common and our relationship, right at the start, was a wonderfully creative experience.

On the day we met, I was caught totally off guard. Of course, she did arrive drowning in skintight pink silk and Monroesque platinum tresses, but as we talked, a very different person emerged. Unlike Marilyn, Jayne was bawdy in a Mae West kind of way. With her 36-D bust, hourglass figure and pouty, programmed smile, Jayne epitomized glamour and sex appeal in a far coarser way than Marilyn.

Jayne wasn't shy or reclusive, and her humor bubbled forth constantly. In between fittings, she ran around in the models' room in her "all-together," which produced a privileged sight indeed. Beneath the persona—a hymn to every B-movie star who ever lived—I soon discovered she was also a devoted mother, wife and businesswoman. Jayne never asked for complimentary clothes; she paid her way—and I mean in every way. Her struggle to stardom was tough and treacherous and left her wary of relinquishing control to anyone she didn't implicitly trust. She had never forgotten the hard times, and I understood that emotion all too well. I hadn't forgotten mine, either. Both of us orchestrated our careers based on outrageous behavior, an eye for the press and critics-be-damned talent. Jayne was to bosoms and moist lips what I was to acid wit. We were two peas in a very privileged pod.

I began designing a dazzling new wardrobe for her—a total turnaround from the cut-to-the-navel, rhinestone-studded disasters she sported around town in her pink Cadillac. I didn't want to camouflage her gorgeous body. I merely wanted to add a touch of mystery to her appearance. One of my first creations for Jayne was my naked-illusion dress, which—I am the first to admit—I shamelessly copied from the great designer Jean Louis. This gown—her favorite among the many I eventually created—was a caviar sheath that began with a shimmering platinum hue at the neck and descended to a deep, pearly gray at the heel. Hand-stitched jewels and pearls covered the gown's strategic areas, causing bedlam whenever she appeared. The dress revealed little but promised a lot—as did several other flesh-toned dresses I created for her that literally dripped with crystal and gold appliqués, sprayed on only the most fantasized-about areas of her legendary figure. Jean Louis may have begun the look, but I took it a step further, and today, Bob Mackie and Cher have single-handedly kept the look alive, but nobody did it better than Jayne. After all, she had something to back it up with.

I was proud to have her as one of my most devoted clients—who, as 1962 progressed, included Dorothy Lamour, Yvonne De Carlo, Ann Blythe, and a long list of society and political figures. I was completely amazed. Women believed in my fashion outlook with the kind of zeal usually reserved for football fanatics. They wanted to look beautiful, and I did my very best to fulfill those fantasies.

Designing an entire wardrobe for a star—especially one as visually demanding as Jayne—involved hours of fittings, sewing and re-sewing. After we became close friends, I'd take the completed dresses to her pink mansion on Sunset, which she had decorated entirely in gold, white and pink, pink, pink. Her pool, in the shape of a heart, was inscribed "I Love You, Jaynie" in hot pink tile, a gift from her mild-mannered, massively muscled hunk of a husband, Mickey Hargitay. Olympic-sized Mickey, one of Mae West's chorus of body builders who served as window dressing in her nightclub act, had dropped Mae the minute he met Jayne—causing quite a few hard feelings between the two sex sirens of Hollywood.

Jayne confided in me and I in her. Personally, she was on the verge of filing for divorce—an action she threatened nearly every other month. God only knows how many times she told me the marriage was over, only to exclaim several days later that the proceedings were off—and all was perfect again in her pink palace. Mickey and Jayne had a relationship that seemed to feed on passion, fighting—and making up. Professionally, her life was also in a state of turmoil. She desperately wanted to be like Marilyn, who had written off fluff roles for more meatier parts in pictures like *Bus Stop* and *Some Like It Hot*. Jayne would be less fortunate in her career decisions, which would include an exploitation film called *Promises, Promises* in 1963. In that movie, and in *Playboy*'s pictorial glorifying its star, Jayne actually appeared nude—something I had no idea would occur and would have advised her against. Why bother to create the illusion of nudity if Jayne was determined to reveal the real thing? But the worst was yet to come.

Eddie Fisher (above left) kept a close eye that Lily Pons (above) and I didn't kill each other before the show as I fixed the gown I designed for her. Everyone could feel the tension between us.

An early celebrity client, Irene Ryan (right), tried to convince me the "Granny" boots she wore on her show "The Beverly Hillbillies" went well with the dress I had created for her. The inscription in the photo reads, "Dear Richard, I'm sure the shoes helped your lovely gown. Love, Granny Irene Ryan."

My first "Worst Dressed List" ran with little fanfare on October 30, 1960 in *American Weekly*, a Sunday supplement magazine published in newspapers around the country.

I knew the List had made the big time when none other than the queen of gossip, Louella Parsons, headlined it in her widely read syndicated column.

Milton Berle (above left with Laird Cregor) holds the honor of being the first man to make the List.

By the fifth year of the List, it was an international phenomenon, and Mr. Blackwell was a household name around the world. I even gave out trophies to the top ten, but none of the "winners" showed up to claim them. I often wondered why.

I was flattered when Jane Russell, Connie Haines and Beryl Davis (left, l to r) asked me to design their on-stage wardrobes for their Las Vegas act, but it turned into a clash of the titans with me as the ringmaster. Taking time off in Palm Springs (below).

I designed for Jayne Mansfield for years, but with her taste for headline-making publicity stunts, she had a hard time keeping anything on. Jayne was a free spirit who would surprise everyone by walking around the fitting room totally nude as if it were the natural thing to do.

Two of my most dramatic design innovations were the elegant "above the table" look (left), high fashion gowns exploding with glistening jewels, and the most extravagant hats (below). Both are modeled by actress Charlene Holt.

This is the dress that saved my business. I drew this sketch (right) after my nervous breakdown and stroke, the dress was a sensation, and our business flourished.

Branching out from fashion, I asked actress Amanda Blake to present my new perfume, Blackwell Number 11 (left), at a star-studded debut party that made the front page of the *LA Times* in the early Sixties.

Talk-show host Regis Philbin (right) was a tremendous influence in my becoming a television guest. He really seemed to appreciate my brand of humor.

It was a sign of having arrived when Faye Hammond (right), the influential fashion editor of the *LA Times*, and G.B. Giorgini invited Spencer and me to the Pitti Palace in Florence. I found her subsequent overtures to be shocking and unwelcome.

"What did I do right?" asked Phyllis Diller when I took her off the List. (l to r) Mr. Blackwell, Irene Ryan and Phyllis Diller at a formal showing to the buyers.

I began living in a manner that befitted my already lavish lifestyle: a baronial mansion in Hancock Park that soon became a mecca for clients like Goldie Hawn (above) and Michelle Lee (left), both of whom are posing for fashion layouts. Spencer and I lived in a whirlwind of champagne parties, cocktail receptions, heady dinner parties and formal soirees (below left). Our presence in Bloomingdale's (below) was a major boost for our line.

Presenting the dramatic fashions of
Mr. Blackwell

the Mr. Blackwell Show

I decided to introduce my new line not just with a fashion show but with a television extravaganza: "The Mr. Blackwell Show," with a host of guest stars such as Agnes Moorehead (right, second from top) and Eartha Kitt (below)—and yours truly as the master of ceremonies. All fashions by Mr. Blackwell.

Spencer and I were traveling in Europe. We had decided to take a much-needed vacation to get away from the daily grind of the garment district. What happened on that trip was certainly no grind, nor was it a real vacation, either. It turned out to be yet another series of rather incredible events packed into several short weeks. Par for the course for me. Did I mention we ran into Jayne?

Italy

We stayed at the lavish Excelsior Hotel in Rome, and from our marble balcony watched the parade pass by. There is an air of magic about Rome, an incredible blend, like some rare perfume filled with romance, beauty, history and happiness. Italians— Romans in particular—are open and emotional and, more often than not, wear their hearts on their sleeves. I absolutely agreed with that attitude. No one had ever accused me of concealing my feelings—although many, I fully realize, wished I had. But I felt at home in Italy, because everyone, even the priests, yelled as loud as I did.

We had been in town for what seemed like a mere minute before the press discovered I was there. Ordinarily, I would have been more than happy to converse with them, but since I was in Italy to escape controversy—not create it—I made a few innocuous comments about Sophia Loren and the gorgeous weather and left it at that. They weren't satisfied. Shouting for more, they pounced on me like basil on pasta as I tried to leave the hotel. We got as far as the hotel lobby before running back to the suite. I loved the attention—but I also wanted to see the damn city. Famous last words in the land of Lucrezia Borgia.

Once we managed to sneak out the back of the hotel, I discovered the Roman streets literally teemed with life, lust and luxury. Like a scene lifted from *The Roman Spring of Mrs. Stone*, Tennessee Williams' brilliant film starring Vivien Leigh and Warren Beatty, the avenues were alive with beautiful boys—the famous "Ragazzi di vito" fraternity—who strolled seductively along the rows of hotels, cafes and shops, smiling for the American women and men.

Naturally, they were available—for a price. With their dark, swarthy good looks, tight, muscular bodies and flashy grins, they could be found loping along the boulevards, scanning the streets for prospects. Their shirts were unbuttoned casually, pants pulled tight at the crotch. These young flesh brokers charmed everyone with their polish and wet-lipped, dreamy-eyed stares, melting their targets in minutes as they ran their fingers through wavy black hair and pretended nonchalance. I knew the act by heart—I had been like these hungry young boys so many years ago, and despite the change of locale, certain conditions of the heart never change. Lust is a universal emotion—and the Italian street boys knew it better than most.

Being in Rome was heaven—until one glorious morning when I opened up the newspaper and read the boldface headline: JAYNE MANSFIELD LOSES DRESS IN WRESTLING MATCH! My dress! I nearly strangled on my espresso. I knew Jayne was traveling in Europe, lugging her Blackwell gowns with her like some sort of Ziegfeld road show, but I never imagined she would use my beaded illusions to create this kind of publicity. Stationed in Venice, Jayne had obviously gotten out of hand with some unknown gentleman at a local nightclub and proceeded to cause a stir when she began wrestling with him on the dance floor and all my beautiful beads burst into a thousand scattered sparks across the room. I was livid—and I screamed furiously at Spencer that Jayne would be forever banned from the showroom. I wasn't going to spend weeks on a dress only to have La Mansfield—in one of her madcap stunts—rip it off at a moment's notice. Again bothering to create an illusion of nudity when Jayne was determined to reveal the real thing? Wiping up the espresso I had flung dramatically across the room, Spencer muttered his agreement.

The next morning we left for Venice—not necessarily to confront Jayne, but if the occasion arose, I could at least give her my if-looks-could-kill glare. Walking into the exquisite Danielli Hotel for dinner on their romantic roof, who did I spot but Miss

Wrestling Queen herself. Mickey Hargitay was nowhere in sight—and a good thing, too. She was making a spectacle of herself, kissing and cooing over her newfound friend to the point of near pornography, rubbing his chest and clinging to him with reckless abandon. A moist sheen clung to her skin, and her platinum hair was badly tousled as if she had just gotten out of bed. Maybe she had, for all I knew. When I went over to say hello, she could tell I wasn't happy with her behavior. Still, I held my tongue. After Argentina I felt it was best to be back in the United States before making a scene of epic proportions. And God knows, I had no interest in being caged up with her in some Italian jail cell. She might have gotten more attention than me.

I survived my fit of rage over Jayne by concentrating on Venice—a fairy-tale city if there ever was one. St. Mark's, the Bridge of Sighs, the Grand Canal looking down to the elegant Academia Bridge, the Moorish mystery of the prison-like Doge's Palace, the thousands of Venetian cats that darted and dashed through the stone palazzos—a mesmerizing, mist-filled fantasy rising from the water. Gondolas floated along the canals while white stone buildings seemed to float on the water like temples swimming in the sea. Soon, however, water transportation began to make me ill—all that rocking and rolling—and we retreated back to the terra firma of Rome. I didn't have a chance to say goodbye to Jayne, but I can only imagine how many times she "accidentally" fell into the canals—only to emerge dripping wet as drooling tourists, jealous gigolos and crazed paparazzi worshipped her every jiggle. I was furious—so what's new...

Recovering from Jayne's assault on my now-denuded gown, Spencer and I were in the midst of a lavish breakfast in the Excelsior's Garden Room when, to my utter surprise, I received a note from Faye Hammond, fashion editor of the *Los Angeles Times*, who happened to be in Florence. She invited us to pay her a visit and to attend the lavish summer fashion extravaganza at the Pitti Palace, one of the most exclusive events in all of European design. I smugly assumed I had made the big time, since Faye, a very influential fashion voice on the Southern California circuit, wasn't even an acquaintance, much less a friend. She had certainly never called me before. After our trek to Florence together, would she ever call me again?

At the Palace

The Pitti Palace showings were, without question, the most opulent in the world. As the train pulled into the ancient, vine-encrusted town of Florence, I wanted to be a part of that golden aristocratic atmosphere.

The president of the Florence Fashion Design Organization, G.B. Giorgini, met us at the station with Faye by his side. A short, stocky, gentle man with a cropped crown of white hair and a Romanesque profile, Giorgini resembled a modern-day Julius Caesar. Miss Hammond was far less imposing in a bright cotton print and mousy, flyaway hair. She looked more like a midwestern Sunday-school teacher than the fashion power-house she actually was. To greet Faye and G.B., I dressed the part: all black, no jewelry, severe and chic. Very Italian. After our hosts deluged us with open arms, lots of smiles and hugs from Faye, they proceeded to take us on a tour of Florence before the Pitti Palace showings the following day.

Florence was as beautiful as Venice, filled with priceless treasures, ancient monuments and villas, all merging into Florence's central piazza. Cobblestone streets led to wondrous sights—the Santa Maria Novella, an enormous black-and-white tiled church that gleamed in the golden sunlight; the Uffizi Galleries, where the world's greatest Renaissance paintings are displayed; the sparkling Arno River; the Pont de Vecchio, leading into the incredible gallery of goldsmith shops and the elaborate Medici Chapel, which contains the most famous sculpture known to man: Michelangelo's "David." I was in complete awe, standing before the marble masterpiece Michelangelo had sculpted hundreds of years ago. The sheer power, artistry and emotion in those curved white lines are unforgettable.

Equally unforgettable was the Pitti Palace showing, which was a nearly religious experience for me. As we sat waiting for the show to begin, I glanced around the huge tapestried room, gleaming with crystal and gold lights, fresh flowers and richly colored tile floors. God knows Hollywood could never match this in beauty or scope. The crème de la crème of society sat perched in special golden chairs with hand-carved arms. The rest of us sat in simpler seats. Already I realized there was a definite class system within the hallowed halls of the Pitti, not unlike America, where the buyers and attending celebrities sat in the choice first rows bordering the stage. Of course, the American shows didn't have 15th-century paintings adorning the walls, nor did the viewers have champagne served to them by liveried servants in regal attire. We were in a different world here, and I loved it. I felt like I was attending a royal wedding, not a fashion show.

The presentation began with a fanfare of music, filling the huge stone hall with magic. The dark ramp blossomed with a thousand tiny lights, adding a necklace of rainbow shimmer around the T-shaped stage. As elegant melodies wafted through the Palace, the room, ablaze with silks and satins, seemed to glow with color and glamour. Diamonds, emeralds, sapphires, rubies and pearls caught the light that streamed through the arched windows and danced around the wealthy wrists and necks of Europe's elite.

Lines of models appeared in a series of dazzling confections. As they sauntered down the runway, my mind raced back to California and the caustic press who panned the idea of mixing theater and fashion. Well, I reasoned, if it was good enough for the Pitti Palace, it was definitely good enough for me. I loved the drama, the props, the pacing, the people. In a very important way, these showings freed me to continue to do what I do best— create show-stopping events.

The next morning, the four of us toured Florence again. During our walk down quaint streets lined with terra-cotta pots filled with flowers, Giorgini invited me to show my collection at the Palace the following year. I was stunned. No American designer I knew of had ever been invited to appear onstage within those hallowed walls. I stammered a thank you, but basically I stood speechless and just stared open-mouthed. Faye smiled, G.B. shook my hand and Spencer, nearly apoplectic with excitement, grinned enthusiastically. Thank God we'd come to Italy—and how ironic that I had to leave America to find the confirmation I craved.

The only dark cloud that marred an otherwise sunny trip was Faye's insistence that we visit a street of jewelry makers on the Bridge of Sighs. It sounded exciting, so off we went, unaware of what she had in mind. I wanted to window shop—but Faye had other ideas. Strolling past a shop, she pointed to a stunning diamond bracelet in the window, ran in and asked to try it on. Like idiots, Spencer and I traipsed behind her like lambs to the slaughter.

Lady Hammond let it be known she would love to have this exquisite trinket—and implied that the fashion editorials in the powerful *L.A. Times* might reflect her deep appreciation. Although I'm positive the *Times* knew nothing about this flagrant bribery demand, I was appalled by her suggestion—a request, I might add, that I politely declined. This distasteful episode was the first of many such deceits I experienced over the years—more commonly known as "gifts of gratitude." Well, no one could be that grateful, and besides, the damn thing cost more than we spent on the entire trip. Anyway, I reasoned, what assurance did I have that Faye, after adorning her greedy little wrist, would fulfill her end of the bargain? It wasn't worth the trouble or the possible scandal if word leaked out.

My anger soared higher than the sky. I hated the "payoff" way of doing business, whether it was dinner, theater tickets (first five rows, center, naturally) or diamond bracelets. Spencer and I sent flowers to Lady Faye on our return. It was our way of acting as if nothing had happened, other than a gloriously fun meeting in Florence. After all, we still wanted to do the Pitti Palace showings the next year. It could be the making of our career internationally. So we decided to act as cool as possible. But Faye Hammond was absolutely frigid: She rarely covered my work again. C'est la vie.

As the year drew to a close, the business had grown to 129 staff members and production was at an unbelievable peak. Even higher were our spirits, which were floating at least ten feet off the ground. Our success was still rather incomprehensible to me, but I had no intention of arguing with good fortune.

Success usually gives birth to more success, so I decided to expand further. And what better way to expand than with the perfect finishing touch to any wardrobe—perfume.

The Sweet Smell of Success

Introducing a new line of perfume and toilet water was almost unheard of in American design circles. In 1963, perfume was still a French monopoly: Chanel No. 5, Arpege, Shalimar, L'Heure Blue and Joy—classic, celebrated and costly. Why shouldn't American designers enjoy a piece of the perfumed pie?

As usual, everyone said it was an impossibility. If such highly successful California designers as Adrian, Helen Rose and Edith Head hadn't entered the perfume industry, what chance did I have in succeeding? I didn't care when the doomsayers hit me with a litany of drawbacks. Advertising would cost a fortune; the crystal bottles I envisioned had to be created in Paris; marketing a brand-new fragrance would be next to impossible, considering the competition; and the actual scent would have to be created, mixed and packaged in Paris. I heard it all—and went ahead anyway. Spencer shook his head and prayed.

Sexy, sophisticated, provocative and privileged—that's how I saw my fragrances for women and for men. Coming up with the name was my first priority—I wanted a classic sound with a twist of humor, so I decided to number them Mr. Blackwell #10 and Mr. Blackwell #11 in a backhanded tribute to the greatest scent ever created—Chanel No. 5.

Creating a perfume is one of the most fascinating and time-consuming procedures on the planet. Extraordinary perfumers are as difficult to find as platinum-plated hen's teeth, but I knew where to go—Roure Du Pont, whose factory of fabulous fragrances was internationally famous for its creativity, quality and, most importantly, the best bunch of noses in all of New York. When the nose knew at Roure Du Pont, success was a sweet sniff away.

I flew to Manhattan and supervised the mixing, matching and measuring of hundreds of precious oils into what I thought was an incredible fragrance. Number Ten was an elegant, brisk blend of floral and Oriental notes that evolved into #11 just by adding a masculine overtone of spice. By basically keeping the same formula for both men and women, production costs were minimized and by bringing out both scents simultaneously, I'd hit two markets with one ad.

After Du Pont completed its work, five-gallon cans of my undiluted oils were shipped to Los Angeles and sent to a mixer in East L.A., of all places. There, Blackwell #10 and #11 was poured, packaged and prepared for sale. Who needed Paris?

Cyril Magnin called and wanted the fragrance for Joseph Magnin in San Francisco. I said yes—if he would carry my fashion collection as well. He agreed and we debuted the perfume to the Northern California market in July, followed by a masterpiece of promotion at the Continental Hotel on Sunset in L.A.: an X-rated sniffing party. The sophisticated fashion press was in for a shock—my favorite emotion.

Held in a beautiful suite high above the Strip, each guest, upon entering, was given a list of suggested body parts for perfume usage. It was good for a laugh and a blurb. After being seated at round tables, my assembled sniffers were presented with my latest brainstorm in tiny crystal bottles by sexy models who asked them to smell and rate. After a symphony of sniffs and snorts, and several "oohs" and "aahs," #10 and #11 were pronounced triumphant. To clinch the fragrant finale, a Pink Pussycat stripper burst into the room and "entertained." The press loved it.

Mere hours after the party, we were on the front page of the *L.A. Times* with a half-page spread and two photos, actually overshadowing the headlines. Murder, money and mayhem are nothing compared to a perfect perfume press party. What that tells you about society's priorities is up for grabs—but the front-page article sent sales soaring in the nearly 300 stores that had already ordered the fragrance, scent unsmelled. Every bottle sold out in less than a week.

If I had known what was coming next,
I might have taken a little extra time to stop—
and smell the perfume.

Within two weeks we were on the front page of the *L.A. Times*—not once, but twice. Short of being a serial killer, it was an absolutely unheard-of accomplishment. Our perfume party was heralded as the "most stunning event of the genre this season—mad in concept, flamboyant in execution and galvanizing in denouement."

The other front-page story included a quarter-sheet photo of me with Jane Russell and singer Beryl Davis modeling two of my gowns for their upcoming appearance in Las Vegas. It was million-dollar advertising at a price I liked best: free!

Three Crosses to Bear

In a weak moment I had agreed to design the onstage wardrobes for Jane Russell, Connie Haines and Beryl Davis, who had decided to put together a song-and-dance act for Las Vegas' late-summer season. Designed as a singing showcase for all three stars, the Jane/Connie/Beryl show was scheduled to open Louis Armstrong's Riviera Hotel engagement on August 5. They wanted clothes, lots of 'em. What they got, and I in return, was a comedy of egos and errors that could only, it seems, happen to me.

It really started out as a great idea—and ended up a smash. I guess that's all that should matter, but the period between the beginning and the end was, to put it mildly, a hodgepodge of confusion that rivaled *The Three Faces of Eve* in personality conflicts. At least with Eve there was a reason for her madness. I'm not quite sure what Jane Russell's excuse was, or Connie Haines' for that matter. Only Beryl Davis remained my connection to the rapidly vanishing realm of sanity that soon enveloped my days and nights. If I imagined diva Lily Pons as a low point in my career, then Las Vegas proved to be positively subterranean by comparison.

The cast of characters was as follows: Jane Russell, the former Howard Hughes discovery who shot to fame via *The Outlaw*, was darkly voluptuous, ravishingly sensuous and didn't give a damn about Hollywood, images or publicity. She had endured all that "star-making crap" years ago under Hughes' heavy thumb and had no interest in repeating the process. Jane was the ultimate "broad"—she drank a bit, laughed a lot, swore a little and basically couldn't care less. She hated fittings, despised rehearsals and was the only real claim to international fame this trio had. Appearing in Vegas should have excited her somewhat, but Jane was at the stage in her life where she'd had the midnight glamour—and was now spending half her life sleeping it off.

Connie Haines—short and petite with dark, curly hair and pixie-cute eyes—looked a little like Rebecca of Sunnybrook Farm. In reality, she was aggressive, devious and fancied herself the spokesperson of the group. Once a popular singer with Tommy Dorsey's band, she could still belt 'em with the best—but her loudest and longest notes were usually saved for offstage. With an uncanny ability to keep situations stirred up, she was the veritable bee in everybody's bonnet, and there was no doubt when Connie's stinger had stung. Miss Haines, if I'm honest with myself, always fought for what she truly thought was best for the group—although, mysteriously, the pink spotlight always seemed to find her profile first.

As for Beryl Davis—well, she was the oasis in a fiery desert. Tall, elegant and striking in a Dietrich-like way, she was also a fabulous singer. And a born diplomat who did her best to keep the peace—a challenge Gandhi in his most serene moments would have found hard to achieve.

If Jane gave the act pizzazz and Connie offered vocal vitality, then Beryl wrapped it in a sheen of elegance. Her ballads, which she performed in a beautifully intimate, mesmerizing way, stopped the rehearsals cold. Beryl was—and is—a gorgeous lady; she comes as close to being perfect as anyone I've ever known, with a voice that would make Samson happy to lose his hair. The other two in the group made me want to pull out mine.

After meeting with the good, the bad and the egotistical, I frantically wondered what I had gotten myself into. Judging from the few rehearsals I had seen, things were in disarray at best. We got down to serious work in mid-July, when the trio descended on my showroom one rainy afternoon. I can't really recall if it was actually raining, but it certainly was in my memory book. In fact, it was more like a tropical typhoon.

Such diverse types created a real design dilemma. What might work on Jane's showgirl figure would cheapen Beryl and caricature Connie, who stood a good six inches below the others. But these were costuming problems I could eventually solve with enough time, seamstresses and aspirin. What I didn't anticipate was the eternal, infernal ringing of the phone between meetings. Calls from Connie in particular did little to brighten my day; in fact, they threw me into a tailspin. Accusations that I was secretly sabotaging her costumes in favor of Jane and Beryl were daily events I was forced to endure.

Before all of us flew to Vegas, I witnessed a three-ring circus of jealousy, backstabbing, egomania and showbiz insecurity. Connie knew it was impossible to compete with Jane's glamorous image, so she made doubly sure my costumes for her were as flawless as humanly possible. The only saving grace was the fact that I managed to use less material for her stage outfits—and still charged her the same price. A rather pathetic consolation prize, especially since my profits most likely would go to the services of an accomplished psychiatrist after the August opening.

Las Vegas has always seemed like a crazy dream to me—all neon-lit, starry-eyed, roulette-spinning madness. Staying there for any length of time convinces even the most bizarre character that even stranger people not only teem but thrive amidst this burst of gaudy brightness scattered across the desert floor. Watching Bible-toting schoolmarms slamming slot machines with the machismo of Muhammad Ali was enough to make me think I was nearly normal. In Las Vegas, every person has a story and every dollar has its price. It's Disneyland gone bad. Jane, Connie and Beryl were quite at home in this cuckoo-land of craps, cleavage and casinos.

For my trio of stars, I created what I would later dub my "above-the-table" look. Each gold- and jewel-embroidered dress was elaborately beaded from the bust upward, creating a lavish necklace effect from the stage. Jane's gold gown was so delicate, in fact, that I had to book an extra seat on the flight to Vegas just to carry it—a fact that the press dutifully reported. Upon seeing the photos, of course, Connie's paranoia hit new peaks.

The Riviera swarmed with tourists eager to see Jane onstage. With rumors that Howard Hughes might show up for opening night, the pressure intensified. We were all skipping across a tightrope without a net—and pre-show jitters punctuated the meeting I had with Jane, Connie and Beryl the night before opening. The sole exception was Jane herself. Sleepy-eyed as ever, she just dismissed all the chatter with a bored toss of her head and a sip of her drink. Connie, talking a mile a minute, remained forever lost in her own cloud of self-adoration, informing everyone from bellhop to maid that the queens had arrived. Beryl managed a fatigued smile from the corner of the room as we discussed the last-minute details.

After what seemed a year, Spencer and I escaped the madhouse to catch Liberace's closing-night performance. I heard he was his usual outrageous self, but that his opening act, a young girl from Brooklyn, was the real eye-opener. For once, the hype proved to be true. Watching her sing a revamped "Happy Days Are Here Again"—in a horrible red-and-white checked tablecloth dress—sent chills down my spine. We sat transfixed, as did the rest of the captivated crowd. She was given the longest standing ovation I had ever witnessed. People screamed and cried and begged for more, more, more. But this girl knew when to stop. No encore.

The tiny 21-year-old gamine causing all the musical commotion was named Barbra—Barbra Streisand. I knew from the very first note that she would become a legend. And she has. Stories about her spectacular talent raced across the nation and then the world. After struggling to be accepted—on her own terms, I might add—she was already basking in the glow of sudden stardom. Although not conventionally beautiful, she became a star among stars and, as she grew older, would even bring a new sense of style to the fashion world. As I watched Streisand take her final bows, I also knew nothing would stop her. She was already at a peak most performers only dream about. As the years progressed, she has been awarded every imaginable honor, as well as the dubious distinction of appearing on my list more than anyone. We all have an Achilles heel, and fashion was Barbra's.

Of course, bright and early the next morning, I couldn't wait to tell Connie about Streisand's closing-night ovation. But my trio of sopranos had already heard the news, each reacting in their own unique way:

Jane muttered, "That's fine, who cares?"

Beryl was "happy for Barbra's success."

And Connie—well, Miss Haines was fuming. The more she heard, the more she fumed, and fumed, and fumed. I finally shut my mouth and prepared for opening night.

Moments before the sequined curtains rose, I checked and rechecked the gowns. Then the overture began in a swell of strings and trumpets. Peering out from the backstage area, I saw a room packed to the rafters with smoke, booze-filled glasses and a thousand fans—all waiting for Jane, who was set to open the show with a solo. As a matter of fact, all of us were waiting for Jane while she stood, face to the wall, praying. Sensing a possible disaster, I volunteered to escort her onstage, to which she readily agreed. For all her tough-as-steel bravado, Jane was as nervous as a cat-stalked canary. So, out into the jammed room we walked, me in my tuxedo, pretending to be a member of the Riviera staff, and Russell resplendent in her gorgeous gold dress, which drew a chorus of appreciative whistles from the boys in the back—Jane's kind of crowd.

Our trek to the microphone was a perilous journey in high heels and, feeling no pain, Jane couldn't walk a crooked line, much less a straight one. Shouting, stomping and screaming, the audience couldn't have cared less. Jane Russell, I suddenly realized, was a real star. Somehow, some way, Howard Hughes' publicity machine had created someone American audiences adored. Despite her lack of rehearsal, she was the standout in a show that was sold out. Wonders never cease. Neither did Connie's phone calls.

While I was head over heels in a deluge of work, Spencer was in the painstaking process of opening our new showroom in New York— a major business decision that caused lots of excitement, and lots of second thoughts.

Between my Las Vegas trio, designing the regular line and making personal appearances, I was swamped. We'd been thinking of opening a New York branch since 1962, but the question remained unanswered: Could I succeed on infamous Seventh Avenue? The risks were enormous, the rewards unknown.

Seventh Avenue

Ever the gambler, I did the unthinkable: moved "Mr. Blackwell" to a small showroom located through the back door of a firm called Hannah Troy. But Hannah Troy's designers, aware I spent most of my time in Los Angeles, "borrowed" most of my designs and put them in their own line. Needless to say, we didn't last there long—just long enough to test the waters, which were shark-infested indeed.

Spencer then found a large, cement-walled cutting room on the 21st floor of 530 Seventh Avenue. Basically, it was little more than a hollowed-out shell of a tomb—cold, damp, old— but we felt that with enough time and imagination, we could turn this barren barn into the city's most elegant showroom. Spencer took over refurbishing chores, and the results were spectacular.

Filled with 18th-century French furniture that he purchased on a quick trip to New Orleans—beveled mirrors, huge crystal vases, a black baby-grand piano, damask draperies—the show-room had every amenity anyone would ever need. We had trans-formed our 3,000-square-foot cement box into a shimmering showplace, a room where mirrors reflected a thousand sequins in the soft, spot-lit air—where, to be honest, I had the ultimate stage to present my very own fantasies in fabric. With a new line of clothes that paid homage to the legendary look of Garbo—tai-lored wools, slouch hats, even "Queen Christina"-like gowns— my opening was a thrilling moment. Our elaborate invasion had worked. I only wish I'd taken time to enjoy our hard-won success, but life in the sixties moved at a frantic pace, and a tidal wave of work threatened to engulf me at any moment.

That summer of '63 was hectic, nerve-shattering, often infuriating—and one of the most artistically fulfilling periods I've ever experienced. What mattered to me—beyond my ego battles—was having a sense of security in an insecure business. The pressure to deliver collections, the challenge of a new perfume and the sobering fact that I knew Seventh Avenue was waiting with baited breath for me to fall on my ass, brought out the fighter in me. I had too much at stake to fail. I could never imagine, during those sweltering days in Vegas, for example, that I would grow to cherish those moments of madness as a summer of innocence—that November would crash around us in a shower of bullets as the political promise of Kennedy's Camelot was shattered forever. Winds of change swept through the United States, but harsh, cruel realities remained.

The assassination happened on the day I was preparing my first in-store fashion show at Moss Brothers in Tampa, Florida. Moss Brothers, a very important account that had gone to extraordinary lengths to arrange a presentation of my collection, was a definite coup. I arrived at my hotel room, excited and hungry for applause. As I unpacked, I switched on the radio. Suddenly, without warning, the walls of my room seemed to tumble down around me as the choked voice over the airwaves announced that President Kennedy had been shot. I was devastated. Angry. Frightened. Frantically I flipped the dial as the horrible truth spoke to me in a dozen different voices on a dozen different stations. And all of them, just like me, were wondering why.

I arrived at Moss Brothers in a near state of shock and went directly to the store manager—a tall, emaciated toothpick of a man with tight lips and an arrogant, officious manner. Before I managed to speak, he instructed me in a lonely, distant voice that reflected years of emotional turmoil in an unforgiving industry: "You must go on."

"I have no intention of doing the show—not now."

Something as frivolous as fashion seemed damned empty in the face of the international tragedy that had just occurred.

Standing over me like a high executioner, the manager demanded that I perform as scheduled. He reminded me tensely that all the top customers were already seated. Too much had been arranged to call it off now. "You will go on," he finished with bitter force.

Reeling from his indifference, I felt numb. I decided to take matters into my own hands. Ten minutes before showtime, I walked backstage and told the sullen-faced models hired by the management not to bother changing, and we walked onstage together in our street clothes. In a hushed voice, I confided to the audience that I couldn't go on.

"How can a fashion show override the death of our President? Surely none of us can be that superficial"—not even your store manager, I wanted to say.

I glanced to stage left where he stood, grim-faced, not knowing what I planned to do next—or how his cherished clientele would react. But before I could continue, the audience rose as one—many crying openly for the loss of our great leader—until I, too, was lost in the raw emotion of the moment. Tears streamed down our faces, and none of us bothered to wipe them away. I couldn't help but think: How could a beaded bodice possibly make a difference in these troubled, deadly times? Outside, the Florida sun splashed a golden glow over the city, but here we felt as cold and gray as an unforgiving winter night. A feeling of powerlessness enveloped us.

I returned to my hotel room and stood in the darkness. In the still hush, the silent radio and the blank television screen beckoned—but I had heard enough. Too much. I didn't want to know any more. After stuffing my clothes haphazardly in a suitcase, I put the bags by the window.

Peering out into the streets below, people moved in slow motion, frozen in fear and sorrow. I lit a cigarette in the silent room, then watched several petals fall from a bouquet of roses someone had sent to me. They floated forlornly to the floor, soon to wither and die. I realized I hadn't even bothered to turn on the bedside lamp. I felt comfortable in the dark melancholy that wafted over me. Images of John Kennedy flashed through my mind. It would be a very long time before anyone would recover. And we would never be quite the same.

My voyage home, trapped in a web of depression, was a flight I honestly don't remember. The land beneath my window looked dirty, joyless, ugly. Staring into the void of the sky beyond, the horrible awareness that time is so tenuous made me realize that life was too short, too fragile to waste. All we really have are our dreams, however tattered they become as the years speed by. Life as it really was had a desperation, a callous cruelty I couldn't accept—not then, not now, not ever.

By February of 1964, my desire to fulfill those locked-away desires, hopes and wishes grew stronger. I had endured the wrath of indignant movie stars, pricked my fingers on spiteful pincushions, gone nearly blind examining bugle beads, suffered hearing damage from an opera star's high-pitched shrieks, been savagely bitten by the press and viciously barked at by the fashion industry itself. If I was going to make it to the top in this cutthroat business—and stay there—I was bloody well going to do it in a manner, and a manor, that I could be proud of.

The Burglary

I was ready to start living some of that glamour I was always talking about. When we spotted a huge white mansion for sale on Windsor Boulevard in Hancock Park, one of Los Angeles's most beautiful areas, I had to have it. Spencer typically pleaded poverty, pronouncing me "absolutely impossible" about any kind of financial responsibility. But money had little meaning to me when I wanted something. Spencer had always provided both the necessities and luxuries of my life. I rarely had—or have—more than a quarter in my pocket at any given time. Whether we could afford the house or not had no bearing on my decision to make an offer on it. Everyone needs a fantasy, and this place was mine. Spencer finally agreed. But it would be tough. Cash was not our biggest commodity; nerve was.

After weeks of negotiating, manipulating, borrowing and praying, the escrow finally closed. It would be a continual struggle to maintain the house the way I felt it should be kept, but we never let on; it was our secret. The upfront image of well-manicured wealth looked great, and our new home was indeed a palace.

The 28-room, 12,000-square-foot, 45-year-old Mediterranean villa resembled an alabaster temple—a romantic study in sweeping arches, pale stone terraces and column-studded porticos. Through the curved front door, a 40 x 60 foot entrance hall loomed in old-world splendor as a grand staircase, in rare old mahogany, spilled down from the second floor in a tide of bottle green carpeted steps.

Sunny rooms ran the front of the house—drawing rooms, salons, a dining room seating 40 or more, complete with an elaborate, hand-carved painted ceiling over one hundred years old. Rare French and Italian antiques filled the rooms. Delicate French doors, ten feet high, opened onto acres of sculpted grass and clipped gardens covered with pink and white roses, irises and gardenias. Huge, fan-topped palms dotted the sloping lawns.

With a house like this, decorating took on a new dimension—and dementia. As fast as I could, I furnished my home with art, 18th-century crystal and giant bronze chandeliers. Now I had the chance to see if the fantasy would bring happiness—or something else. I was too excited to worry about the enormous upkeep a place like this would require—but Spencer would see to that. During those first months, I wanted to experience the illusion of an enchanted life filled with grand mansions, glittering parties, evenings of music, champagne and laughter. My new home would provide the perfect Hollywood backdrop for the flamboyant role I had chosen to play.

Between designing the interior of the house and designing my new line of clothes, I immersed myself in entertaining. Sit-down dinners for 40 were not uncommon during those Windsor Boulevard days, and these enchanted evenings brought back memories of earlier times, growing up in the glitter that was Hollywood.

I thought it would be a great idea to premiere my fall line of clothes at the house. I planned to hold my first outdoor evening fashion presentation beside the gazebo that stood at the side of a formal walled garden, bordered with beds of pale spring blossoms. The setting, I hoped, would be as dramatic as the clothes I had designed for the occasion. I had no idea just how dramatic the final show would be. How could I? I'm no masochist.

The week before the show was a saga that ended in an epic tragedy rivaling the worst of Tennessee Williams. I worried: Was the house ready? Who knew how much food should be ordered from Perino's? Should we hire live musicians and risk the wrath of our blueblood neighbors? Would we dare to disturb their boring tranquility? Would the models show up? Where would we put the press? And finally, the most serious question of all: What about the seating arrangements?

In Hollywood, this particular thankless job is an art form. Stroking egos always is. Seating nearly 300 celebrities, socialites and fashion buyers is no Roman holiday. Who sits where and with whom?—that's the question. If we made the mistake of placing one too many ex-wives at the same table, I could kiss my peaceful gathering goodbye. Countries have been overthrown with less violence than the riotous possibilities presented by this social gaffe. So Spencer and I spent days fine-tuning our battle plan.

Social enemies and buyers were placed at different ends of the garden, a limit of two known adulterers to a table, and at least one big star to a seating. The rest of the group had to have someone to whisper about. That was, and is, the real secret of good table seating. Speaking of tables, Spencer and I knew ours had to be round. Stylistically, they were a vast improvement over the boring square designs, but round tables, most importantly, managed to avoid quite cleverly the problem of who to seat at the head. I knew that everyone in this egocentric crowd would expect to have that seat of honor. To avoid an uprising, I did what King Arthur did so many centuries ago: I ordered round tables and scattered them around the garden.

Saturday, three days before Judgment Day, I put the finishing touches on the line my seamstresses had slaved over for weeks. The new collection was heavily beaded: gowns, evening capes, cocktail costumes and mink-cuffed theater coats—gorgeous, dramatic, excessively opulent and extremely expensive to create. That cost, unfortunately, showed up on the rapidly growing price tags of my clothes. But I refused to cut corners—or ideas— and if ranch-mink piping sent the cost skyward, so be it. I had grown as a designer.

Downtown, we carefully wrapped the clothes in plastic bags, organized the jewelry and numbered each outfit. There were 52 styles in all. Even I was amazed at the intricate, time-consuming effort that went into each dress: sprays of handsewn jet, showers of crystal flowers, bows of beads. When the work was complete, Spencer arranged for the clothes to be packed in our station wagon. We planned to take them home for safekeeping.

Minutes after the car was locked by our shipping boy in the garage of the building beneath our showroom on a Saturday afternoon, he returned to the showroom for a brief moment to pick up more samples. But in that moment, tragedy struck. When Spencer and I walked down to the parked car, the station wagon was empty! At first, the hideous ramifications of that sight didn't sink in. Then, suddenly, as if scalding water had been thrown in our faces, we realized that the unthinkable had occurred: The collection had been stolen! I scanned the backseat desperately—and saw a mile of car upholstery. The scariest sight of my life. Naturally, I became totally hysterical. I poked myself to make sure I wasn't dreaming; no luck. Desperately, I prayed we were the victim of a sadistic joke; fat chance.

Mouth open, eyes widening, Spencer scoured the area while I sat in a daze. Nothing turned up except my temper. I pulled myself out of my trance and began screaming. What was I going to do? Someone in Los Angeles had a fabulous new wardrobe, and I was the unwitting donor. This was not my idea of clothing the poor, I can tell you that.

With hallucinations of my future vanishing in a vapor of tragedy, I racked my battered brain. There was no alternative: The collection would have to be duplicated by Tuesday evening. Spencer threw up his hands and sighed, "Impossible." I shouted back that nothing was impossible. My life was proof of that!

I lurched for the phone quicker than Jayne Mansfield created hysterical headlines, and told everyone the news. The reaction remains one of the most astonishing moments of my career. The entire fashion community—seamstresses, cutters, beaders, finishers, even designers—came together for the first and possibly last time. Volunteering their time, talent and invaluable services, they began working to save my show and my reputation. I had no words to describe how grateful I was. Certain feeble-minded fools implied that the robbery was yet another Blackwell publicity stunt; I informed them in bloodcurdling shrieks that if I needed attention I certainly wouldn't destroy my own collection for a few tired lines of copy in the morning paper. I was much more creative than that.

For the next 72 hours, fingers flew, tongues wagged, seamstresses sewed, cutters cut, beaders beaded—and I prayed. And screamed, "Please, God, deliver me from this disaster." No one would believe this in a movie. Only reality—and my own brand of emotional bad luck—could wreak this kind of nightmare. But deliver me He did. By Tuesday afternoon every dress, cape, gown, hat and scarf had been completely re-created, with one sole exception; the mink-cuffed ball gown. Unless I wanted to cut up my own fur coat, mink was unavailable. No single dress was worth that, so I dropped it from the line, happy for what I— and everyone else in town—had accomplished. No movie studio at the height of its costuming powers could have matched our tour de force of fashion sorcery that infamous weekend. Even in 1964, miracles could happen.

The night of the show, the house was polished and primped and primed for the assault by the guests, who had by this time heard about the Blackwell fashion robbery. Jane Russell and Beryl Davis arrived bravely to salvage what they assumed would be an unsalvageable show. God bless them for being there. I'm sure half the crowd was waiting for me to introduce my models wearing sketches of the collection, but what they got was the real thing, and the reaction was electric. Also electric was Jane and Beryl's act: Russell stopped the show with a fabulously suggestive version of "Big Bad Jane" while Beryl, ever the lady, sang "The Bluebird of Happiness." Connie Haines was nowhere in sight, which proved to me that some prayers are answered.

Onstage, I managed to make light of the entire robbery— while Spencer smiled unconvincingly when guests remarked how well I had taken the catastrophe. His left ear was temporarily deaf from my bombastic screams—but he never let on. In Hollywood, appearances are everything.

I went on with my life, designing and selling and planning my next Hollywood project: Amanda Blake's wedding. Amanda, the famed Kitty on TV's "Gunsmoke," was a friend and client, so when she called one morning to tell me she was planning to marry, I attempted to express my pleasure, although inwardly I thought, Oh, no, not again. Amanda was very unlucky with men, and I had a deep feeling that her latest paramour wasn't going to end her uninterrupted string of strike-outs. But she was adamant: This was the love of her life and just this once, would I host this dubious affair? She wanted her wedding to be out of a fairy tale, and my house, she raved, was the perfect palace. What could I say? I certainly didn't want to tell her I thought she was headed for disaster, but in retrospect, I should have.

The Beatles Are Coming

The marriage was nearly over before it began. To say that Amanda and her groom fought constantly before the nuptials was the understatement of the century. Theirs was an extremely passionate physical relationship that left Amanda, even on the day of her betrothal, badly bruised and requiring massive makeup.

"The press must never know," was the recurring theme on that infamous day. And despite the hollering from my French bedroom where Amanda attempted to dress, they never did.

If only she could have been more like her on-screen persona, and less the incurable romantic who, once she fell in love, threw all caution to the wind. But I was powerless to stop her. When Amanda made up her mind, especially in the realm of romance, that was it. She was in love with love, and that was her great downfall, both emotionally and financially.

My house was becoming a hotel, and I was getting fed up with it. Every socialite in town wanted to use the garden for parties, receptions, teas—even, God forbid, cookouts. I wanted a little peace and privacy. But some things are not meant to be, and my serenity in a quiet house was one of them.

I barely had a week to recover from the wedding when I received a phone call from a real estate lady representing Brian Epstein, who managed the Beatles. As it turned out, he wanted to rent our house for "the boys," as he affectionately called them. They were on the second leg of their groundbreaking American tour, and would hit Los Angeles in August. For once, I was speechless.

"The Beatles? At my house?"

The thought was a bit disconcerting. Would they tear the place down? Hold all-night jam sessions? Or be content to sit around and burn a few irreparable holes in the carpet? I had no idea, and at first I was unwilling to find out. But it's hard to turn down the hottest stars in the universe, especially when everyone I knew practically frothed at the mouth with envy when I told them about Epstein's request. Admittedly, the Beatles did interest me. Anyone with that kind of talent always does. After talking to several people who knew the band, I discovered that these four boys were really quite gentlemanly, and had no interest in vandalizing anyone's home, much less mine. Feeling a surge of relief, I agreed to let them stay at our house. As the days grew closer to their arrival date, the web of secrecy around the group's travel plans grew harder and harder to keep. I felt like royalty was coming to stay—which, in the sixties, is exactly what the Beatles were. I began a cram session on their music, and despite my initial reluctance, I must admit they were incredible. People who didn't know that the Beatles were planning to stay with us wondered about my sudden interest in rock 'n' roll, and I'm sure they thought I had gone over the edge as "I Want to Hold Your Hand" blasted out of my speakers for the fiftieth time.

Then, two weeks before they arrived for their August 23, 1964, Hollywood Bowl engagement, some smart-ass on the ten o'clock news leaked where the group planned to stay—and World War III began. In a scene straight out of *The Day of the Locust*, vast throngs of frenzied fans, like armies of camera-carrying ants, surrounded the house in a siege of celebrity mania.

As the circus-like atmosphere escalated to Felliniesque proportions, we had no alternative but to admit defeat—much to the relief of my terrified neighbors. Over a loudspeaker, police blasted the news that the Beatles would be staying elsewhere. But like true believers in that age-old Hollywood credo, "Don't believe anything until it's been officially denied," thousands of fans remained camped out in front of the house. Unfortunately for them, the news was true—and at the very last minute the Beatles retreated to a home in Bel Air to avoid the melee.

Spencer and I were disappointed not to have met them, but we did attend their sold-out-before-it-was-announced performance at the Bowl. The music—if we could have heard it—was drowned out in a storm of shrieks, sighs, screams and squeals. I'm surprised they even bothered to play, much less sing. The noise was deafening, and quite self-defeating, in the long run. Because of scenes like this, the Beatles would eventually give up concert performing. With that kind of adulation, I couldn't blame them.

In 1965, things began to change. My career became an obsession, and the obsession was quickly devouring me. With the success Spencer and I had enjoyed for the past seven years, my friends assumed my happiness and stability were as certain as my next collection, my next acerbic one-liner, my next glittering party. On the shiny surface of my life, the image of contentment fooled most of the people most of the time. But in the land of illusion, realities are not what they seem. As I grew more successful, I grew less satisfied emotionally. I began to feel a pervading loneliness creep over my days. To be alone—or worse, to feel alone—in a world of millions of people applauding my career made me realize that success can be a tough place to live. I began to sink into my work schedule like a robot, without any hope of climbing out into the sun that never stopped shining in Southern California.

The Big and Small of It

Like a slowly worsening case of the flu, I became tired of working. I didn't know if it was my impossible schedule, or if it went even deeper, but I knew I felt powerless to stop my bouts of depression. I was sick of being taken for granted. My workrooms were not the cheeriest places to be. The idea that designers spend all day sketching clothes under great crystal chandeliers while reclining on tufted chaise lounges is a misconception. For me, there were no lavish private offices, chaise lounges or a dozen errand boys at my beck and call. My own staff consisted of one assistant who doubled as a pattern maker, two sample makers and a finisher who also served as a model-dresser if a customer should appear on the scene, requesting an impromptu fashion show. Stuck with my now-infamous fluorescent lights, a phone so antiquated I felt like I was talking in a bottomless well and four stark walls that were suffocatingly windowless, my office was as boring as an old B-movie.

Spencer's frugality continued to reach new heights when it came to my own needs. Today I appreciate his less-than-spendthrift ways, for what we have is due to him, not me. But by controlling the firm, he also controlled my life, and sacrifices had to be made. Spencer taught me about the mundane facts of the fashion business: Even after a spectacular season, we had to hold on to as much of our money as possible. Sample fabrics had to be bought at a minimum, since the bills were due long before we shipped the product. And profits were the paper kind that had to go back into the cost of the next collection. A line of new dresses ran no less than $50,000 to create, not to mention publicity, office upkeep, salaries. The list seemed to grow longer and longer as we grew more successful.

But I worried if we could hang on to our success. We were now living in the land of love children who hated glamour, in a world where the young elite rejected tradition. The fashion of the day was a bizarre mix of Beatles-type accessories and pop-art clothes—absolutely horrendous unless you were superstar model Jean Shrimpton, who actually looked good in a sack dress. The Carnaby Street influence would soon rock and roll the fashion world enough to make me add that extra beaded bodice in a flash. The Beatles ushered in a new generation that wore beatnik boots, ill-fitting tops and tight peg-legged pants. The music was the work of genius, but the clothes were the work of a madman.

The days of the little black dress were over. Would my clothes still sell? Or would I become as outdated as many of my other designing rivals? I didn't know, nor did anyone else in the precarious world of fashion design. Everyone was frightened, nervous and jumpy, searching for a new look. It hit me like a thunderstorm.

It was more than obvious that the larger lady was totally left out or ignored in the eyes of the "fashion world." There was a terrribly wrong belief that if a woman was larger than a size 12, she was either older or couldn't afford the best of high couture. I always said "big is beautiful," so it was then that I decided to produce for larger women the identical line I had created for smaller women. Little did I suspect that many buyers would assume my styles would be matronly and old-looking because of the lady's size. But since when did a larger woman lack the ability to look just as smashing as a smaller one?

Since simplicity was the Blackwell signature, this was an exciting new adventure for me. I was off and running with a whole new concept, and loving every minute of it. Lane Bryant was the only retailer to work with. In spite of being the highest-priced line in the store, we had almost a 100 percent sales record. The distribution was sensational because of their dozens of stores. Our shippings soared and the profits were ringing like church chimes.

For me it was another opening, another show: I had given birth to the above-the table look. Above the table was a phrase I invented, and it simply meant that most of your investment in a dress should be the most visible part of it for an evening. After all, at most black-tie affairs, you are seen mostly from the waist up. That's why I created the "illusion" bustline, often jeweled with the most magnificent crystals money could buy. With the cream of European seamstresses, we hand-beaded everything right here in L.A. Everything from the waist up was emphasized, creating a totally new look. There wasn't any way a woman could say, "Let me think about it. I have one similar to that at home"—unless she'd just bought one from us the week before.

The mid-sixties, however, were the beginning of John Fairchild's reign of terror over American fashion, the dawn of an empire that would ultimately destroy several talented designers' careers through his poisonous, power-mad decrees on who was "in" and—more importantly—who was "out." As head of the fashion trade journal *Women's Wear Daily*, Fairchild wasn't quite omnipotent yet, but heads would soon roll and reputations would be ravaged ruthlessly. In 1965 the signs were there and I watched, knowing full well that one doesn't stand under a falling wall without running for cover if you possibly can. My fellow designers mocked my wariness of Fairchild, but I had a hunch he would prove to be the fashion dictator of our time.

The fashion scene in Europe, meanwhile, was hopeless at best. Lots of press, no lasting sales—typical of designers intent on creating fads, which, by definition, never last beyond next week. I wasn't about to subject the American woman to such fatuous fashions, and in my efforts to buck the tide of the current stream of one-hit-wonder designers, I became more and more obsessed. But this obsession was slowly fraying the edges, tearing away at the fabric of my life. I felt Spencer slipping away from me—or was I slipping away from him? It was time to focus on a new direction.

Television was the answer—kind of getting away from myself. Being on camera, saying the most outrageous things, playing the "Blackwell part," I became the world's most infamous talk-show guest. And with all this incredible exposure, the Worst Dressed List simply exploded.

The Television Years

I really loved the television medium, but contrary to most people's perceptions, my appearances didn't affect sales. If anything, my celebrity became a negative. How can an entertainer be a designer? That was the standard question. TV did, however, add a glow of humor to my controversial ways, and taught me how to communicate with millions of people with the wink of an eye or a toss of my head. I was offered literally hundreds of bookings. The List had taken off worldwide, and my television appearances over the next few years gave me the kind of controversial credibility I desired.

Spencer kept toiling day and night, while I spent much of the late sixties in front of a camera, uttering outrageous put-downs that made women across America whisper, "Oh, my, but he's so right." For example, I dubbed Phyllis Diller a "scarecrow hung on a clothesline after a heavy windstorm"—which, by the way, she loved. And as my bookings increased, so did my popularity with middle America. They loved the idea that I didn't fall prey to the standard Hollywood "doesn't she look fabulous" routine. TV producers quickly realized my good-natured barbs meant ratings.

Most of the talk shows were thoroughly rehearsed and scripted down to the last gasp, each question and answer carefully prepared. I would have preferred going out onstage and being as outrageous as possible—hanging myself on my own terms, so to speak. But that kind of freedom was as hard to find as Shelley Winters' waist. Through the art of the unexpected ad-lib, however, I managed to raise more than my fair share of eyebrows, especially when it came to critiquing the host of the show and the visiting celebrities who sat on the obligatory sofa—which was always bumpy, caused heat rash and, I feared, was wired to electrocute me when I went too far.

The cruelest aspect of some of these appearances was the insistence of a few sadistic producers that I "rip up" the guests. My usual question, "Do they know it?", was followed invariably by the reply, "Oh, of course they do—and they're thrilled." But of course I only succeeded in making an enemy. Little wonder my dressing room felt like Siberia after some shows. But if I was going to get used, so be it.

In January of 1967 I was booked on "The Joey Bishop Show," little suspecting what kind of nightmare was about to follow. All I knew was that Joey's show was great exposure, had exciting guests and was co-hosted by Regis Philbin, who I had known since his early television days in San Diego. Regis, short, snappy and street-smart, was Joey's catch-all; I heard he caught all the hell Joey threw his way if things went wrong. I sympathized with Regis, since Bishop was as tough as he was talented. But regardless of his reputation, I hoped my appearance would be a big moment—and, was it ever! The biggest moment of professional near-suicide in my entire life.

At the Vine Street ABC Studio, I met with the show's pre-interviewer, who naturally wanted me to talk about my recent Worst Dressed List, which had been released just a few days before. The deal was that Joey would feed me the names of my List-makers and I would give him my prescribed line. Whatever comments Joey made were okayed by the watchdog producer and included in the script. No ad-libs allowed. Before my spot I didn't have the opportunity to see how the show was progressing; the "Green Room" television set didn't work. It was only later that I realized the blank TV screen was intentional. Like a blindfold before a firing squad, Joey's guests were kept from witnessing the other executions taking place onstage.

Joining us on the dais were Zsa Zsa Gabor and Gomer Pyle himself, Jim Nabors, whose homespun looks and gosh-darn manner belied the fact that when he opened his mouth to sing, he sounded like Alabama's version of Pavarotti. With a grin, Joey asked me to discuss my List, which included such fashion fiascoes as Mia Farrow ("A Girl Scout cookie in a martini at Arthur's"), Julie Andrews ("A plain-Jane Pollyanna playing Peter Pan at half-mast"), Elizabeth Taylor ("A boutique toothpaste tube, squeezed from the middle"), Liza Minnelli ("Pop-art picture of a fried egg at sunrise, eaten by Auntie Em") and Ann-Margret ("Marlon Brando in a G-string").

As I snipped off my lines, Regis chuckled dutifully, Joey laughed and Jim Nabors sat on the sofa with a grim-faced stare. At first I assumed he was suffering from a gas attack, but when I got to my next target, Governor Lurleen Wallace—the wife of archconservative George Wallace of Alabama—whom I referred to as "next Monday's wash in a broken washing machine," I found out otherwise.

Jim Nabors was livid—Gomer Pyle was getting ready to blow up on national television—and he started his assault by shouting, "As a boy from Alabama, I resent your criticism of my Governor." And he demanded that I apologize.

Well, no one tells me to apologize for something written in a script and okayed by Big Joey Bishop himself—so I refused. I still believed it was all part of the act, but it wasn't—and the battle really began. Nabors called me rude, among other things, and I responded with a frozen smile and turned to Joey, who immediately cued to a commercial to avoid a further blowup. During the break, Jim sat like a stone pillar of rectitude, glaring at me with his angry, hound-dog eyes while Joey whispered to a group of producers at the side of the desk. Regis, who sat at the opposite end of the set, turned the other cheek—something he was quite used to doing, working on that terror of a show. He knew I was damned mad, but neither of us had any idea what Joey planned next.

Back on the air with less than three minutes to go before signing off, Joey blurted out that I must apologize to Jim Nabors, Mrs. Wallace and, I assume, the world at large for daring to live up to my part of the scenario. For a moment I thought he must be joking, but he was dead serious.

"Are you kidding?" I asked, and I really thought he was.

I was determined to stand my ground. But for the clincher—and the ratings grabber—he ended the show by announcing that since I had refused to apologize, I would never be invited on the show again! The color drained from my face and my mouth went desert dry. Pretending to be exasperated, Bishop said good night. But on my end of the sofa, though we were off the air, the show was just beginning.

I was in a rage. Joey laughed and said he thought the segment was very cute.

"Cute!" I bellowed. "Cute my ass! This is the biggest double-cross I've ever seen. What the hell kind of show is this?"

Three stagehands quickly veered out of the line of combat. In venom-drenched tones, I reminded Joey that it was his idea to have me on—and he knew damn well what I was going to say. To publicly ban me from his show was humiliating—and a pathetic attempt to stir up controversy. I yelled for Spencer, who had been sitting in the audience, to call our lawyers.

The word "lawyers" sent untold numbers of producers scurrying around the set like confetti in a hurricane. In the corner, two talent bookers asked for cyanide pills. I would have been happy to accommodate them. The legal department, dazed and distraught, appeared next. I said we wanted a retraction of Joey's line about never appearing on the show again, plus a guaranteed booking to prove to the public that his inane comment was an overzealous slip of the tongue. Without another word, I left the room as Spencer followed behind, shaking his head in dismay.

I would have preferred having the head of everyone involved served to me on a platter, but Spencer and our attorney decided to drop the whole episode, accept Joey's apology the next night on his TV show and leave it at that. Fortunately for me, "The Joey Bishop Show" was certainly not representative of the vast majority of national talk shows I appeared on. For every Joey Bishop there was a Phil Donahue, a Mike Douglas, a Merv Griffin and a dozen others who managed to win their own ratings battles with a lot more class and a lot less subterfuge.

Phil Donahue, then stationed in a small Dayton, Ohio, studio with an even smaller studio audience, was a dream to work with—although my campy humor, who-cares attitude and colorful ad-libs did manage to shock his sometimes conservative, good-Catholic-boy persona. I don't think Phil knew too many flamboyantly theatrical Hollywood designers before meeting me. His wariness was not only understandable but rather amusing. I liked him because, like me, he was a pioneer of sorts: His show was one of the first to utilize the studio audience as part of the act. That kind of participation with the public not only helped his ratings but, more importantly, boosted my ego. I loved dishing the dirt with his wide-eyed, open-mouthed studio crowd. The more outrageous I got, the louder the applause.

Of course, Phil could get away with quite a bit more than a huge network extravaganza like "The Joey Bishop Show," but even when he did go coast-to-coast years later, I always found him more than willing to take chances, to allow me the proper forum to do my thing. Phil had real integrity, was honest and completely professional, and always kept his cool. I'll never forget, many years later, when I was booked to do his show in Charleston. Due to a less-than-observant travel agent, I flew—accompanied by models, crates of clothes, etc.—to Charleston, South Carolina. Imagine my surprise, and Phil's, when I discovered his program was being broadcast from Charleston, West Virginia. I barely made it to the correct state before showtime, but Phil was as unruffled as I was exasperated. Such was life on the road, hardly boring to say the least.

I appeared on Merv Griffin, Mike Douglas, Johnny Carson and every morning, mid-morning and afternoon show on the planet—and I enjoyed every minute of it. Entertaining, making people laugh, creating through humor a unique stage personality audiences responded to was an achievement I felt proud of. I came to life when the cameras switched on. Whether on television, in public appearances, or in black and white on the pages of a newspaper or magazine, I had all the answers. The lines flowed, the punchlines zinged, the laughs were timed to perfection. I was in control. But as the sixties flew by, my offstage life began to suffer by comparison, and all the hard work began to take its toll.

My relationship with Spencer had lost its once-bright luster. We weren't kids anymore, I knew that. We had been in business for a decade, gone through hell together, endured sexual criticism and bias from ultraconservative elements throughout the country and still managed to survive unscathed. Yet why had some of the closeness faded? I still loved him, but his inability to give me the kind of attention and confirmation I craved depressed me. I understood the fact that he was busy 24 hours a day managing my career and running the business, but maybe that was the problem, not the answer. To hell with fame if there's nobody to share it with. Spencer was hardly ever there, and when he was, he seemed distant. So did I.

I hated the fact that people asked for my opinion and often ignored his—not just strangers, but friends, too. Like a broken record, always "Mr. Blackwell" this, and "Mr. Blackwell" that. But insincerity clouds the air like smog. If you're not rich, famous, thin and well-connected, forget it. And far too often I felt Spencer was unfairly relegated to the sidelines of my public life, a situation I tried to correct in vain. I stressed to anyone who would listen that Spencer had absolute control over my career. But my protests might have been whispered in a tornado. No one listened, no one cared. I worried he might be losing his self-esteem, and I prayed my creation of "Mr. Blackwell" wouldn't desecrate the only completely honest relationship I had ever known. I became obsessed with the fear of losing him.

Television, no matter how time-consuming, was only a small part of a career that seemed to revolve more and more around chaos. Between designing in Los Angeles and flying to New York to work the showroom, I was in the air more than I was on land—and the skies were growing decidedly darker. Sitting alone in countless planes forced me to think about my life.

But it was too late to turn back time; I had hundreds of commitments to keep, a job to continue, new collections to design. But an old adage hit hard and true: "Don't wish for what you want or you might get it."

The Warwick

In 1968 my frustrations finally surfaced in New York at the elegant Warwick Hotel, where I was staying in preparation for yet another television appearance, this time on "The Tonight Show."

The Warwick, located at 54th and 6th Avenue, was my home away from home. I loved the ornate gilded lobby with its cut-glass doors, Oriental rugs and silk-flocked walls. It was a multi-storied mirage of a hotel where people came and went in a flurry of sleek alligator luggage and purring limousines; the rich played here, sipping champagne in fluted crystal glasses in the lavish dining rooms and shopping extravagantly among the row of boutiques situated like secret treasures along 54th Street. The Warwick was one of the few remaining bastions of elegance and civility in an uncivil world and, in a way, was a shimmering oasis where I could retreat to find the peace and quiet I longed for. But now, even the ingratiating smiles of the bellhops did little to raise my spirits. I felt like I was sleepwalking as I entered the Warwick's dining room on my first night in New York.

Sitting in the darkest corner I could find, I found myself staring into the flame of a candle, oblivious to the waiter hovering over me.

"Mr. Blackwell," he began, eyes narrowed with concern. "Are you all right?"

I tried to answer. "Yes, I'm a little tired, that's all. I need some rest."

Please go away, I thought. It's too late to wonder if I'm all right. Much too late. My life felt like it was slipping away.

"Will there be anything else?" he asked gently.

"No," I muttered unconvincingly. "I'm fine. Really."

I wanted to call home, but I was afraid to. Afraid of hearing a cold, unconcerned voice on the other end. I wondered if I had anyone in L.A. Who was here for me to confide my fears to? I thought about visiting Dad, but I didn't want him to see me this way. Wasn't I the tough survivor? Why was I coming apart now? Feeling short of breath, I opened my tie and unbuttoned the top button of my shirt. My throat felt tight, constricted, as I choked back tears.

I left the dining room as fast as I could and wandered into the brittle night chill of the streets. Loud voices called out to me, but I wasn't listening. I walked faster and faster down the sidewalks, past hundreds of faces that melted from view as my eyes blurred. My face felt wet and salty. As I wiped my eyes in front of a store window, the warped reflection mocked the image I saw there. My face was ravaged, bunched up in deep lines. I ran a hand through my graying hair. Where had the years gone? Taxis zoomed by, their horns screeching in ugly squeals. I stared deeper into the glass. I barely recognized the haggard man staring back. I lurched across the avenue and down a gloomy side-street where groups of boys stood talking in the shadows.

How familiar they looked with their wet smiles and inviting glances. I stood against the walls of a building, invisible. No one cared that I was there except for one teenager with blond, sun-streaked hair. He looked my way, passed by, then looked back. His skin glowed under the harsh neon glare, but he wasn't offering what I needed. I stared at him with hatred for his youth and beauty. Now I was the hunter, not the prey. Tonight it was my turn to pay. But I couldn't. I still had a sliver of pride left, and I turned away from his hungry stare.

Blinded by the lights of the city, I wanted to hide. Veering back up the noisy street with a sudden, nearly serene calm, I knew what I had to do. Walking into the Warwick, I was met by the short, dark-haired Puerto Rican manager, Angelo, whose wiry body—so compact beneath the starched white shirt and pinstriped pants—walked towards me. He took my hand in greeting, and I felt his fingers cover mine, his teeth glittering like pearls. I felt naked, raw, driven by an overwhelming desire for someone to hold me, touch me, for a kind voice to tell me that he cared. Angelo smiled. He knew I was distraught. The marble lobby seemed as still as a crypt.

"I don't think you're feeling well, Mr. Blackwell," he whispered. "Please, let me take you to your room."

"No," I stammered, "I'll be all right."

Why should I bother a stranger with my problems? What good would it do in the end? I still had to face myself—a creation I hated, an illusion I wanted to destroy. Now.

I stood in the elevator alone; my breathing grew louder as the glass tomb rose toward the sixth floor. Fumbling with my key, I swung the carved mahogany doors forward and walked inside my suite. I didn't bother to turn on the light. Summoning up every ounce of rage and regret, I walked into the bathroom and threw open the medicine cabinet. I heard glass shatter and fall in a shower of silver shards. Grabbing the plastic bottle filled with Dalmane, a potent barbiturate prescribed for sleeping, I swallowed 30 of the slick red-and-yellow capsules and wandered out into the living room.

No more hurt, I reasoned, no more loneliness. I wanted Blackwell to die. Forever. But I wanted the kid from Brooklyn to live—again. The room began to spin and my body crumbled to the floor. I grew closer to finding the peace I craved.

I felt my eyes droop, yet my heartbeat was quickening. I tried to stand up. Instead, I fell over a chair and back to the floor. Bracing myself against the bedroom door, I struggled to reach the bed. My vision blurred, grew clear, blurred again, like windshield wipers in the rain. I saw quick images before me, and then the dizziness began. The murky outline of a phone grew nearer. My hand shot out to grasp it—my only connection to a world I wanted to leave behind. I looked back. And then something happened. I didn't want to die. I picked up the receiver and asked for help. The voice on the other end was kind, concerned. I felt weak and the room suddenly went black, and I was alone. The world seemed to stop.

I remember waking in a room with glaring white light: voices from the bottom of a well, vague shadows of faces staring down on me, trying to help. My thoughts gradually grew more coherent. I realized Angelo was clasping my hand. I wanted to thank him, but I couldn't. Out of the confusion I heard the words "we love you" whispered in my ear. Why hadn't anyone said that before—and if they had, why hadn't I stopped to listen? My eyes opened wider; the light stung.

I mumbled finally. I hoped they could hear me. I fought to speak louder, but I was still too weak.

Seconds later I slipped back into a deep sleep.

The next morning, I awoke weak, embarrassed and completely ashamed. My suite was filled with strangers peering at me from the side of the bed with a concern I will never forget. I was riddled with guilt. Angelo and the rest of the Warwick staff had, thank God, reacted quickly and called a doctor, who had the unpleasant task of pumping my stomach. I remember feeling disoriented, as if I were trapped underwater, struggling in vain to reach air. But now my depleted energies were slowly returning. As I fought to clear my mind from the haze of sedatives, the horror of what I had done—or tried to do—suddenly hit me. How could I face anyone in the hotel? I imagined the sympathetic faces of the staff, their eyes averted, embarrassed over my own weaknesses, my own unhappiness. I was humiliated over my inability to deal with life. I had always thought of myself as strong, even indestructible; yet something had snapped and I had been powerless to stop the deathly pall that had enveloped me. There is such a fine, nearly transparent line between life and death, and I had nearly crossed it.

The harsh truth that I had almost died—by my own hand—chilled me, and forced me to brutally confront myself. I knew a lot of tough questions needed to be asked, yet where were the answers? Why couldn't I enjoy what I had fought so hard to achieve? Few had received so much acclaim in so short a time. Why couldn't I be happy? My life was like a merry-go-round, twirling faster and faster until I could barely hold on any longer. But through the freeze-frames of my life, I had caught the brass ring more than once, and it had shone as bright as pure gold. I would catch it again when I learned the lesson I should have accepted so long ago: to appreciate what I had already accomplished. Without developing that sense of personal confirmation, I feared I would forever remain a victim of my own insecurities—and of the role I had, perhaps unwisely, chosen to play.

I assumed Angelo had called Spencer, but the telephone in my room lay like a silent weapon, inexpressive but deadly, in the deathly stillness of the room. Why didn't he call? Was he too busy? Too embarrassed? Too angry? I wanted to know—but dialing Spencer's number was a task I was emotionally incapable of handling. I couldn't listen to his voice, I couldn't face what he might say to me. But I couldn't face not knowing, either. Hours crept by, and the phone remained silent. I was used to that by now, I told myself. But I still needed him.

> I wondered if he still needed me...
> if anyone needed me.
> I didn't know.

If it had been up to me, I would have just disappeared and gone away, perhaps forever. But I couldn't do that to Spencer. I couldn't desert him, his entire life, everything he had brought into my world, and just walk away. Despite my personal problems, I had an obligation to go on. Spencer had made a commitment for me to appear the very next day with Johnny Carson on "The Tonight Show," and somehow, with whatever was left in me, I intended to go through with it. The show, they say, has to go on. But at that moment, for the life of me I couldn't imagine *why*.

Johnny and Me— and Shirley

The Johnny Carson show was a program I appeared on regularly throughout the late sixties. Johnny has always been an enigma to nearly everyone who knows him, or rather, thinks they know him. Because, like me, no one really does. Intensely private and reserved, Carson is the opposite of the jubilant, quick-humored, good-ole-boy-from-the-Midwest persona he so carefully projects. There is an air of sadness about him, even of frustration— a feeling I knew all too well from dealing with his booker, the legend-in-her-own-mind herself, Shirley Wood.

Shirley's power was rivaled only by the show's producer, Freddy DeCordova, and Carson himself. Shirley's job was to book the guests, set up all the pre-interviews and, I suppose, take the heat from Carson if anyone turned out to be a dud on the air. Of course, he had the power to override any decision Shirley made concerning a guest. If Johnny liked you, the Carson show could catapult even the most ordinary entertainer into an international celebrity: Look at Charo. But if he didn't like you, watch out.

In my opinion, Shirley was devious, selfish and took advantage of the guests like few bookers ever had. If she got you on, you were expected to give something back. I've been told by many people that most of the guests got away with sending her a bouquet of flowers, theater tickets or a piece of costume jewelry. I never got off that easy. Since my strengths as a designer revolved around my evening clothes, and being that Shirley loved my clothes, she decided that she simply couldn't live without that incredible gown. It infuriated me, but what was I to do? Ever since I'd rebuffed Faye Hammond's apparent shake-down in Florence, I'd learned the hard way how to play the game. But to be fair, I had also won dozens of new clients after just one appearance on Johnny's show. Still, I hated being used in the Shirley Wood tradition of you-scratch-my-ego, I'll-scratch-yours.

Shirley's disposition left a lot to be desired as well. After I arrived at "The Tonight Show" offices, Shirley put me through a question-and-answer session that made a murder trial seem like the story of Cinderella without the happy ending. This is what you will say, this is what you will not say, repeat after me. I felt I was back in reform school. Maybe I was. She had a never-ending list of do's and don'ts: Never step on Johnny's jokes, never discuss anything not approved by Carson's staff, never dare to break out of the sanctimonious mold of the show, and never argue, object or disagree with His Honor on the air. Shirley encouraged me to be my normal, acid-tongued self—but only with stars Johnny hated. God forbid I trashed one of his personal favorites like Angie Dickinson, Suzanne Pleshette or Lucille Ball. My career would be, as far as television went, seriously damaged. So I listened to Shirley and bit my tongue.

Every talk show, from Douglas to Donahue, had its own back-stage intrigue, but the Carson show, with its high stakes and even larger egos, was teeming with personality conflicts and personality flaws—none more so than His Lordship, who smiled sweetly to your face and grimaced behind your back. His job was one of the most difficult in all of television, but I never criticized his professional talent—only his inflated self-image. I was in no mood to go on the Carson show, but once you were scheduled to appear, the booking was solid as granite. If you were a no-show—as Barbra Streisand was in 1975—you were blacklisted...and to be black-listed from Johnny's forum was the equivalent, in show-business terms, of being sent to Siberia. Barbra's stunt didn't hurt her career in the least, but she was, and is, one of the few stars who were immune to Carson's wrath. I wasn't.

Sitting in my dressing room before showtime that night, I looked tired, puffy and dispirited, but as the makeup artist slid the thick pancake makeup over my sallow skin, the image began to gel. With a deep breath, I forced myself to grin—the sly, sinister Blackwell smile that announced someone was about to be axed. My fingers shook as I put on the sapphire and emerald rings I was expected to wear. I wanted to run out of the mirrored room, down the scuffed tile halls to the streets beyond, but tonight was an all-important appearance.

Armed with my usual list of targets, I walked out onstage and was warmly greeted by Johnny. But by the end of my spot, Carson's eyes had glazed over. I could tell he wasn't happy. It seems I had upset one of his guests, a second-rate TV star whose name escapes me, but who was a Carson pet. It had taken me all of 60 seconds to go from the A-list down to D-minus domain. My outrageous comments had already been approved by Shirley, but His Nibs was not amused. Even Freddy DeCordova looked the other way when the show finally came to an end.

Needless to say, I didn't stick around for the goodbyes. I went directly to my dressing room, sat in a chair and closed my eyes, the entire evening replaying before me. As I sat there, I began to grow angry, because Shirley had known exactly what I had planned to say. Finally I was mad enough to call her office from my dressing room. With visions of a dozen of my glittering evening gowns hanging in her closet, I dialed her extension. After introducing myself to the voice on the other end, I was told Shirley had left for the evening. How amusing, I thought, that her secretary sounds exactly like Shirley. A moment later I heard the click-clack of feet pattering down the hall. I instantly recognized the voices that filtered through the door, which I had left ajar: Shirley, Freddy and Johnny. They were discussing me.

My heartbeat quickened as they grew closer to my room. Their voices grew louder.

"Boy, that Blackwell sure has a big mouth," remarked Freddy.

Shirley did not say one word in my defense. "Well, I'll never allow anything like that to happen again," said Shirley. I nearly fell through the floor. How typical of Shirley to let me take the heat. Johnny said little. He didn't have to. It was clear that I had been demoted to the bottom of his list of guests—right down there with the singing dogs and the dancing penguins Shirley booked when no one else was available. The more I thought about what she had done to me, the harder it became to hold my temper.

Without thinking, I walked to the door and flung it open.

"Thanks a lot, Shirley. Thanks for everything," I said bluntly.

Freddy and Johnny turned for a moment and stared a bit blankly before they turned back and continued walking. But Madame Wood stopped and glared at me. She knew I knew—and that was enough for me.

I wanted to say a hell of a lot more, but I held my tongue with utmost restraint—a next to impossible task. Even though Shirley was a vicious hypocrite, I wanted more Carson shows in the future. Besides, how else would she acquire a new wardrobe? But one day things would change. Shirley Wood wouldn't last forever.

As I walked back to the hotel, I took deep breaths of the cold night air, my attitude improving with each step. The bookers weren't going to get the best of me. I figured I had survived far worse—and I'd probably survive worse in the future. I was right on both counts.

Someone always has to be the pigeon.
It was my turn.
Thanks for nothing, Lady S.

The next day, despite all the craziness, I flew back to L.A. feeling better about the bond Spencer and I shared. We were in a state of transition—and so, too, was the industry. By 1969, fashion was nothing more than a mini-skirt and a see-through blouse. The real fashion business seemed light-years away from the "Lights...Camera...Couture" myth fostered by the media. Behind the perfect patina lurked a very different reality, and its protagonists were far less exciting than anyone would care to imagine.

The Other Side

The other side of the industry—a side few have the misfortune to experience—can drive anyone with even the tiniest mind absolutely crazy. As a designer, I loved creating clothes, making statements about the direction of feminine fashion, attending chic openings, making women look and feel beautiful. But the business isn't all satin bows and feather boas; there's a lot of polyester to deal with. Dealing with certain buyers, stores and salesgirls became an unwanted and unappreciated part of my life, and after dealing with me, I'm sure the store representatives had some regrets of their own. We may have been stuck in the same brocaded boat, but we didn't have to be bosom buddies. We all had egos and we all wanted to be right.

The stores that bought the Blackwell line made a fortune on us; our sales record was about 90%, not including shoplifters, who brought the figure closer to 100%. Actually, having one of my gowns shoplifted right out from under the snooty noses of the salesgirls was the greatest honor that could have been bestowed upon me. At least with a shoplifter I didn't have to see how the dress looked on a customer—an experience that at times can be pretty frightening.

I have always felt that the right dress on the wrong woman—or the wrong dress on the right woman—can be quite devastating. A dull matronly type shouldn't even try to pour herself into one of those Monroe-esque, sequined seductions. But just try to tell her that and watch the fireworks begin. Trying to be a clone of someone else spells disaster with a capital D.

But many of the ladies had no idea that time stands still for no one. That's what mirrors are for. Regardless, they often refuse to accept the fact that Shirley Temple curls simply don't work when you're past 50. The Joan Crawford dancing shoes are also a fetish one can do without—unless you really dance. And what about those Miami springolators—perfect for the bleached-blond, gigantic-bosomed temptress who has absolutely no taste, but wants her plastic pumps decorated with rhinestones anyway. I had to deal with these questionable types every day, and I had to bite my tongue so often I rarely ate solid meals past three in the afternoon—the favorite fitting time for the "ladies who lunch" bunch. With one less martini and one more exercise class, they might have been able to squeeze into the gowns they so desperately coveted. But really, why bother? They bought them anyway, and worried about the bulges later.

At any rate, my designs were selling faster than the stores could buy them, and I personally felt our success was based on quality, creativity and, sadly for me, underpricing. Our prices had risen since 1960, but in comparison to the rest of the market, a Blackwell gown was a coup. But you wouldn't have known it from the salesgirls' attitudes in the high-priced boutiques that handled my line. The snob appeal of selling a big-deal French haute-couture gown for many times the price of mine appealed to the girls behind the counter. After all, it didn't take any longer to sell a Givenchy than it did to sell one of my gowns—and the commissions were better. But I have never understood why a woman would pay three-quarters of the price of a dress for a label—and 25% for the dress itself.

If I thought that was really true, of course, selling labels instead of dresses would have been a better business—and far easier to accomplish. I already knew dozens of socialites who owned bad imitations of designer gowns with real couture labels sewn inside for effect. What the hell? At least half the women I befriended over the years thought if you wore a Bill Blass or an Oscar de la Renta, life would suddenly take a dramatic turn for the better—never considering if the dress in question was right or wrong for them. The surest way to find out is to ask the salesgirl.

If she beams, "Oh! Miss Gotrocks, that dress is you!" you're in trouble. Simply set fire to her wig, run for the nearest exit and pray the bitch goes up in flames as penance for her lies.

Fashion folly on Seventh Avenue is as omnipresent as John Fairchild's ego. The streets and restaurants of Manhattan are filled with women who wear what's "in"—even when they forget to read *Women's Wear Daily* to discover, 30 seconds later, that it's now "out." You can be sure that if a certain style is hot today, someone on the *Women's Wear Daily* staff will, just for fun, decree it's no longer fashionable tomorrow.

I spent much of the next years on the road, each trip a duplicate of the one before. Out-of-town fashion shows, usually held in the local department store, sound relatively pleasant. But in the real world, these "trunk shows" are backbreaking bores that require frazzled designers to act happy, speak sugary bon mots and—most of all—control themselves. It's not easy, but we all try...

On the Road

These road-show extravaganzas require elaborate planning and nerves of bonded steel. First, models need to be hired for the trip. Dealing with the Beauty Brigade is the first potential headache, since the magnificent majority feel they're as important as Moses on the mountain. Then, of course, airline tickets need to be purchased for a flight that is always three hours late in arriving. When the traveling circus finally lands, one is always greeted at the airport by the Local Social Queen, hereinafter generically referred to as the "LSQ." Trust me, they're all the same.

But some trips are worse than others, and one in particular ranks high on my list of unforgettable nightmares. It began on a sour note—and went downhill from there. Our flight arrived late, as usual, and the LSQ was livid as we stepped off the plane—since the press had already left before snapping that once-in-a-lifetime shot for the society page. Her physical attributes weren't any cheerier: body drenched with the dizzying aroma of Jungle Gardenia, face made up with a trowel, feet swollen the size of grapefruits from wearing those oh-so-chic Italian pumps.

With my stomach still lurching from rancid airplane "food," our LSQ stunned me with the news that her friends, whom we'll dub "Ladies of the Club," had decided to model the collection themselves. My fuming models were not amused, and neither was I. Horrific images of twenty middle-aged society women, ranting and raving and reaching in unison for their "favorite" dress—translation: the one that looks the absolute worst on them—forced me to snap my mouth shut lest I stun her with a series of screams.

When we reached the rented "limousine"—a black Cadillac borrowed from the local funeral home—the LSQ then sweetly announced yet another change of plans: She'd drive us to the hotel herself, and I was invited to sit up front and "chat." I agreed with the enthusiasm of a vegetarian visiting an abattoir. Careening into town, I was told for the fiftieth time just how "thrilled" everyone was—and: "By the way, dear, I've arranged for us to have dinner."

"We'd love to," I lied. An invitation to sit in an electric chair would have been more welcome.

I could only imagine the hot spot she'd selected. Perhaps the local coffee shop, where the mouthwatering "special of the month" was, no doubt, "Jumbo Deep-Fried Shrimp." You see, those jewels from the sea can be saved for weeks: Just drop them in boiling grease and they're as good as frozen. The obligatory lemon wedge on a wilted lettuce leaf always added the final frightening touch. Voilà! Heartburn City for the low fee of $5.95. And the apple pie à la mode was usually "on the house." That's where it belonged.

And we hadn't even arrived at the hotel yet. Our home away from home looked like a ten-story Turkish bath. As we pulled up to the entrance, the drunken doorman, in a suit two sizes too big in the shoulders and three inches too tight in the waist, took one look at our mountain of baggage and disappeared into the plastic palm trees. Our oblivious hostess bade us a cheery farewell, swerved out of the drive, hit a curb and, exhaust fumes billowing, careened around the corner.

My models, uttering curses fit for a truck stop, pitched in and helped an elderly bellhop carry the collection to our "suite." It was a magical mix of my favorite color combinations: turquoise carpets, red drapes and buttercup yellow walls. Twin beds. A Gideon Bible. And a packet of moldy mints for that touch of class atop the polyester pillowcases. A paint-by-numbers "African Sunset" adorned the bathroom, which contained the worst shower this side of the Bates Motel—dribbling a quart of water every hour whether it was turned on or not. The best I could hope for was a quick splash in the face before my dinner date. The models proceeded to retreat to their own hovels, professing sudden "exhaustion."

I hung the collection from the shower rod, since the closet, in a past life, was a towel rack. In a last-ditch effort to freshen up, I sent out for egg white—and gave myself a quick "instant surgery" facelift. When I arrived for my dinner date, my skin was so tight I could barely talk, much less smile; but I hadn't planned on doing much of that anyway. As a special treat, my LSQ has brought along two of her dearest friends, whose coiffures resembled havens for hungry moths. I couldn't resist complimenting them on their creative use of hair coloring. "When you decide which one to keep," I heard myself saying, "let me know." They didn't seem to appreciate my wit, so I laughed at my own joke. It was the mistake of the evening. My face, drum-tight from the egg white, cracked, and I suddenly resembled an antique painting resurrected from a fire. Talk about character lines! As I began to peel, the entire table stared at me in horror. I don't know whether they lost their appetite, but I certainly did. It was time to say goodnight, and I excused myself.

Back in my room, I tried to sleep—only to realize that my next-door neighbor must be the local callgirl—or boy—and, mon Dieu!, was she fast. The door must have opened and closed twenty times that night! I think she made more money that evening than I did on the entire trip. Needless to say, dawn arrived before sleep did, and I looked like the wreck of the Hesperus. My wake-up call was late, and the operator apologized that she was so busy; maybe she had been my next-door neighbor.

When room service finally came with coffee, served by the same geriatric bellhop from the night before, I could see why he was so late in arriving: He'd been busy eating breakfast down at that trough in the kitchen; he was ballooning out of his uniform with what had to be 50 pancakes. It was a thought as chilling as my coffee, which had obviously been poured into the pot directly from a sinkful of last night's dishwater. Spencer wisely decided to wait for the coffee shop downstairs to open. But we soon discovered that it was closed for the day—perhaps by the Health Board, or maybe the chef was out sick from eating his own food. On second thought, what if *he* was my next-door neighbor? These morbid thoughts were interrupted by a call from our hostess: She was waiting for us in the lobby.

Dressed in her Junior League outfit—pastel suit, pearls, matching shoes and handbag—she announced that she'd arrived to escort me to the showroom, where I had given specific instructions on the equipment I needed for the presentation: two spotlights, a piano (with player) and a ramp of sorts decorated with lights. I held my breath as we entered the room.

If I had possessed a gun at that moment, I'd be writing these memoirs from San Quentin. The piano was a dilapidated upright Spinet placed at the far end of the cavernous room; the spotlights were 75-watt bulbs; the ramp was a plyboard sheet on two cement blocks, covered with indoor/outdoor carpet; and the lights were someone's string of Christmas tree sparklers timed to blink just like a Vegas billboard.

Images of Olivia de Havilland in *The Snake Pit* flooded my mind. I started yelling, "Nothing is right! Nothing will work! This is an outrage! A disaster!" The LSQ clutched her purse, pursed her lips and called me neurotic. With my life flashing before me, Spencer tried vainly to reassure me that everything would work out fine.

"Maybe," I bellowed, "if a tornado passes through town ten minutes before showtime and takes us all with it!" But for now, make no mistake, I was the local tornado—and the damage was already done.

She finally retreated to the manager's office, in a rage herself, while another member of the Junior League set approached me, crying she's done everything I've asked for and she just can't understand why the piano on the other side of the room won't do. Just to shock, I explained that I often go through strange changes during a show, and I might imagine I'm Judy Garland and want to sit on the piano and sing "Over the Rainbow." She giggled, hoping I'm kidding. Little did she know. Next, I was reminded that the Club to which I'm presenting my collection was "restricted." I didn't dare ask "Against what?" I had a strange feeling I knew what they meant, so I decided to change my opening song to "My Yiddisha Momma." I had a deep suspicion these Wasps wouldn't be happy with my choice of material. But there was some comfort in the thought that the poor department store that sponsored my show would be banned for years to come by this peroxided legion of lunatics.

Well, ladies and gentlemen, with "showtime" looming before me, I was a walking wreck. The room was beginning to fill. My models were sulking in their dressing room 50 yards away, with two hand mirrors and one makeup table among them. I wondered if my refusal to allow the local ladies to model my clothes had anything to do with the Lilliputian dressing area that had been set up for them. My models knew so. And they were threatening mutiny, sending tubes of mascara flying across the room, and plastic hair rollers careening through the air while I raged unprofessionally about their lack of professionalism. Only Spencer managed an air of serenity as he reassured me that everything would turn out beautifully.

Since our entire audience had visited Bloody Mary land beforehand, they absolutely loved me, my clothes and my models. Many, I'm sure, thought I was Judy Garland doing "My Yiddisha Momma" to the tune of "Over the Rainbow." After the show, Madame LSQ was visibly relieved that the ordeal was finally over. Thus did another road show come to a triumphant end.

As we headed for Los Angeles the next day, our plane felt like a vessel of divine deliverance. And Spencer, for the first time since I've known him, complained to the stewardess about his tea. I was proud of him and the models. As the plane glided through the peaceful clouds, I leaned back in my seat, never forgetting that behind every cloud—is another cloud. For it would all soon begin again, like a bad movie with endless sequels—all starring me.

By the spring of 1970, a fashion revolution was brewing, and I was at the center of the storm. After years of breezy, youthful clothes—mini-skirts, transparent tops, jeans—the fashion industry was at a financial standstill. Although the public at large, and especially men, were happy with the "less is more" sexuality of the thigh-bearing styles, the newly crowned dictator of design, *Women's Wear Daily's* John Fairchild—ably assisted by his cohort in couture crime, publisher James Brady—decreed that a new look and length be introduced: the midi dress, the ugliest, dowdiest and dumpiest ankle-length look since the bustle. No one was pleased with this latest Fairchild discovery—least of all me. Fashion houses across America, which had invested collective millions in minis, were livid—and so were the women wearing them, who were now being told, in imperious tones, that their clothes were hopelessly outdated, and entirely new wardrobes would be necessary. The power of the press continued to amaze me—but never more than in 1970, when *Women's Wear Daily* began its PR campaign to redefine the look of the well-dressed woman.

A Fashion Revolution

Women's Wear Daily started out as a trade journal that was strictly for the industry. Articles on designers, collections and fabrics evolved into a bitchy, elitist, gossipy tabloid that catapulted New York's jet-set society into the consciousness of mainstream America. As Women's Wear Daily's power grew, so, too, did John Fairchild's—until he began to believe his own publicity. The columns of Women's Wear Daily, odes to the "Beautiful People" who dashed from Le Côte Basque for lunch to Twenty One for dinner, were nothing more than fancy tabloid journalism—but by illuminating an industry that had always been rather mysterious, Women's Wear Daily became a powerful force in fashion. If they dubbed a style "out," the garments in question disappeared from the sales racks as fast as the salesgirls could pack them up and ship them back to the displeased manufacturer. Women's Wear Daily was the equivalent of Hollywood's Louella and Hedda: They could make or break you with one of their editorials. John Fairchild had arrived.

His latest power play, the "Long Live the Midi" campaign, was embraced by the industry with the same enthusiasm that vampires feel for sunlight, crucifixes and wreaths of garlic. According to Time, a protest by 335 angry clients of the Dallas-based Sanger/Harris Store stated that they objected "strongly to being suppressed into buying the midi exclusively. We like looking feminine and intend staying that way." The problem was nationwide, the reverberations worldwide, and the culprit couldn't have cared less. Like Zeus on Mount Olympus, Fairchild waved his stumpy fingers and demanded subservience from designers, buyers and the public alike. I was in no mood to join the brigade of sycophants who bowed desperately to his whims. I was ready to fight in spite of his front-page intimidations.

Called the most feared man in the fashion publishing field in *Time*'s devastating 1970 profile of his sanctimonious kingdom, Fairchild began pushing "the longuette" just in time to confuse every designer and buyer preparing for the fall collections—collections that would, if he had his way, inaugurate the new midi look. But who knew if the midi would sell? I knew it wouldn't, but practically everyone else, frightened of being banished from the hallowed pages of *Women's Wear Daily*, threw up their arms in exasperation. Should they go for the long look or stay with the short? They went with the midi, of course. In the meantime, the spring collections were dead on arrival. Who wanted to invest in short skirts now? The industry lost untold millions in revenue.

To make matters worse, the United States was in a recession, and fabric mills ground to a halt, clothing manufacturers went out of business, retailers were devastated. No one knew what to buy or sell. The months before the midi arrived were an endless nightmare involving millions of dollars and thousands of jobs. I was sick that one person could wreak such havoc on an entire industry, but I knew, as far back as 1965, that Fairchild was dangerous. In my opinion, he was beginning a long line of arbitrary fashion decisions to indulge his egomania.

Women's Wear Daily announced that the whole look of American women would change, and die-hard miniskirt adherents were going to be out in the fashion cold. This, by the way, was the same fashion tabloid that had praised the mini look about a day and a half before.

Infuriated with Fairchild's hold on the American woman, I took action. Decrying him in every interview, public appearance and television spot I participated in, I let America know just how hideous the new look really was—and how irresponsible it was for a paper with *Women's Wear Daily*'s stature to intimidate by constantly editorializing their decision about what fashion should be and not reporting with equal prominence the many other looks. Since the midi made any woman under 5'7" look like a female Toulouse-Lautrec cross-bred with a demented munchkin, I continued these tirades until my feud with Fairchild became the topic of conversation at every pretentious party across town.

"Women want to look like women," I raved, "and men want women to look like women." It was just that simple—and that complex. Defining femininity can be, I'll admit, a difficult chore, but one thing I did know was that the midi would flop—and flop big—but not before thousands of fashion victims wasted good money on a trend that wouldn't last beyond next week.

Unlike his fashion whims, which he perpetrated seasonally on a helpless public, Fairchild's vendettas against a coterie of disobedient designers lasted—and continue to last—for years. I, too, would taste the Fairchild freeze-out for my refusal to conform to his high-handed commands. But I was in good company. Over the past 30 years, *Women's Wear Daily* has fought with a Who's Who of international designers. Some were relegated to nonexistent status for their independence and their refusal to release advance sketches; others merely dared to question Fairchild's methods. Great designers like Pauline Trigere—one of my closest friends—and Mollie Parnis and Bill Blass were early casualties. Later, St. Laurent and Lacroix tasted John's mercurial disapproval. They had fallen prey to *Women's Wear Daily's* build-you-up, tear-you-down syndrome. Once Fairchild's darling sun kings of fashion, they fell in and out of favor on a recurring basis with the viper's nest at *Women's Wear Daily.*

Seething over the entire scenario, which was beginning to resemble a Seventh Avenue version of *Bonnie and Clyde*, as Fairchild and Brady shot down anyone who stood in their way, I decided to call him up. The conversation was short—but not sweet. When I inquired if Mrs. Fairchild planned to wear "the longuette," the silence from the other end was cold enough to chill the Plaza's champagne supply for a decade. The one-way conversation reached deep-freeze stage when I demanded to see a photo of his wife wearing the midi in question. The next sound I heard was a dial tone. The audience was over, along with any chance of my being covered by his newspaper ever again. I couldn't have cared less.

Women's Wear Daily had always ignored California anyway and invariably turned up its snotty snout at us rebels. I could stand the heat, but others were less thick-skinned and watched their pride slip away by acquiescing to Fairchild's decrees. The *Women's Wear Daily* regime still flourishes today. Like a mutant Venus's-flytrap, it feeds on the tender flesh of out-of-favor designers, movie stars, socialites and, most importantly, a gullible public. But if I learned anything from the whole midi brouhaha, it's this: Trust your own instincts, not theirs.

It seemed no one had any instincts to trust, though, as I looked back on the decade in fashion. Glamour had given way to the Flower Child look, which had given way to the mini, which had given way to the midi. Like dazzling dominoes, styles fell from grace in rapid, uniform succession—while the smart ones, including Givenchy, Chanel, Oscar de la Renta and Mainbocher, refused to become bedazzled by the style of the moment. They continued to show elegant, classic couture—couture not even *Women's Wear Daily* could kill even if it wanted to. That's why my own collections sold over the years. I never gave up on elegance, either.

While Halston minis were being returned to the factory from Bonwit Teller in record numbers, or so the gossip said, and Seventh Avenue braced itself for the inevitable disaster of the midi, I threw all caution to the wind and presented my most glamorous fall collection ever. No pants, no mid-calf lengths, no Fairchild fads for me. I wanted the glitter of the forties, the elegance of the thirties, the drop-dead Hollywood sparkle of the twenties—and I wanted to bring it back in the middle of the worst massacre of the garment industry since the Depression. Outside, a polyester wasteland loomed: Pants that mysteriously stretched became the vogue while a new micro-mini style, dubbed "hot pants," became a reactionary fad against Fairchild's midi if there ever was one, proved that fashion was no longer just a look—it was a state of mind, and a pretty misguided mind at that.

Everywhere I turned—at fashion shows, movie premieres,

theater openings, television shows—the pantsuit reigned, with the "hot pants" look a close second, often worn by women who should have stayed home. By being out in public, they risked being picked up by the dog catcher.

The early seventies wallowed in the mire of bad taste. Women were caught in the battle of what was "in" and what was "right," and never the twain shall meet. Everyone lost—except the very rich, who stuck to priceless originals while the rest of America faced the sight of Granny's lime green jumpsuit at all hours of the day and night. The matching shoes and purse were an additional shock effect for those with stout hearts. Little wonder I had no trouble coming up with one-liners for my public appearances. Truth is always funnier than fiction. So let this be a lesson to anyone who's willing to forsake common sense, the savings account and one's reputation to buy the fashion flavor of the month. Remember: What's hot today will be like ice tomorrow. You'd be a lot smarter to invest in a good three-way mirror and take a good, long look at what you're putting on your body. It might surprise you, it might scare you—but it will definitely improve you. Learning what's best for you is the only real fashion question worth studying.

In the meantime I was drowning in a world of shapeless sacks, polyester prints, patent-leather boots and drab cover-ups. Was I crazy, or was America losing its mind? The women's movement—which I wholeheartedly supported—mistakenly thought defeminization was the answer to sexism in the United States. I always thought it so ironic that many of the early feminists dressed like the very sex they supposedly rebelled against. Many of the liberationists only managed to alienate and confuse men even further. Husbands began looking elsewhere, and "working late" became a national buzz phrase for millions of disgruntled men.

Lines and curves were suddenly something to be ashamed of, while proper makeup became a sinister symbol of the bubble-brained bourgeoisie. Chic meant having two backs, and designers like Bill Blass—to the profound detriment of women everywhere—encouraged the flat-chested waif image of glamour. I absolutely hated the tacky clothes being shoved down the

American woman's throat; in this country, I felt like I was the sole dissenting voice in a sonata of schlock. Fashion trends spread like wildfire in a bone-dry forest: Once the match was lit and the first flick of flame found its way into the welcome air, mass destruction wasn't far behind. That's the way I felt about the state of fashion as we entered the seventies. It was, for all intents and purposes, dead. Or at least comatose.

I continued to design as creatively as I could. As long as the collection was elegantly timeless, I enjoyed experimenting with new colors and fabrics. I enjoyed the drama of fashion, the sheer power of a perfect gown. But since I was labeled the "King of Glamour," I wasn't expected to sidestep the beads and bows for even one collection. Store buyers discouraged me from trying new looks. "Don't argue with success" was the battlecry. I agreed—up to a point. After all, even traditionalist-to-the-core Coco Chanel, who was quoted as saying she hated any type of fad or trend, updated her classic suits and dresses. In less than honeyed tones, I asked the buyers what the hell they came to me for. Did they want the same dress, year in and year out? I wanted to scream from frustration—and I always did.

Since your reputation rests on your last collection and how well it sold, of course, pleasing the buyers was a necessary evil. The store buyers were the double-edged swords of the industry; You can't live with 'em and you can't live without 'em. These women are the kind who—after years of success with your clothes—finally get stuck with a few items and go berserk.

After they allowed every woman in town to mutilate the once stain-free fabric with lipstick smears, hairspray and makeup blotches, buyers never understood why I refused to accept such war-weary returns. Threats were hurled over the phone like hand grenades, and relationships once based on goodwill and trust crumbled like old eye shadow. Welcome to the wonderful world of former pals who cross to the other side of the street after spotting you. The ones who said how wonderful it would be to have your collection in their boutique. The ones who paid after six months and 600 reminder phone calls. The ones whose checks bounced all the way to Brazil and back.

These were the same women who called you "darling" last season. Who flocked to your dinner parties and wiped out all the caviar in one extravagant swoop. Who ripped you off for theater tickets. Who now, after a couple of dress losses, refuse to return your calls.

There was always some woman, puffed up with self-importance, who couldn't "review" the line until midnight or so—when the only thing this aging fashion acolyte really wanted to review was your body. I guess I looked the type. And at times, I'll admit, I surrendered to their clammy hands. In fact, I even led them on. I abandoned my dignity as they made demands and expected me to satisfy them. My memories of those unfortunate evenings are like slowly developing photographs, revealing faces and rooms I'd rather forget. Their one-sided passion seemed to last longer than it really did. I let them touch me, use me. Some took pleasure in seeing me forced to please them, while others—so old, alone, pathetic—made me feel the weight of the world's sadness rested on their humped shoulders and mask-like faces.

And not all the buyers were women. The potbellied, toupee-clad "gentlemen" of the trade had their own way of doing business. Their seductive arts were far less romantic than their female counterparts; they expected sex from any designer with a collection to push. It was fifteen minutes of fantasy for them and fifteen minutes of hell for any of us.

The public, fooled by the glamour, had no idea what went on behind the scenes. Prostitution was a more terse—and honest—term for the "little favors" requested of us, but God help me, it was just as much a part of the job as choosing the fabric. I was a prisoner of a business I desperately wanted to escape.

Although many of the buyers were some of the most aggressive people I've ever met, several experiences with important would-be clients left me wondering if I shouldn't just open a bordello and get it over with. One such encounter occurred during one of my trunk-show excursions. I was going to show the current collection at San Antonio's Joske Brothers, one of the most successful department store chains in the country. The setting for the presentation, the elegant Menger Hotel—located directly across the street from Joske's and the national landmark, the Alamo—seemed perfect.

San Antonio

If I thought the Alamo was the oldest monument San Antonio had to offer, I was proven wrong when we arrived at the airport. The doddering dowagers who met us, Instamatics dangling from their necks, were a sight only Methuselah could appreciate.

We arrived in Texas in a flurry of overstuffed bags, tons of trunks and the usual frazzled nerves.

"Here we go again," I whispered to Spencer. I could only pray that the remainder of our trip would be more promising.

It wasn't.

Despite the fact that my appearance was being heralded as one of the social events of the season, the Menger Hotel ballroom was still in an alarming state of decorating confusion. The ramp, approximately two feet wide, emblazoned with dime-store reflectors for that showbiz effect, was about as safe as walking Captain Hook's plank for my stiletto-heeled models. How on earth they expected anyone to turn around and pose on a makeshift plywood runner that wasn't big enough to hold a pygmy Chihuahua was beyond me.

"The show goes on," Spencer grinned.

"It sure as hell does," I agreed, shaking my head in exasperation.

The audience was respectably impressive. Since San Antonio is situated a short, dusty drive from Mexico, the crowd I serenaded resembled a host of Mayan princesses, all darting across the border to buy their seasonal wardrobes. Although I sang flatter than Dinah Shore on a bad day, one brilliantly striking woman, with arrow-straight black hair, brandy-colored skin and jet eyes, couldn't stop staring at me, seemingly transfixed. Her fingers absently fluttered around her rubied throat, where an extraordinary fireworks display of glittering scarlet gems encircled her neck. Even from the stage, I knew those boulders were the real thing. Her husband sat by her side—an imposing figure of dark, brooding good looks. Both pairs of eyes were riveted not on my face, but on my body. They made me feel naked standing there. I assumed every performer's nightmare had finally happened to me; glancing down with as much subtlety as possible, I was relieved to see things were definitely closed. But their stares continued, and as I sang the lyrics, "That's why this designer is a tramp," the number suddenly took on a whole new meaning.

Despite the fact I was the center of a rather unsettling voyeuristic fantasy, the show went well. My act, designed to give the audience what they want in terms of outrageous, bitchy and campy one-liners, was a far cry from the boy next door. As I continued my standard soliloquy, I could feel myself become increasingly wary of encouraging any wrong ideas. God knows I had no desire to involve myself in a matrimonial ménage à trois; I gave that up when I left my escort days in New York. But finally the curtain fell, and I was left to face what I knew would be a sticky situation back at Joske Brothers.

The collection was quickly packed and rushed back to the store, where lines of women, like crazed scavengers, waited to grab whatever they could. Of course, not all my audience raced across the street. A few, I knew, saw their husbands and sons in my demeanor, and that reality never failed to shake them. Some—shocked at my nerve onstage—simply denounced me as hopeless. But I already had my hands full with my dedicated duo—who, I suspected, would be waiting for me at Joske's, determined to get a close-up view.

Entering the crowded store, I retreated immediately to the designer salon dressing area, where I was supposed to greet the customers, charm them as best I could, and help select a suitable ensemble for their wardrobe. Since most of the clients would have looked better in a monk's robe than my particular designs,

I viewed this dubious duty with as much enthusiasm as walking over a bed of red-hot coals. Still, I did what was expected of me. I was so wrapped up in the barrage of society matrons circling me that I scarcely noticed, at first, my two distinguished admirers hovering near the fitting rooms, surrounded by fawning store assistants.

Before I could manage a graceful exit, the head of merchandising sidled up beside me and whispered that one of Mexico's most prominent socialites had requested a meeting. I didn't have to guess who the interested party was. I knew what was coming, and it wasn't a situation I looked forward to.

I approached the private dressing room with the trepidation of a guillotine victim. Keeping my eyes fixed on the fluttering curtains that separated the cubicles, I passed by her husband, who sat like an emperor on a red velvet wing chair, sipping a scotch. In the afternoon light, his face belonged on a Roman coin—sharp features with a nose that protruded defiantly from his coppery skin, and a set of bottomless black eyes. But his aristocratic manner didn't fool me. I felt a proposition coming on. I knew the script, the scene and the dialogue by heart, so I braced myself for the inevitable.

Pushing back the curtain, I was shocked to find one of Mexico's most elegant women standing stark naked in front of a three-way mirror. Although only five feet tall at the most, she overpowered the room. Her skin was coffee silk, smooth, firm and flawless. I found myself embarrassed for staring, but I was too intrigued with this stunningly sensuous display. She was absolutely gorgeous—petite but full-figured in a ripe, Rubenesque way. My eyes drifted to her open mouth, wet with champagne. Her breasts were perfection; Rubens himself could have painted them. Whether through the miraculous gifts of nature or the help of a plastic surgeon, Madame was a stunning statue regally resurrected into the real world.

I pretended to be indifferent—and my nonchalant attitude clearly bothered her. A subtle pout played across her lips. I had the distinct impression that she was used to getting what she wanted—from servants and store owners as well as her own family. I began to grow a bit indignant; her vast reserves of money didn't impress me. Believe me, I'd rather help some girl who had saved her hard-earned pennies for one dress than flit around this modern-day Cleopatra, who could afford to buy the entire collection. But the name of this glitzy game was sales. Joske Brothers hadn't paid me to trek halfway across the United States to kill a single $50,000 order. Like the costumed court jester, I was expected to perform and amuse—only on a professional level, of course. But Madame's far from coy sexual come-on raised the stakes. While her husband waited outside, I stood with my feet frozen to the carpet and continued to stare. She began to smile and moved among the racks of evening gowns that had been wheeled in on rollers for her private inspection. Her celebrated rubies, strewn across the glass-topped dressing table, flashed crimson sparks into the air. The atmosphere was heavy with dense perfume, old money and unanswered questions. She had hers and I had mine.

"Which one?" she inquired imperiously, holding up two lace-embroidered capes.

My daze lifted a bit and I became aware of her voice, a husky musical whisper that filled the mirrored room. Her legs curved toward her rounded waist in a stream of polished, silky skin.

"I think the blue," I stammered, still more than a little off guard from her lush nakedness. "It may be a bit small since it's a model's sample."

"Small?" she asked. "I doubt it, judging from what I saw on stage. I think it would fit me perfectly." Her double talk wasn't lost on me. I got out of there as fast as I could.

Some people have nerve, I thought. But what a package to display it in. As I waited like a salesgirl for Madame to emerge from her sequestered self-absorption, I mentally took bets on how long she would take to leave her reflection that was dazzling yet immobile, beautiful, timeless yet fragile.

Several feet away, her husband motioned for me to join him. I wondered if he had any idea just how brazen his wife could be. I found out in a hurry. After only the briefest of greetings, being the consummate businessman, he drove directly to the point. He was prepared to offer me a very generous amount of money if I would consider moving to Mexico and living with his wife! His deadpan, confidential delivery, punctuated by sips from his drink, seemed surreal—like a cartoon of an adventure I had no interest in pursuing. I quickly declined his offer. His face tightened as he rose from his crimson throne. This is surely it: Now he plans to strangle me with his bare hands. But he merely walked past me and disappeared into the sequin-lit shadows of the fitting room beyond. I heard low whispers, the rustle of silk and Madame's voice calling my name as she stepped out into the hall. Parading to my side, poured into the most revealing silk top she could find, she took my hand. With the tone of a sympathetic professor, she smiled and said she understood my hesitation.

"Would my husband be of interest?"

"What? Are you joking?" Surely I was hallucinating.

"Hardly."

"Well," I managed to say with as much aplomb as possible, "I'm afraid that won't be possible."

Glowering, Madame disappeared in a blur of blue, only to return moments later with her husband in tow. They proudly produced a photograph of their son, a thin, wiry Portuguese bullfighter dashingly dressed in red and gold silk. They must have spotted my temporary admiration, for they hastily jotted down his address and phone number and placed it in my hand. I must admit I didn't say no to their final offer—but I didn't say yes, either. As a token of gratitude for my consideration, I suppose, Madame bought all ten dresses and swept out of the store. But not before I embraced her affectionately, now more amused than annoyed by her attention.

Shoppers began to fill the room again, my temporary diversion shattered by a thunder of chattering women, descending upon me with alarming speed. Through a sea of painted faces, ill-fitting wool suits and strands of yellow pearls, my two new suitors slipped out the side door and into the interior of a waiting limousine. My eyes followed their path. Madame waved through the window. I waved back, shot with a desire to follow them to their place in Mexico. But the moment passed, and in a flash of polished chrome and black steel, the car leapt forward and disappeared into the amber afternoon.

I had been spending so much time at out-of-town fashion shows and commuting between New York and Los Angeles that I was beginning to feel that an airplane was my second home. Our continued success only brought more work, longer hours and shorter tempers—at least on my part. Even though Spencer usually accompanied me on these trips, I relied heavily on him to take care of the day-to-day activities back in Los Angeles. No matter how much work was piled on his shoulders, he never complained. Spencer was too even-natured for his own good. Often I was concerned for his health because he always held his emotions deep inside—a quality we definitely did not share. While I spoke my mind, usually without thinking, he was always under control and could shut me up with a simple stare. Spencer was able to practice this fine art when I was invited to Sacramento to create an outfit for a great lady.

Nancy

Every designer would love to say they designed for the First Lady of our Land, Nancy Reagan. I really did—but she wasn't the First Lady then. She was a mere Governor's wife, ensconced in Sacramento at the Governor's mansion, which the Reagans inhabited for eight years before moving to more illustrious quarters on Pennsylvania Avenue. But design for Nancy I did—unlike many couturiers who sent her a gift and then called a press conference to announce that she was wearing their clothes. It was a great publicity sham, and if I were the First Lady—don't laugh, I've thought about it—I'd be furious. But frankly, while Nancy was in the White House, I didn't feel I had the right to discuss what I had or hadn't designed for her. To me, it was a matter of discretion; every public figure has a right to some privacy.

Of course, I could also claim without too much hesitation that the President and I were friends. After all, we had appeared in *King's Row* together decades earlier, and relationships have been built on far less. But that's really so much nonsense. Even during his years in Hollywood, Ronald Reagan was on a much higher branch of the tree than me, a lowly bit player. I probably spoke twenty words to him during the whole shoot. In the rigid hierarchy of a Hollywood soundstage, even that was risking it.

As for Nancy, I never knew her during her salad days as Hollywood actress Nancy Davis. Our first contact took place many years later when the Bakersfield branch of the Cotton Council of California called me. The girlish voice, in a drawl as wide and deep as the Mississippi, was as deeply Southern as a magnolia blossom, a columned portico, a stiff bourbon on the rocks.

"Would Mr. Blackwell be interested in designing a cotton ensemble for the Governor's wife?"

I immediately knew her Southern sheen disguised the fact she had no idea who the hell Mr. Blackwell was. After all, she was talking to him and didn't even know it. Heaven knows, my voice was recognizable to most anyone who did more than work and sleep. Unfortunately for her, I had a feeling she did both simultaneously.

After introducing myself, I listened to her request with increasing interest. She explained that they wanted to photograph me against a huge bale of cotton which, according to the hundreds of press releases dutifully delivered, would be woven into the fabric of the very gown used for Mrs. Reagan's ensemble.

Being the showman that I was, I thought the idea was great; a coup for the Cotton Council and a coup for me. Although the widely publicized bale of cotton was basically a prop, I knew the value of publicity and never let on that the fabric I really used was a gorgeous cotton brocade I had discovered months earlier.

Spencer and I arrived by plane in California's capital on a sunny spring morning. Leaving the plane, covered in every diamond I could beg, borrow or steal, I was a sight to shock Sacramento. A gathering of Senate wives, cotton representatives and local press choked the terminal lobby as we entered; I especially enjoyed watching the Cotton Council members nearly knock each other out for a photo opportunity. The phrase "steel magnolias" took on a new dimension. With women this energetic, I began to believe the South just might rise again. After the initial crush of mint julep'd hellos, I hoped—for my stomach's sake—that their hospitality would include breakfast. I was famished—but my hostesses were frowning. There simply wasn't enough time, they explained. Mrs. Reagan was waiting. Well! As Mae West once muttered, "Pardon me for breathin'!"

Unwilling to create a controversy five minutes after landing, I climbed in a car and off we drove—a caravan of camp if there ever was one. The streets turned into boulevards, well-manicured and

lined with sweeping, stately trees—I had a feeling we were entering Reagan country; the chatter of my debutante driver grew
louder as we turned a corner and pulled into the driveway. I must
say the "mansion" that appeared before us was anti-climactic, to
say the least. It resembled a dolled-up tract house—set for auction
on Sunday.

I always thought a Governor's mansion should resemble a
small-town palace—lots of sweeping stairways, white marble and
glittering chandeliers. Well, there was a stairway—but it hardly
swept anywhere, and as for the glittering chandeliers and marble
floors, I settled for a few condominium-style floor lamps and tiled
halls. After being ushered into a "drawing room," which was decorated in Early Funeral, I listened in vain for a fanfare of trumpets—or a bugle, at least—to announce our arrival. On second
thought, after examining the dreary, Spartan surroundings, I was
more in the mood to hear "Taps," the only appropriate theme. My
grumbling stomach did most of the announcing anyway.

I glanced around the room for a coffee pot, a crust of bread—
anything! Sensing a possible outburst, Spencer shot me a look of
extreme warning—that please-don't-mortify-me-here glare he
had been known to deliver. I didn't care—I was starving. If
Nancy Reagan didn't show up soon, I was about to bribe a maid
for a cookie from the kitchen. But then I heard voices from
another room, the patter of feet and a side door sliding open. The
photographer started snapping at the empty doorway. Then
there she was, floating toward me.

"Good morning, Mr. Blackwell," Mrs. Reagan murmured
softly.

Petite and elegant, she smiled at me. I smiled back. The
Cotton Council ladies smiled, too.

It was all too cute for words—especially the speech in which
I heard myself saying how proud I was to be chosen for this
great honor. I barely knew what I was saying, I was so dizzy from
hunger, and as for meeting Nancy Reagan, I didn't know whether
one curtsied or bowed or just stood there. So I decided to
ask her what any self-respecting designer would ask on a day
like this:

"May I have your measurements?"

She smiled.

I smiled.

The Cotton Council did not smile, nor did the Senate wives.

One doesn't ask the Governor's wife such intimate questions in front of the press. Those details are for a private secretary to dispense—not Nancy at a media party.

Actually, it was a line meant to break the ice, and break the ice it did. It nearly sunk the room. But ever-savvy Nancy, no stranger to on-camera improvisation, laughed and said:

"Of course. Send for a tape measure."

The crowd loved it, Spencer visibly relaxed, and the Cotton Council, assured of a spot on the evening news, congratulated themselves on a job well done. As for me, my job was only beginning.

Nancy's voice, nearly lost in the swirling confusion of the moment, was polite, controlled and to the point.

"Shall we go to my room?" she inquired pleasantly, obviously more than willing to star in my rather theatrical scenario.

Thank God someone was.

"Naturally," I responded as coolly as possible, watching her ascend the drab staircase to her private quarters on the second floor.

Before I could join her, two husky bodyguards appeared, seemingly from the woodwork, and stepped between Mrs. Reagan and me on the stairs. For a moment I was startled. Did I look like some kind of terrorist? Surely I had no intention of becoming a security threat—unless I wasn't offered a cup of coffee soon. Regardless, to make matters even more formal, I felt the hot breath of one of them behind me as the other bruiser led me up the stairs. The gray-suited guards parted as we reached Mrs. Reagan's boudoir, one of the few tastefully appointed areas of the house. The door was left open. Just beyond it, the muscle-bound men stood like silent sentinels. I had a strange feeling they wouldn't take kindly to a request for some bacon and eggs, so I disguised my stomach rumblings with quick, loud coughs. I'm sure Nancy thought I had a serious congestion problem or a bad case of nerves.

The fitting began well, despite the constant but discreet peering of the security guards from the hall. The door remained open, I suppose because she wasn't about to close herself up with a man she had never met before. She needn't have worried; if she had paraded stark naked in front of me, for once I wouldn't have noticed or cared. I was too busy worrying about whether I was going to fumble this glorious opportunity. The bust-size question, one which I had no idea how to approach elegantly, waited to be asked. I jumped in head first and simply asked what size bra she wore. Not the best idea in the world, but I wasn't about to wrap the tape measure around that specific spot. I wanted to vote in the next election.

Nancy laughed. She was no doubt amused not only by the hectic proceedings but by my obvious uneasiness. When I asked her, in hushed tones, if we might close the door for some privacy—if not for her, at least a little for me!—she mercifully agreed. As quickly as I snapped the door shut, a trio of tenor cries shrieked through the woodwork.

"Are you all right, Mrs. Reagan?" I couldn't believe what I was hearing.

It was immediately obvious that these supposedly "butch boys" were not quite the monuments to masculinity I had imagined. In fact, their sssssscreeching from the other side of the door was at least as sibilant as my own voice has been known to be. This time, I smiled. Things aren't always what they seem. Even in the Reagan household.

Mrs. Reagan assured her bodyguards I wasn't a threat, and we continued the fitting. After fumbling with a tape measure I still, after all my years of designing, never really figured out how to use, I suggested another approach. Why couldn't her secretary call me in Los Angeles and give me the particulars over the phone? She graciously agreed. Feeling increasingly intimidated about this entire escapade, I flew out of her room past the rather startled security men and down the stairs, where I was greeted by the waiting ladies who sat chatting on the living room sofa like the casting couch for a Fellini movie. I suppressed an urge to ask where Federico was. I certainly didn't want to alienate my hostesses before lunch, which was the only activity I was looking forward to.

As politely as possible, I inquired if some refreshments might be in order.

"Sorry, Mr. Blackwell—still no time. We're due at the Capitol Building in just a few minutes."

I had almost forgotten: We were set to meet Mr. Reagan for a noon summit. I whispered to Spencer that I would rather stop at the House of Pancakes. He was not amused.

Reagan, surrounded by the political splendor of the marbled halls and towering ceilings of his office, didn't disappoint. He was everything a Governor should look like, and more. Tall, commanding and strong—with movie-star charisma to burn— Governor Reagan was an impressive combination of charm, vitality and Irish vigor. We were introduced briefly—for some reason, he didn't immediately recall meeting me on the *King's Row* set—and after a few well-positioned photos for posterity's sake—and the Cotton Council's press kits—we said goodbye. Feeling like I had been through World War III, I hoped I hadn't embarrassed myself too badly. Would I ever learn to behave, ask the right questions, say the correct lines—or was I always going to be, somewhere beneath the diamonds, that street kid from Bensonhurst, unable to feel comfortable around such power?

Before I could think about it, our whirlwind tour of Sacramento took us down the Capitol Building's cascade of steps and into a waiting car, which deposited us at the airport. I've never been so happy to see a coffee shop in my life. But naturally, it was closed for remodeling.

On the bumpy flight home, as I listened to Spencer speak about how rude I had been, I fretted for once that maybe he was right. Perhaps I had been a bit chilly compared to the rest of the Cotton crowd; perhaps I had been a bit brusque with Mrs. Reagan; perhaps I had just plain blown it.

I needn't have worried. I got back to Los Angeles, received Nancy's mythic measurements, and set to work on a brown and white dress and short jacket that would make the ups and downs of our journey worthwhile. After sending her my creation several weeks later, I received a warm letter from her thanking me for the lovely visit and the outfit. I suppose she, too, understood the rather theatrical circumstances of that day and looked on the events surrounding it as the epitome of high camp. Who says First Ladies don't have a sense of humor? At least Nancy did— and probably still does.

Whether in Texas dealing with a millionaire "princess" or in California dealing with a future First Lady, I looked upon these experiences as temporary diversions from what I liked to do best: design. Creating new collections excited me the most. All the other accouterments of fame were a distant second by comparison. I began to appreciate the little things that happened day to day—a customer calling to tell us how wonderful our clothes were; a hundred reorders from boutiques across the country; landing accounts in Australia, Canada and Germany; finishing a knock-out gown to my satisfaction. These moments gave me real pleasure. I cared about satisfying my clients—and it felt good to hear they cared, too. Not especially headline-news material, but it began to be just as meaningful to me—maybe more.

Of course, if I had been strapped to a business ledger or tied to a boring bank book, I am certain I would have gone crazy—or crazier than my critics already thought I was. Thank God for Spencer. Taking a cue from the Billie Burke-type housewife who pretends she can't cook so her husband will hire a housekeeper, I happily let Spencer take over that unwelcome task while I concentrated on the collections. Spencer, I must say, always did a hell of a job running the company. Although at times I became infuriated with him for certain decisions. When fabrics would arrive damaged, ever the peacemaker, he would pay the bill anyway. Factories that had originally given us estimates on a full production cutting inevitably seemed to raise the final bill, and despite protests, that bill would be paid as well. Spencer knew it was best to pay the 40 thieves—or lose them as your labor. So we paid the price and went on—while I was told, in no uncertain terms, that the real problem was my perfectionism. Well, my critics were damn right. I demanded excellence—from the fabric houses, from the seamstresses, from the pattern cutters, from the factories that put the line together. And I expected to receive it.

I knew that the tiniest detail, such as the way a button was sewn to the silk lining of a skirt, could make or break any dress. Jokes persisted in fashion circles that more time was spent on the inside of one of my gowns than on the outside of most of my competition's. I always laughed the loudest because it was true—and a compliment, in my opinion.

> Being a perfectionist is an absolute necessity...
> That's not being temperamental.
> That's being smart.

Each passing year brought new collections, new fashion shows, a new List and another appearance on "The Tonight Show." But thanks to past experiences, my feelings toward Johnny and company remained mixed at best.

January 5, 1973, would mark my final appearance on the show. Another backstage power play was to occur that left me determined to survive without the hard-won exposure this show guaranteed.

Goodbye, Johnny!

On January 4, 1973, the day before this fateful appearance, I released my Worst Dressed List for the previous year. Raquel Welch, Julie Andrews, Lauren Bacall and Yoko Ono were just a few of the honorees. I knew the only reason Johnny wanted me on the show was to rehash the winners, of course, but when I arrived at the studio for taping the following afternoon, a string of strange events led me to believe that something was brewing.

After I was led to my dressing room—a cramped, ugly, four-by-four cell devoid of any glimmer of cheer—I was told to wait for my dear friend Shirley Wood, whom I hadn't spoken to recently. In fact, as I looked around the dreary room, I felt as if an execution was about to occur—mine. Minutes crept by as visions of death row clouded my mind. Mysteriously, the adjacent toilet door was locked; coffee, that most common of beverages, was unavailable; the guard informed me that the Green Room was off limits and that mingling with the other guests was a definite no-no—something about spoiling the spontaneity, they said. I got the message, all right: Someone was freezing me out—or getting ready to.

The door finally flew open, and there she stood. With that gargoyle smile and droning voice, there was no doubt that the High Priestess had arrived, armed with a list of "suggestions" jotted down on a scrap of stationery. Here came the fun part.

"We have a few changes we need to go over," she puffed, unfolding the white memo with exaggerated formality.

"What's wrong now?" I asked, not even attempting to disguise my sudden displeasure. I hoped I was just being paranoid. After all, Shirley was still smiling.

"Nothing—nothing that can't be corrected," she advised with the well-rehearsed pleasantness only the most devious types project. But this particular episode wasn't Shirley's idea—not even she would dare suggest the ridiculous request that followed.

"Johnny doesn't like your list. He wants you to change some names for the broadcast."

I stared at her wide-eyed, not quite believing what I was hearing. The List was already out. Every newspaper in the country had printed the names, from the Associated Press, to U.P.I. wire-service stories and more.

"Here are the names Johnny wants you to include."

I exploded. "I won't do this! The List has already been released. Everyone knows who's on it!"

"Johnny won't do your list if you don't add these women."

"You mean he won't do the interview?"

"That's correct. He will not do the interview." Her voice had gone from sticky sweet to arrogant ice in a matter of seconds.

Like pieces of a perverse puzzle, her conversation began to make sense: It seemed to me that Carson wanted to use my list to trash his own enemies—women who included, for some reason, Carol Channing and Zsa Zsa Gabor. Perhaps Johnny had an aversion to diamonds; most likely they reminded him of marriage, the only contract he's been unable to successfully negotiate.

So Mr. Wonderful wanted me to do his dirty work. Hell, no! I told Shirley to put me on one minute before the show ended and that would be that. And that was that. When I walked out to greet Johnny that evening, the show was virtually over, he read the List—and lo and behold, Carol Channing and Zsa Zsa Gabor were on it. Johnny gave me the cold shoulder on the air, said goodnight to the viewers—and said goodbye to me.

Little did I realize that that goodbye was forever!

My attitude was simply good riddance, c'est la vie and all that jazz. But the exposure I continued to receive from Carson's frequent put-downs of me generated far more publicity than my annual appearance ever did. I suppose I should be grateful for his backhanded attention. I felt a little like Carson's former wives—gone, but certainly not forgotten.

Lucky for me not all talk show hosts were so arrogant and not all bookers so conniving. They can still be devious, however, as was proved by my upcoming appearance on Merv Griffin. While Johnny had managed to surprise me, I managed to surprise Merv on a show that involved, ironically, one of Johnny's most disliked women—Zsa Zsa.

Late one afternoon, I received a hasty phone call from one of Merv's bookers, who needed me that night for a taping. I was happy to appear. Unlike other hosts we know, Merv is a real gentleman. His interviews might have been on the bland side, but that was fine by me. By comparison, I seemed more outrageous than ever. Watching his chubby Irish face crinkle up with exaggerated horror when I ripped into Elizabeth Taylor for her hideous hotpants fetish was priceless. His audiences loved it—and so did the sponsors who counted on me to spice up the proceedings.

On this occasion, the anticipated fireworks revolved around the booker's erroneous idea that Zsa Zsa Gabor despised me. After all, I had put her on the List more than once. What could be better for ratings than two bitches tearing into one another while Merv uttered his patented "Ooooohh's" with every barb? But the booker—who didn't inform me or Zsa Zsa about our respective appearances—set off a dud. On the air, the heralded slug-fest dissolved into a mutual admiration society as Gabor kissed me fondly when I stepped up onto the dais. Merv tried his best to rev up a controversy by reminding Zsa Zsa of her checkered fashion past.

She just smiled and said, "He's such a naughty boy—but I love him anyway!"

Merv's face fell a foot, the backstage booker most likely started clearing out his desk and Zsa Zsa and I had a ball. She knew what marvelous Merv was up to—and she enjoyed turning the tables on a typical Hollywood situation. Whatever you may think of Miss Gabor, she's never been anyone's fool. In fact, she's one of the most intelligent women I've ever known—a master manipulator of the press and the public in general. Her dizzy Hungarian beauty queen routine is strictly for the cameras.

I continued appearing on "The Merv Griffin Show," but I never did see that scheming booker again. He's probably working for "The Tonight Show" since Shirley Wood has retired.

If 1973 was my swan song on the Carson show, so be it. I was too busy to worry over such nonsense. There were other shows to guest on, and other avenues of the media that I had yet to explore.

My truly provocative years
were just beginning...

Two years earlier, on January 10, 1971, the greatest fashion designer of the 20th century had passed away—Coco Chanel. Her death would mark a turning point for the fashion industry as well as a turning point in the Blackwell career. One can only imagine what she would have said about the hot new looks of the year: battle fatigues, Chinese Mao uniforms, sleeveless T-shirts. Need I say more?

In 1971, fashion had hit an all-time low when even the former First Lady Jacqueline Kennedy started wearing tight jeans, braless undershirts and thongs (not to mention her marriage to Dumpy Daddy O). The glittering myth of Camelot was definitely over. A real Greek tragedy—and I was in the mood to bitch about it.

What better way to vent the venom than on radio? No tyrannical TV hosts to deal with, no crusty critics to please, no trunk-show terrors to confront—just me and my microphone.

Radio Days

My entrance into radio began quite by accident. Bob Walsh, the program director of L.A.'s KABC all-talk radio station, with its huge listening audience throughout Southern California, called the office one morning and inquired if I might be interested in doing one-minute spots for broadcast. I was intrigued—even more so when he told me each 60-second spot would run ten times a day. The idea was perfect. For a minimum of studio time, I would receive maximum exposure to the California market—not to mention the fact that Walsh—along with head of sales George Green and station manager Ben Hoberman—gave me free rein to stir up the city in any way I thought best, as long as I didn't resort to "tastelessness." Me, tasteless? A bit camp, perhaps, but never tasteless.

I knew from my years on the cocktail party circuit that if one really wants to get noticed, especially in a one-on-one conversation—which is exactly what radio is: an intimate tête-à-tête with the listener—one doesn't raise one's voice. A near-whisper, delivered in a lethal, low-pitched purr, forces audiences to listen to every word. In a short minute, I knew I could capture a sizable market with my quotes, quips and one-liners. I definitely planned to be my outrageous best, but the delivery would be much softer, almost understated.

I quickly stirred up a hornet's nest during my first few weeks on the air. While my detractors carped that I was fast becoming radio's most outspoken voice, I just laughed and wondered why it took me so long to gain that reputation. After all, two or three

With close friend and longtime client Ann Blyth (left). Ann was there with me every season, and if ever a designer needed confirmation, it was me.

I met Elton John at a Hollywood party on the Universal backlot. It was a battle of fashion confusion, but through the maze of mad plaids, we were friends.

Among my most memorable designs were my provocative illusion dresses (left); my "big and small" line of elegant evening gowns in larger sizes for ample-figured women (below left); with actress Beverly Garland, a dress made entirely of paper to poke fun of New York's disposable fashions (above); and the nude look (below).

Daring was a big part of my infamous image at my shows and in my promotion—up to and including total nudity (left), for which I was chastised by the entire fashion industry. Ads for Spencer's line of men's ties (below) were also provocative, to say the least.

When I refused to include Johnny Carson's own nominees on my Worst Dressed List (below), it was, as expected, my last appearance on his show. Other hosts, from Mike Douglas (top left, with guest Kaye Ballard) to Regis and his perky sidekick Cindy Garvey (top right), let me do my thing—and loved it.

A close friend, Cesar Romero, and I (left) go back to the early Hollywood days in in the Forties. Spencer and I enjoyed hobnobbing members of international society such as Mrs. J. Paul Getty (above). Actress Terry Moore and I (below left) had a common bond: Howard Hughes. He'd married her and he'd given me a new name: Blackwell. Greeting and respectfully adoring Nancy Reagan (below).

As host of my own highly rated talk show on KABC radio in the Seventies, I reveled in the freedom to talk directly with the public.

Blackwell wows the women!

Recently Mr. Blackwell made one of his many personal appearances at the fabulous Whittier Quad... and these photos are proof of the loyalty and devotion of the Blackwell audience. At 10 o'clock in the morning over 500 ladies gathered to have coffee, be entertained and win prizes from the guy with the warmest heart and friendliest smile in radio. And, as the standing ovation shows, they really loved their morning with Mr. Blackwell. Your product can benefit from this devotion too... try Mr. Blackwell... monday-saturday 1-3 pm, right here on TALKRADIO 79.

KABC TALKRADIO 79 abc

It was a privilege for Spencer and me to host an unforgettable evening at our Windsor mansion for the legendary Josephine Baker on her triumphant return to America in an SRO appearance at the Music Center.

An unlikely menage a trois (above): Yours truly with the fashion editors of *Harper's Bazaar*, Nancy Dinsmore (above at left), and *Vogue*, Eleanor Phillips. Even more unlikely: Two good-natured recipients of my Worst Dressed award kiss and make up with their tormentor: Zsa Zsa Gabor (left) and singer Barbara Mandrell (below), who welcomed me on her T.V. show—duly bandaged—to accept her award in person.

weeks had passed before the sanctimonious saviors of high society began to raise their eyebrows in horror. But I didn't give a damn what the mavens of good taste said. My audience tuned in to hear me do what I do best: jeer and jest about the ins and outs, ups and downs, wrongs and rights, the good, the bad and the ugly on fashion, celebrities, openings, shows—a gamut designed to raise the faint-of-heart's blood pressure, as well as the station's ratings.

Joan Rivers was one of the first stars I discussed on the air in less than reverent tones. Rivers, whom I'd befriended in New York during her nightclub days at the Upstairs/Downstairs, had opened in one of Beverly Hills' hippest spots, Ye Little Club, with a new comedy act the station asked me to review. I prepared my dialogue with my nose severely out of joint because, inexplicably, I hadn't been invited to her opening. I always thought she was one of the most fabulous comics around, but I walked into KABC ready to do unto Joan what I thought she had done unto me. If it's provocative they want, I said to myself as I inched up to the microphone, it's provocative they'll get.

The Rivers spot lasted one minute; the reverberations lasted quite a bit longer. I began in a deadly whisper: "I'm supposed to review Joan Rivers at the...well, it seems I've forgotten the name..."

I could imagine the club owner throwing the radio against his office wall right about now. "Anyway," I went on, "she's somewhere in Beverly Hills...I wish I could remember what street. And she has a new comedy act—but I can't imagine what I could say about it in a mere minute, or for that matter, why I would want to. So, Joan dear, if I ever do have more than a minute to talk about you, I will. But I don't—so I won't."

To say that listeners somehow thought they'd missed the point was putting it mildly. The phone lines lit up in KABC's switchboard room like endless alarms, all wondering if I'd finally lost my mind.

I quickly buried the hatchet when I discovered on the air, much to my red-faced regret, that Joan had no intention of turning her back on a friend; it was an oversight that she had been completely unaware of. As I thought about the situation, I realized that Rivers was just like me—although I did have a better wardrobe. Joan was abrasive on the outside but incredibly sensitive underneath; she had her act and I had mine—and we were doing pretty damn well for ourselves. Our gimmicks became our images, whether we liked it or not, but those gimmicks weren't as easy to create as they looked.

Joan was one of the most dedicated artists in the business. She understood the pulse of the American public. After years of playing backroom bars the Hell's Angels themselves wouldn't frequent in broad daylight, she had finally arrived. And her ride to fame sure as hell wasn't in a shiny Rolls: Joan had come a long way from her humble stage beginnings, playing a lesbian infatuated with another unrecognized talent of the time, Barbra Streisand, in the Off-Off-Broadway show *Seawood*. It was only a short decade or so later that Joan had catapulted to fame by running her mouth at breakneck speed. I could relate!

As the weeks scurried by, the one-minute massacres I delivered became wildly popular. Bob Walsh was ecstatic and George Green sold my spots for more money than even I thought I was worth. There were no clouds in sight—until one infamous morning when someone decided to air my cozy chats on "The Michael Jackson Show." Not only did clouds suddenly appear; a veritable monsoon materialized.

KABC's Michael Jackson (not to be confused with the other Michael Jackson—you know, the one who has talent) was and still is a popular talk-show host whose strangely affected British accent and reserved style make him a favorite of the anal-retentive crowd. His interviews with politicians and various other dignitaries visiting the L.A. area were as dry as a Chasen's martini—but harder to swallow. Not to mention the fact that he took an inordinate amount of pleasure being related to Alan Ladd, the Shane of movie fame. Jackson was married to the daughter of Sue Carol Ladd, who had been married to Alan Ladd—but that's another story. I never understood too much about family trees anyway, and I didn't really care who Michael Jackson was related to. He was egocentric just the same. As I've said before, the gimmick that makes you a star can also destroy you—or at least get you in trouble with a Personality like Michael Jackson, who did not share my sense of humor.

This horror show began in a completely innocent fashion. Well aware that my spots were going to be run on his daily sermonette, I invaded camp territory with a little 60-second bit on his prim and proper veneer. In jest, I simply stated that he looked like he sucked lemons and his voice seemed to be squeezed out of him. "I bet he even wears Alan Ladd's old jockey shorts, too," I added. Everyone laughed but Jackson.

Absolutely infuriated that I would dare besmirch his exalted reputation on the air—and on his very own show—Jackson ran to anyone who would listen and demanded I be taken off the program, the station and the universe. KABC promptly increased my 60-second spots to two hours a day—six days a week. When Jackson discovered this dollop of information, the fires of hatred burned brighter than Times Square lights on New Year's Eve. To add fuel to an already out-of-control blaze, my fan mail increased from a mere trickle of letters to a downpour so deep my mailbox had to be enlarged, while Mr. Jackson's cubicle continued collecting the occasional Historical Society newsletter, political this and that and endless miles of cobwebs.

Actually, our off-the-air, on-the-air squabbles kept the listeners with their ears to the loudspeaker and their jaws to the floor.

I spent months and months at KABC meeting, talking to and befriending lots of wonderful people—many of whom were the listeners themselves. A devoted, disarming and delightfully delicious bunch, they called in with questions, problems, comments and lots of outrageous quips themselves. With my extended format, which gave me ample time to call a spade a spade, the phone-in regulars became fast friends—an invisible but omnipresent family—and it felt as if I had found a new life.

Radio proved to be the platform I'd been searching for. I especially enjoyed the fact that, for a change, I could come to work dressed down—no suits, ties worn over choking shirts or the rest of the Blackwell trappings. On the radio, I didn't have to concentrate on appearances, as I still had to do in the showroom downtown. Sitting in the studio with a mike, a glass of water and my thoughts, what came from within was all that mattered. I spoke my mind and, shock of shocks, tens of thousands of people listened and reacted.

Like the outside audience, the guests I had on the show felt like family, too. I encouraged them to forget their Sunday best and come on down to the studio, have a cup of coffee and talk, talk, talk. Sometimes they even managed to get a word in edgewise. That's not to imply that the interviews were completely one-sided. And other details, like commercials, took up more time than anyone could imagine. After all, I found it impossible to read the copy thrown in front of me in 60 too-swift seconds. It takes me ten minutes just to say hello. But the slow pace turned a dull spot into a Blackwell editorial. Often, after finishing half the commercial, the clock on the wall would remind me I was hopelessly out of time, and in sheer panic, I would ad-lib the finish. After I began rejecting commercial copy altogether—unheard of in the world of radio—and simply chatting about the sponsor's product in my own way, George Green, head of sales, told me my instincts must be on target, since his department was swarming with new accounts. Soon the sponsors told me to make it up as I went along—so I did just that, and their sales increased. This was great news, because with sponsor satisfaction assured, I could concentrate on my in-studio guests.

I was less enraptured with the occasional crank callers who ranted and raved and carried on. I liked our phone-in format up to a point. But having an hysterical voice call up on the air and mumble phrases Marlon Brando wouldn't understand was a bit frustrating. So, too, were the ones who tricked me into thinking they were intelligent and civilized, only to end their discourse with some of the coarsest four-letter words I knew—and a few I didn't!

But the professional haters were the worst. These were people who had total disdain for anyone on the radio, and they didn't call just once. Like a never-ending nightmare, their voices, often thinly disguised, said the most hateful things. Obviously emotionally erratic, they moved from show to show, spouting truly tasteless trash to any and every talk-show host in Los Angeles. I suppose they felt threatened by our power of expression, or perhaps they simply craved an outlet for their venom. I'm no shrink, but I knew when to hang up on someone—and I did with the speed of a streaking bullet.

My guests were a wide variety of fascinating, controversial, high-profile people—which is probably why I received more than my share of bad apples on the phone lines. No one gets too excited over the local garden club president discussing fertilizers, but they definitely react to a loud-mouthed sex therapist—and believe me, I had my share. The titles of their books, were always as snappy as possible—you know, *Loving in the Loo*, that kind of thing. But what surprised me most about the libido experts was their less-than-romantic appearance. Most of them were the most unattractive people alive, ancient enough to have forgotten how to do whatever it was they were talking about. And even if they remembered, I suspect their list of willing partners was minuscule at best.

Others masked the salacious tones of their books by claiming to be psychiatrists. I have no doubt they were. One such example was a woman who'd written a book in which she said it was okay to expose every feminine sex secret in the land, but when it came down to discussing her own love life, wild horses couldn't have pried her mouth open. Referring to her book's title, I asked if she had any secrets she'd like to share.

"Secret what?" she asked.

Well, if she couldn't recognize a sex question when she heard it, how on earth could she write about it? Smiling, I held the book to my chest and said, "Secrets like husband swapping."

Dead silence. If looks could kill, I'd be ten feet under.

Madame Psychiatrist turned a very bright shade of purple before exploding, "I'm not discussing myself! I've written a book! That's why I'm here!"

"Not anymore!"

I clicked off her mike and went to a commercial.

I must say that the book had been written in good taste, but I felt it was important to know if the information in it was "do as I do" or "do as I say." The audience was curious, and so was I.

I also remember the generic girl authors who, at war with society, wrote how-to books urging women "to do it all": have a family, edit the Encyclopedia Britannica, cook gourmet meals, cut a hit record. I almost grew dizzy from the list of accomplishments the female sex was expected to complete. What one didn't hear about these girl-authors, however, is that 80% of them were in the midst of messy divorces, couldn't organize a grocery list and wouldn't know how to turn on a stereo. They wrote about achieving the impossible because they were impossible. They understood the problems of the everyday American woman about as well as I understood Einstein's Theory of Relativity. But these know-it-all ladies sold books to every impressionable woman in America, so I felt it was my duty to help sell the authors themselves—right down the proverbial river.

No talk-radio show format—especially not mine—would be complete without a weekly appearance from either an astrologer or a psychic. I always got a cosmic kick out of tempting the fates with insider information from modern-day seers on the airwaves, and everyone else loved these media-age prophets as much as I did. Telephone calls jammed KABC's switchboard whenever they appeared; I guess if I'd been home wondering how I was going to pay the light bill, I'd pick up the phone for a little free advice as well. I had a sense of humor about it all, but others took their advice as if Moses was delivering the Sermon on the Mount—as long as Annie the Astrologer or Sinbad the Psychic told them what they wanted to hear. Many members of my audience were looking for a rainbow to brighten their lives. They all wanted to know when Prince Charming would appear, when that million-dollar job would be offered to them and, most importantly, why it was taking so damn long. Some were spoiled kids looking for instant gratification, but others were almost haunting in their desperation, their loneliness, their craving for guidance and understanding.

Listening to them speak in dark, pleading tones about their broken lives was devastating to me. I wanted them to have their prince on call 24 hours a day, an unlimited Swiss bank account—whatever made them happy. What the astrologers and psychics did, however circumspect, was to offer hope—and that belief in a better tomorrow, whether through horoscopes, holograms or hand reading, proved to be a tonic for thousands of lost and lonely souls. If ever there was a public-service spot, this was it.

Of course, not all my experiences with psychics were so emotionally fulfilling. I recall one incident in particular that left me leery of relying too heavily on their supposed sixth sense. I booked an up-and-coming young female psychic once, only to discover that her abilities were questionable at best. Luckily, I had discovered this bit of disconcerting news the day before her appearance, and as mad as I was for booking her in the first place, I managed to employ a calm tone—just in case she had a voodoo doll with my name on it—when I called her office and canceled the interview. I shouldn't have worried: This pseudo-psychic wouldn't have recognized a voodoo doll from a Barbie doll.

Imagine my surprise when the following afternoon I recognized her flashy face entering the studio, looking like something the Ripper had dragged in. Mysteriously, she had not received my cancellation message—and all hell broke loose when our Lady of Lunacy realized I was denying her that blessed microphone. Screaming, shouting and shrieking that she had been counting on this appearance, I finally got fed up. With a short but sweet quip, I silenced her for good:

"If you're such a good psychic," I said, "you should have known you were canceled!"

If ever there was a moment in my life when I knew I was in the right place at the right time, my stint at KABC radio seemed to be positively heaven-sent. In September of 1973, Josephine Baker was coming to town—and you can bet every banana tree this side of South America that we at the station planned to celebrate. I was in a fortunate position to publicize Baker's return—and publicize it I did. I felt I had to. Just a week before her opening at the Ahmanson Theater, ticket sales were less than spectacular—and I told my radio audience just that. Summoning up every glowing adjective I could think of, every fabulous song of hers I could play, every incredible story I could tell, I went on a one-man public relations campaign to remind Southern California what a national treasure Baker was. Within six days, her one-woman tour de force was totally sold out.

Josephine

Born in 1906 to a poverty-stricken black family in St. Louis, Josephine Baker always wanted to be a star. But in America at the turn of the century, elegant black entertainers were about as visible as a ghost in fog. They simply did not exist; society did not allow them to exist. Undaunted, Baker struggled as a young, scrawny, saucer-eyed chorus girl on Broadway before she realized America wasn't ready for her—yet. Fleeing to Paris in the 1920s, she blossomed like a rare, ebony rose, elevating artistry to a new plane, charisma to a new height.

As a trouper in the Folies Bergère—wearing a string of bananas that caused a sensation—she sang and danced for Europe's aristocracy, and became the toast of an entire continent. She went on to adopt what she called her "rainbow tribe" of eleven children, representing every race under the sun, then participated in the French Resistance during World War II, made several hit films, suffered financial setbacks, and finally was elevated to mythic status by her adoring French. Now she was coming home to America—and Los Angeles had her. I regaled my listeners with those stories and more—and I regaled Spencer with my own ideas on how we should best celebrate her arrival.

We decided to stage an evening in her honor that she—and Hollywood—would never forget. And believe me, Spencer knew how to throw a party. Since this was a celebration of the highest order, we planned every detail with meticulous care, and on that star-studded September night, when the music and the laughter and the joy of it all bubbled like French champagne in the warm wind, I knew my memories of those next few hours were to be some of the most beautiful in my life.

The festivities began early in the evening at the Ahmanson, where Miss Baker's regal entrance electrified a packed-house audience. Awash in feathers, jet black chiffon and endless, deafening applause, Josephine was, as she would later demurely say, "au point." But she was much more than merely to the point; she was a pinnacle of radiance in an often dark and dreary world. We clapped until the women split their white-kid gloves and the men's hands were stinging. When she encored with a dramatic, anguished rendition of "My Way," sung draped across the floor like an exhausted but still unvanquished lioness, the lyric never seemed as powerful—or true.

The celebration continued at our Windsor Square home, which we transformed through weeks of work into an American version of Versailles. We hoped for perfection, and on this night the fates were kind: We actually achieved it. A river of black limousines flowed into our circular drive, spotlights glittering on the polished silver grilles like steel sequins. Emerging from their tufted brocade cocoons were society's beautiful butterflies—a moving mosaic of silk, satin and sable, organza, ostrich plumes and gold spiderweb net, all sweeping up the steps leading into the foyer. It looked more like a royal wedding than a champagne supper party, and even I was held spellbound by the opulence and luxury of it all.

The 200 guests Spencer and I invited filled the house the first hour. Then hundreds more continued to stream through our front door with each passing minute. Each black-tied gentleman and resplendent lady was out-dazzled by the next. Like the glorious parties Scott Fitzgerald attributed to Jay Gatsby, this gathering was a sea of splendor that rolled through our candlelit salons, past the dozen violinists lining the grand staircase and into the garden, where a huge white tent lit with crystal chandeliers from The Great Ziegfeld awaited us. Beneath their soft shimmer, on tables covered with deep red roses—Josephine's signature flower—pearl-gray caviar, chilled golden champagne and sizzling French crepes were served beside silver bowls of fresh strawberries and tiny, lace-edged trays of Parisian pastries and petit fours. Sprays of diamonds, emeralds and sapphires circled the powdered throats of dozens of waltzing ladies. The rustle of swaying silk filled the perfumed air as color enveloped the senses in patterns of kaleidoscopic motion under the silver light. Live peacocks, iridescent in brilliant blue, green and gold, trotted through the garden, plumes held high.

Along with everyone else, I waited for Josephine's arrival with mounting anticipation. The guest list was an eclectic mix of old society, new Hollywood and personal friends of Miss Baker. From Hèrmes founder Zavier Guerrand Hèrmes to Gloria Swanson to Sal Mineo to Paul Winfield, the elite of Los Angeles and beyond had turned out to pay a belated homage to this extraordinary woman.

Shortly before midnight, her long white limousine finally slid up the drive. Spencer and I waited beside our front door as dozens of guests inched their way discreetly into the foyer. Slowly, the limo door opened and one silk-stockinged leg appeared. Guests applauded, cameras clicked. Josephine Baker, swathed in black silk and feathers, had arrived. She emerged smiling, then seemed to float toward us, a gorgeous survivor of times now past, when real elegance, glamour and mystery reigned in the rose-colored perfection of Paris in the twenties. Entering the house, she looked neither to the left nor right as she swept toward me extending her thin, fragile hand. My heartbeat accelerated, my eyes brimmed with tears. I was overwhelmed hearing the internationally famous Murray Korda's strings. The violinists lining the staircase began to play "La Vie En Rose." As its poignant notes filled the foyer, she stopped, held my hand tighter and let a tear spill down her still unlined face. I looked at Spencer and then to the guests, who applauded wildly as she nodded graciously, hiding the celebrated face behind a pair of dramatic sunglasses that had become her trademark.

What was she thinking? What was she feeling? Perhaps she flashed on memories from those glorious years spent dining and dancing with kings and queens, memories of her dear friend

Princess Grace, who, it was said, had given her a villa in Monaco after discovering that Josephine was financially strapped. Perhaps she was thinking about her children, now grown and gone, like broken shards of a rainbow dream. Or perhaps she thought about her youth in St. Louis, where celebrations like this one would have been impossible to imagine. No one will ever know. She was a ravishing riddle, an elegant enigma. But Gloria Swanson said it best when she whispered in my ear, "Now *that's* a real star!" I smiled and told her, "It takes one to know one," and in the grand silent-screen tradition, she did not disagree.

Josephine swept majestically into the salon and greeted her admirers like a queen returning from exile. Sitting on an 18th-century Aubusson settee of gold silk under a row of glorious oil portraits and paintings, La Baker seemed to belong beside them. Her presence completed the ambiance of splendor around her. Louis XVI tables, inlaid in pale butterscotch wood; Flemish tapestries studded with threads of purest gold, green and crimson; Chinese porcelain urns, as fragile as a flower petal; bronze and marble busts of the French aristocracy, frozen in time forever—each a treasure, and each a perfect backdrop for her regal beauty.

Glasses were raised in toasts; smiles and laughter lit the rooms. Her soft French-accented voice murmured in appreciation. She turned to me with a slow, gentle nod and asked if the lights that blazed throughout the room could be dimmed. I readily agreed, although I couldn't imagine why. As the room grew darker, now only illuminated by several flickering sconces and the golden flame from the fireplace, I realized she was creating an illusion. Shadows danced over her face, carving her features into a delicate, immortal portrait. Time fell away; suddenly she was once again the ageless figure who had enraptured Europe 50 years earlier.

Her eyes, after she removed her glasses, seemed weary. She leaned over and in a voice that wavered slightly, said, "Thank you. This means so much…" Her words were filled with deep emotion.

A moment passed. Then she took my hand and with her head held high, closed her eyes and whispered, "I'm so tired. So tired…"

Her words were spoken with the crushing weight of years of struggle, yearning for success and, after finding it, discovering that real happiness was as fleeting as a wisp of smoke. I understood and told her so, and for that she seemed grateful.

Then. without notice, she did the most extraordinary thing.

Walking across the room to the violinists, she spoke a few words and turned to stand with her back to the room. The crowd hushed—and I felt the familiar jump in my chest. Josephine was about to sing.

She reprised "My Way"—but here, with her voice backed by a single sad-toned violin, the lyric became a haunting poem—an unshuttered slice of her soul. Moments after she hit the final note, the room seemed to spin into a silent vacuum—until, finally, wave after wave of applause crashed through the house and into the night beyond. She threw a rose to the crowd in appreciation, bid us farewell and left the party. In a theatrical flash, she was gone—disappearing like a dream too perfect to be real.

But I knew I would see her again—and I did. A year later, shortly before her death in 1975, she returned to the L.A. stage and requested to stay with us at the house. Although her visit was brief, it was equally unforgettable. She became fast friends with our housekeeper, Vera, a wonderful, totally devoted woman who seemed to bring a sense of family and roots to Josephine, cooking her a sumptuous succession of down-home Southern dishes. Josephine wanted to remember her youth. The taste and smell of those early St. Louis days were important for her to recapture once again. As we reminisced about her glorious years in Paris, she seemed to be at peace, if only for a moment. Then she would resume her sad-eyed stare, alone with thoughts of a life few would ever truly comprehend.

As her engagement ended, so, too, did her visit with us. I hated to see her leave, but I knew she had other obligations to fulfill, other footlights to cross. She thanked me for all Spencer and I had done for her.

In a final coda to our conversations about her life, she said, "I must go. I don't know when I will return. My children need me." She grasped my arm and corrected herself with a quick, sharp shake of her head. "No, they don't need me. I need them."

I felt my throat tighten as she looked at me with a bittersweet smile and whispered, "Au revoir."

A short time later, I heard the news that she had collapsed in Paris. Like a dazzling dancer slowly spinning a final, breathtaking pirouette, she had simply stopped. But to me—and a million others—Josephine could never die, for she celebrated life as it celebrated her.

For immortals like Baker,
those star-lit celebrations last forever.

During my years at KABC, I enjoyed many such wonderful occasions—although not on such a grand scale. But my everyday involvement with the public—and the open way they reacted to the show—made my life richer and more complete. I still had my nemesis, Michael Jackson, to deal with, but I had learned by this time to avoid him at all costs. After my success in generating ticket sales for Josephine Baker, his jealousy wasn't just out in the open; it was so thick you could cut it with a knife. I tried to shrug off his resentment, but that was easier said than done.

The End of an Era

One morning someone at the station informed me that Michael Jackson was not going to go gently into that good night, as Dylan Thomas wrote. In fact, ratty rumors scampered up and down the halls that Jackson wanted me out—at any cost. It was a predictable pattern; he had been threatening me for years.

In spite of—or maybe because of—the backstage intrigue, I continued my drive to boost KABC's audience share to record highs, and much to Jackson's disdain, I succeeded. Yet by 1974, the thrill was gone. Doing four collections a year was enough work for ten men. I found it harder and harder to keep two high-pressure jobs and do justice to either one. Still, I was too stubborn to give up radio just yet. I simply couldn't give up the relationship I enjoyed with my public.

I suppose I knew I would have to make a choice eventually. But I was slightly surprised at how soon that choice confronted me. My trips to New York posed a problem for KABC: Either I had to give up two weeks of work or I would have to do a remote feed from the Big Apple. Although I didn't have a major problem with that particular setup, KABC did. They disapproved of my extended hiatuses and told me so, giving me all the usual reasons why my frequent trips to New York would have to be curbed: The remote format was too expensive, communication was often garbled, they needed me back in the Los Angeles station with local guests. I argued that my New York guests gave the show an entirely new flavor. I could do interviews from Broadway, Fifth Avenue, even Wall Street. KABC said they would think about it.

But I didn't want them to think. I wanted them to let me do what I did best: stir up controversy, Blackwell style. After one subsequent trip, I returned home to discover KABC had been thinking again—a task they were not well equipped to handle—and found they had decided to make a few major changes in some of the powerful management positions.

I began to see the handwriting on the wall, and the ax finally fell on a Friday afternoon. The program director informed me that my services were no longer required. They told my producer, Louise Tambone, that they'd find a job for her if she wanted to stay, but she said, "No, thanks. You've fired my star."

The two of us cleaned out our drawers, cried a little together, dried our tears and walked out the door with our heads held high. The brass were careful to fire me after my show so that I couldn't use it as a soapbox to air my personal grievances against them. I never would have lowered myself to that kind of cheap grandstanding, but I'll always regret not being able to tell my listeners goodbye. They'd been very good to me, and all I wanted to say was: Love me, and remember me.

It was time for me to be on my way...

During the last few years of frantic days and hectic nights, there had been little time left for family and friends. And even with the end of my days in radio, my schedule was still overflowing with public and social appearances that I was expected to make. Spencer continued to take on the daily burden of running the firm—and understandably, he began to grow sullen, harassed and, at times, remote. I hurt for him. And he continued to suffer an identity crisis, with too many people calling me and making me the center of attention. Few knew how invaluable Spencer was, how he managed to keep the three-ring circus downtown on an even and profitable keel. It was hard; he was tired and I was tired. Keeping abreast of the modern fashion era was a monumental task for both of us—and it took a heavy toll.

"Have I Stayed Too Long at the Fair?"

Billy Barnes

So much had happened since we had opened the showroom in '58. Gone were the innocent, devil-may-care days when we were surrounded by familiar faces and familiar styles. Fashion had degenerated into a hideous parody of its former glory while the world in general seemed to spin faster and faster around us. I rarely had the luxury of retreating to the back room of the office to spend hours worrying over a small detail of a dress, as I had in the past.

The whirlwind of employees we hired were less than what we had hoped for, since many of the old-time craftsmen of the business had either retired or had gone on to that great cloud of chiffon in the sky. In the good old days, when fashion was art, our employees cared as much about the final product as I did, and everyone performed their work with painstaking precision. The cutters prided themselves on producing my patterns perfectly. The seamstresses, who had spent a lifetime creating extraordinary clothes, were proud of their craft—and they were worth their weight in platinum needles and pins. I reveled in the hand beaders we contracted: Except for the occasional garment sent to the Orient for beading, usually with pearls, I would utilize the irreplaceable talents of the women of Europe, who had immigrated to America with old-world taste, talent and the extraordinary skills that had been handed down for generations. And then there were the jolly, hard-working midwestern women who were such pros at trim beading, sewing tiny beads directly onto a finished garment. Unfortunately, this was a fast-fading profession. The work was tedious, difficult and time-consuming, not to mention incredibly expensive.

Still, I refused to cut corners. I continued to demand, for example, that every ten to twelve inches of beading be "locked" to avoid an entire row of beads popping off if one should break free from the fabric. And then to add even more to our bill, I insisted on using multicolored crystal and single gemstones, gorgeous details that required hand-sewing one at a time. All this additional work would result in an abundance of additional costs. But I also refused to raise my prices through the roof; I did not subscribe to the theory that a dress automatically became chic if the price tag ended in three or four zeros. Heaven knows, I was tempted many times to charge $1,000 for a simple silk suit, but my conscience wouldn't allow it. The few dresses I designed that did reach those thousand-dollar-and-up prices were worth every penny. I had never wanted to be an elitist designer—and I wasn't about to start after being in the business for nearly twenty years. My fashions were for American women who wanted to look feminine and beautiful without sacrificing little Johnny's college tuition to do it.

Slowly but surely, as the people who had surrounded me in the showroom for so many years began to retire, either burned out or beaded out, the face of fashion was dissolving into a sea of strangers. Gone were the wonderful old men who spoke in thick Hebrew accents. Gone were the devoted detailers from France, England and Germany. Gone was the sense of real pride and accomplishment these behind-the-scenes magicians created. Their magic was, sadly, eroding into an era of mass production and mass mediocrity. I began to downplay my collections in terms of the unnecessarily elaborate and expensive detail work. Besides, few appreciated it anyway in the Polyester Era.

That quintessential fabric of the seventies posed a plethora of problems. God knows most of it was ugly, and as slippery as a fresh flounder. It was absolute hell to cut and design. Unfortunately, though, even the more classic fabrics I favored were also suffering from the industry's new mass production methods. Patterns failed to be cut with the precision I needed; a mere quarter-inch off in the seam resulted in an ill-fitting garment—and those machines did it every time. As for dress darts, which allowed the fabric to fit like a second skin, we had to stamp their placement in chalk on every pattern and place tissue paper between each separate garment. Without our rather elaborate preproduction process, I knew the factories would just punch holes to indicate the placement of a bust dart or a draped detail and leave it at that. Because of this, no one even bothers to use darts anymore; they're just too much aggravation. How can you complain to a worker who would rather throw a dart at you than sew one for you? You can't, and guilt never works on the indifferent.

I was not surprised to discover that sales of my clothes were declining within the New York market. I thought of several reasons to explain why, and all of them were probably true. I knew that our salesmen catered more to the whims of the New York buyers than in defending what I represented as a designer. New York was so entrenched in following the latest fashion fads that my collections no longer had a place in Seventh Avenue's throwaway society. This was due, in part, to the nearly schizophrenic attitude of both the buyers and the salesmen. On one hand, the showroom salespeople wanted me to design clothes that represented a more contemporary vision of fashion, which I was happy to do. But the store buyers wanted the old traditional "Blackwells," glamorous skintight sheaths similar to the ones that had been so successful in the Sixties, or so they said. But I was simultaneously being told by my salesmen that my designs were hopelessly out of date. The result was ambivalence and apathy from the very people who had been hired to support, understand and push—not criticize—my collections.

If the salesmen couldn't muster any enthusiasm for the clothes, how did they expect the buyers to? It was a no-win situation, and it wasn't helped by the fact that my Worst Dressed List infuriated many of the high-couture stores that purchased my clothes. The snobbish Manhattan hypocrites were not pleased with my annual tongue-in-cheek assassination of the established old guard—and although the world at large was amused, the cloistered cliques along Madison Avenue disliked the "fashion slave" label I attached to them. I suppose I'll never know the real reason or reasons sales declined so dramatically, but I did know we were in trouble. And I was forced to face the fact that our New York showroom was a veritable recipe for disaster.

I could certainly relate to Stephen Sondheim's sentiment in "Send in the Clowns": "Isn't it rich?...Isn't it queer?...Losing my timing this late in my career..." Everything was out of tune now; harsh chords, staccato rhythms and minor-keyed melodies marked my life and work. But I refused to let these discordant notes throw me off my game. I still had a few tricks up my monogrammed sleeve.

I may have lost my cachet within the industry—and my ability to understand what was trendy and hot—but I hadn't lost my ability to design the kind of clothes women across America wanted. And I wasn't the only designer who followed his heart and not *Women's Wear Daily* for creative inspiration. There were many more like me—but we were all considered obsolescent icons of another age by the self-proclaimed high priests who dictated what women would and would not wear. Designer boutiques like Henri Bendel thought anything over a size 12 was an obscenity, and Fifth Avenue had become one long, boring line of impossible-to-wear catastrophes. Elio Fiorucci once had the audacity to state that "to manufacture small sizes is a favor for humanity. I prevent ugly girls from showing off their bad figures." And Bill Blass allegedly remarked that "women must look helpless." Well, that was just plain Victorian and I defiantly disagreed—as did every American woman outside the maddening metropolis of New York. Why should women look helpless? Why should anyone spend thousands on clothes that mirrored the insecurities of the designer?

The real irony is that the A-designer-list in New York was merely the B-list in Paris, the true bastion of originality in fashion. New York ripped off Paris with the swiftness of a professional thief, but with little of the elegance and style many Parisian couturiers still possessed. I used to joke that if Seventh

Avenue decreed greasy brown paper bags to be "in," Fifth Avenue and 57th Street would be a paper parade of brown greasy bags by nine the next morning—an apt description of the garbage on sale in the Big Apple.

Fighting back, I lost some battles—but I won a few, too. I wasn't the only California designer struggling against the tide, but I did fare better than some. I knew there was a market for my work, so I concentrated on the average woman who didn't want to face fashion bankruptcy. I began doing more private shows than ever before, and that decision proved to be the right choice. Women flocked backstage to purchase what was no longer available in most stores—stores that now resembled one long assembly line of single-concept designs for people who must have thought individuality was a dirty word.

The most often heard phrase at my shows was, "Now, *here's* something I can wear!" I relished those words more than I can say. Unable to comprehend the skyrocketing costs of unwearable dresses, I desperately tried to maintain my price, unfortunately not always showing a profit.

Another fringe benefit of my decision to fully concentrate on private showings was the fact that I was actually there—and the women wanted to buy clothes directly from the man on the label. They wanted personal attention, reassurance, advice—and God knows I gave it to them. After years of dealing with every type imaginable—from socialite to schoolteacher—I still enjoyed one-on-one communication with the public. I wanted my clothes to make my ladies happy. And they did.

Though we were inundated with special requests for custom designs, that was something I had neither the time nor the inclination to do. But I still designed seasonal collections for our markets nationwide, oversaw the California showroom—and fretted about what to do with our New York branch. Life was not idle, by any means. The pressures remained strong, but I was encouraged by the fact that there was definitely life beyond New York. My sales jumped to mid-sixties levels—even without many of the major accounts I thought were so necessary for my survival.

Due to faltering sales in New York, Spencer suggested we

branch out into menswear. I thought it was a terrible idea, but he seemed determined. He told me not to worry about it, that the burden would fall on him. To me menswear seemed anticlimactic after a lifetime of satin and silk, but I was surprised to find Spencer truly gifted in this arena. It was a side of him I had never seen before, and his collection of shirts, ties, vests and other men's accessories was definitely ahead of its time. So much so that many of his designs still influence today, including many of the elegant tailored lines made famous by the great Italian designers.

Even though I couldn't seem to generate any interest in menswear, I went along for a while. After all, Spencer had devoted years to my career, so supporting him was the least I could do. Still, appearing at the menswear collection shows was about as much fun for me as going to the gas chamber. Especially at this moment in my life.

I complained continuously—not because it did any good, but because it made me feel better. I vowed if I was going to get ulcers, then everyone else would, too. My reputation for being the most difficult man in town was constantly being reaffirmed. Part of that dubious distinction was true, but part of it was simply a continuation of my act. Being Mr. Blackwell, the outrageous character I invented, required periodic scenes of intense drama. But I usually had no trouble throwing tantrums after seeing what the factories delivered to my showroom. As every day seemed to bring another outrage—and another indignant outburst from me—I began to fantasize about leaving the business altogether. Sitting endlessly on the silver sands of retirement began to appeal to me more and more—and I'm sure to Spencer as well.

Spencer and I had our share of problems, but ironically, our personal woes were almost always the result of a business conflict, not a lack of caring on our part. Stress permeated the office, the house, even the car. I felt taut with anxiety, and lost in increasing isolation. Spencer and I argued over mistakes others made, and we allowed those mistakes to put a wedge between us. I told him that nice guys finish last in Hollywood, New York, Paris and every other city in the world, but he couldn't accept that sobering fact. I knew better. I had seen too many keep-the-peace types bulldozed, and I vowed not to let that happen to me ever again. The Arthur Pines and Irving Mahlers of the world were a fading memory, and they were going to stay that way. Educating Spencer to the wolves in sheep's clothing that infiltrated the business was a necessity, because in the end I wanted to survive. And if fighting every step of the way was the only game in town, I was still ready to play.

Although I had promised myself time and time again to streamline my life, the bottom line was that my schedule was more complicated than ever. In that respect, I knew it would be hard to give up designing, because my deep need to be confirmed professionally was as strong at the height of my success as it was when I was just starting out, fashioning hats in my New York attic. Certain insecurities never left me; in fact, they only grew stronger.

I had lived in the glare of the limelight for a long time, and I had experienced every joy and grief the fashion business had to offer—not to mention the highs and lows of Hollywood itself. All that attention seduced like a drug; but it also alienated and depressed. I lived in a world of extremes. How does one go from a theater full of hysterical women applauding your every twitch to a silent, solitary ride back home after a show? How does one reconcile those two wildly different scenes—scenes like from a movie—within mere minutes of one another? The problem was that life wasn't a movie, and finales didn't end up smothered in rainbows and sunshine, stardust and moonbeams. Sometimes you just end up feeling like hell—and not knowing exactly why.

Although Spencer and I attended literally hundreds of dinner parties, black-tie premieres, midnight charity suppers and God knows what else, I always felt apart from the crowd. Why did I go? I went because I wanted to be recognized, talked about. I won't deny that. Still, in a real-life situation, I wouldn't have minded being treated—and accepted—as a real-life person. I was not, nor had I ever really been, the character the public panned and praised; I wasn't remotely interested in running over to some walking fashion disaster to gleefully point out her blunders in a room full of eavesdropping socialites. But many thought I would—and fled from the room when I entered a party. And there was the intense interest many felt as they held their breath waiting for me to knock 'em on their ass with a bitchy zinger. If it didn't come, they were frustrated all evening. Soon I grew to avoid crowds of people standing in circles, waiting for me to entertain them.

If I force myself to be realistic—an emotion I try to avoid as best I can—I always knew that performers never have it all, because the very nature of fame removes you from normalcy forever. If people perceive you as special or different, they treat you accordingly. That sobering fact was one of the dark clouds in the silver lining of a career I still hungered for. Without it—and the confirmation I received, even at a distance—I was afraid I would be alone. That emotion was unthinkable, but I assure you the feelings were there, stabbing my heart with desolating images of what might have been.

My world was splitting
into a thousand
pieces.

Despite the treacherous pitfalls along the klieg-lit way, despite Saint Theresa's warning that more tears are shed over answered prayers than unanswered ones, despite the isolation and the emotional turbulence, I went on playing the part. Whenever I became really despondent, unable to cope with all the expectations—my own as well as other people's—I thought of a remark made by Bette Davis in the forties, a quote that said it all about accepting your life and yourself just the way you are: "Frankly, my friends, if you don't like where I've been, then you know where you can go!"

Society Is Not My Cup of Tea

The climb is slow,
The ladder's made of dough,
No other sport of queens
Holds half as much intrigue.
But the bluebloods will agree
About my family tree...
Society is not my cup of tea.

The larger problems of my life were hard enough to comprehend, but even more problematic were the dreary social rules and regulations one was forced to follow—you know, the "games people play" on their way up the ladder of respectability. I didn't play the game very well, nor did I feel guilty about not being a member of that Le Côte Basque crowd.

The parties, like the people, were all the same—manicured magnificence in a heavily mortgaged atmosphere. The noisy entrance makers, desperate to show off their latest face-lift, boyfriend, designer gown—take your pick. The gorgeous, the ugly, the slim, the fat, the young, the old—they all were there, all smiling, all hoping, all climbing toward a position few could ever maintain. And the various conversations that oozed from their marbleized faces always focused on the power of acquisition—a new husband, a new Rolls, a new villa in the South of France, a new Harry Winston brooch, a new look—the only prerequisite being that whatever was chatted about had to be bigger and better than last week's thrilling purchase. Like athletes training for the Olympics, the social butterflies had to constantly top themselves and—more importantly—each other. The odor of desperation filled the air as these pathetic human beings, longing for identification and credibility, wandered past me like glittering ghouls.

How these hopelessly selfish women could ever believe they truly had a right to be considered high society was beyond me. After all, high society was something you were born into—not something you could buy, like a refrigerator. The nouveau riche embraced anyone who managed to marry the latest aging millionaire mogul. How else does one explain the proliferation of Vegas showgirls showing up at the "in" events in town? In real high society, money is never discussed—but these gals wouldn't know that. They knew the carat count in every diamond, though. I usually criticized their twisted values and their wasted energies, but since my loud-mouth reputation preceded me, I got away with it. I could be as caustic as I wanted and they still called me "adorable." Adorable? I couldn't live—or accept—such lies and pretension.

I imagine some of you reading this are presently doing a slow burn on the new Aubusson rug—and I know who you are. I wouldn't dream of mentioning your supercilious names, because by the time the page is flipped you'll be waving another banner—and a new set of initials. How many times can you marry and still believe in yourself? How many times can you kill a husband with your arrogant domination, walk away with his fortune and begin the whole sordid cycle all over again? Sometimes I believe men are the weaker sex, at least intellectually. The old saying that the masculine brain is located below the navel and above the knee is, I'm afraid, very true. And a good many women realize it. I should know. I've designed man-catching gowns for my little Venus's-flytraps for many years.

I've often joked that God must be on an extended vacation to allow this kind of insane greed to survive, even flourish, in the Sodom and Gomorrah of society. But even these irreverent remarks were welcome, sought after, much-appreciated put-downs. My insults gave them something to discuss over brunch the next morning while they cursed my name with breathless abandon. "That damn Blackwell" was the phrase. "You'll never believe what he said" became the endless echo.

"Mirror, mirror on the wall. Who is the richest of them all?" Damn it, that was the bottom line, wasn't it? The richest of them all got to be king for a day—unless the little woman blew the bank account that morning on Rodeo Drive or Fifth Avenue.

Image upkeep was the name of the game, and I bought suits for every occasion. My wardrobe was a revolving rondelet of styles and looks, with poor Spencer buried in an avalanche of bills from stores he never knew existed. He reached a point in my spending-spree periods when he didn't even bother to question the mail. He just paid the bills and watched the zeros disappear. Unearthly groans could be heard erupting from his office on particularly expensive days. I would feign a headache and go shopping.

My moods changed even faster than my wardrobe. I was either high or low, depending on whether the limo was on its way to or from another party. And Spencer was always by my side; it was understood that if I came, he came. We had played Dinner for Two for decades and we weren't stopping now. Society simply accepted us as another couple—whatever the last name was. But I know I embarrassed Spencer during my emotional displays—and I didn't help the situation by resorting to a few new habits—habits Spencer knew nothing of. At least not at first.

I started popping uppers. Bennies in particular. The rush of amphetamines kept me in top form; I had the energy, the false sense of well-being, to get through situations I hated. But I didn't stop there. Like deadly dominoes, the uppers I used to get me up had to be cut by Valium for coming down, and then a few reds were required for sleep to complete the cycle. I didn't think about the consequences of such actions then, but although I was very discreet, I'm sure Spencer wondered why my bathroom cabinets began to resemble a pharmacy. I became paranoid that he would find out and confront me with threats and accusations, so I learned to hide my pills—and wouldn't you know it, I'd usually forget where. But I'd get more and the whole damn self-destructive cycle would start all over again.

I felt like I was drowning in Beverly Hills bullshit and didn't know how to get out of the Gucci garbage can. I experimented further with a medley of mood-altering drugs. I realized I had to be in control—a thread of truth that ran through my entire life—and I knew I no longer was. I saw how pathetic some of these spaced-out socialites looked—manicured nails wandering over any thigh within reach—and I didn't want to join that club. Especially when the membership fee was often fatal.

I wonder what would have happened to me if I hadn't had Spencer. Whatever our problems were, the isolation my career created would have been unbearable without him. I realized during those years that I was lucky to have a communication problem; at least there was someone around to have a communication problem with. It's funny how you resent the one person in the world who truly cares, who truly matters. The pressure I felt to be constantly "on" took its toll, and Spencer suffered through the mire. I should have relied on him more. I should have looked over my shoulder, because he was always there, ready to pick me up when I fell. Why couldn't I love him more for the devotion and support he offered? Why didn't I see it? Instead, we lived in silence most of the time. In my moments of insecurity, I thought he didn't care, but, of course, he did. I should have realized that my behavior wasn't defensive; it was selfish, often offensive.

My mirror was beginning to reflect
someone I no longer knew.

A tremendous toll had been taken on me this past decade, both professionally and personally. I never stopped to smell the Chanel, or to appreciate the many true friends and clients who crossed my path. It's strange how we take the people and places we love and need the most for granted. I continued to have doubts about my abilities, my future in fashion, even my List. But such insecurities are the alter ego of every creative person on earth. Stress weighed so heavily on my shoulders that I was left with a feeling of lethargic emptiness, constantly exhausted from the moment I woke to the moment I fell asleep at night, overwhelmed by fatigue, frustration and futility. Then, one morning, the indefinable symptoms became sharper, clearer, more frightening.

A Shock to the Senses

I remember waking, getting out of bed, grabbing my robe—and then, from nowhere, a lacerating flash of heat crossed my body. The pain began in my ears and roared down my chest. I gasped, thinking I was having some kind of breakdown—or worse, a heart attack. I tried to hold on to the bedside table, but I couldn't maintain my balance. The room grew hazy, surreal, lost in shadow. Squinting, I tried to focus my eyes, but the more I tried, the fuzzier the images became. The room began to spin; a sickening wave of nausea swept over me as a pounding pressure erupted inside my head. I remember falling, a loud rushing noise—and then nothing. I passed out, a crumpled heap on the floor for Spencer to find moments later.

Grabbing me, he helped me up, but my legs felt weak and useless. My face had turned a deathly shade of white, and my hands trembled uncontrollably as I doubled over in a dizzying attack of vertigo. I fell to the floor with the room tumbling and whirling around me. I had no control over myself.

Spencer helped me to the car, his supporting arm shaking, and we sped down Wilshire Boulevard toward the hospital. I was quickly brought into the waiting room, grateful to be alive. After experiencing the most horrific sensations of drowning, losing all sense of balance and the infernal heat that stung my head, I barely noticed the doctor standing over me. I felt as if I were standing in a blind, endless tunnel with cars and trucks racing past me, horns blaring, lights flashing. I held my head as tears came to my eyes. When the doctor finally spoke to me, his words came through like a distant echo.

He diagnosed my symptoms as Ménière's disease, an affliction of the inner ear that causes sudden, severe vertigo attacks that last from several minutes to what seems like an eternity. I was terrified. The doctor went on to explain that Ménière's disease is incurable but treatable. What the hell did that mean? It meant, he responded patiently, that although the condition would never completely leave my body, certain drugs and changes in diet could lessen the severity and number of future "episodes"—episodes that could lead to permanent deafness and even end in death. If that failed, there was always a possibility of an operation as a last resort. But that was an alternative I did not want to consider, since it would result at the very least in total hearing loss. Either way, it didn't look good. I was devastated.

How could this have happened? I'm sure all the stress, worry and depression had a hand in it. But I knew I'd better start being a little more careful, because my nine lives were nearly up. Since I never knew when an attack might occur, I was too frightened to even consider leaving my bedroom, much less the house. Retreating into self-imposed seclusion, I was faced with more empty days and nights, laced with anxiety. With the way Hollywood gossips, I could only imagine the rumors that would fly if I collapsed at a cocktail party. I tried not to worry about my career, but I couldn't stop myself. What was to become of me now? I was paralyzed with fear about the future, about the accomplishments I had yet to fulfill, and I sank into a downward spiral of anger and resentment.

I felt as if I had been living life with a dark cloud over my head—constantly threatening to shower me with another terrifying attack. And now it had. Then, just as mysteriously as the syndrome appeared, it suddenly vanished. As the weeks passed and my sense of balance grew stronger, the deep, dull roar I had heard in my ear finally evaporated. Left with dark memories of helplessness and inertia, I prayed I wouldn't have to face them again. If I did suffer another "episode," considering the severity of the damage that had already been done, my doctors later confessed that I would most certainly be deaf.

To this day, I have somehow escaped that silent sentence. I reduced the stress in my life substantially from the moment I heard I might be permanently incapacitated—and even went on a diet rich in niacin and bananas. Lo and behold, it worked, and today I'm lucky enough to still be able to hear every venomous remark my critics utter.

I might have won the battle, but I was still losing the war. My illness had thankfully been arrested; Mother's, however, had not. Rumors of cancer persisted—although she remained silent about the ultimate truth about her condition. She laughed off her ailments as old age, but I knew something was terribly, hopelessly wrong. Pounds fell seemingly overnight from her already emaciated body. I yelled at her to eat—another insensitive action on my part—but I didn't know what else to do.

I knew I had been remiss in failing to devote any amount of real time to her. While neglecting the things that mattered most, I was always on the go to some event that really made absolutely no difference in my life. Weeks passed without seeing or even speaking to her. When we did get together, I found myself growing impatient. I didn't know how to answer the questions she asked—or how to confront the realities of her own loneliness. When she told me she needed me, I cringed. She seemed to be forcing a responsibility on me that I couldn't handle. How could I take care of her? I didn't know how to take care of myself. And when she confronted me with pointed advice on my less-than-amiable activities, I bristled. Accusing her of interfering in my life, I'd wildly hang up the phone—then regret doing it.

Day by day, her health grew steadily worse. I knew that time was running out. She rarely left her apartment anymore, and the outside world all but disappeared. Powerless to stop the cruel passage of time, I felt incapable of giving her the kind of support she needed. Mother was much older now—but, of course, I didn't see her that way. To me, she was still the invincible sparrow, flying alone—but ageless, courageous and indomitable. Wouldn't she always be there for me? Sporadically I tried to plan for a future without her—but I just couldn't do it. She was the one person I never dreamed would leave me.

I found it impossible to handle the truth of Mother's illness. Trapped in a web of painful emotions, I felt like a character in a tragedy, moving inexorably toward the final scene. I knew I couldn't control fate, and what was going to happen was going to happen.

Life had given much to me. It had taken much, too. It was about to do so again. Bedridden at her apartment, achingly thin and silent, Mother seemed to dissolve into the room that surrounded her. The rich vibrancy that had marked her life was fading. Her doctors tried to persuade me to admit her to the hospital on an extended basis, yet I was afraid to. I thought she might completely lose all hope if she felt she was being taken away from her home. But the doctors were right.

I Wanted the Music to Play on Forever

Hospitalization was the only answer. Mother's speech had dissipated into whispered murmurs. But I knew by looking into her frightened eyes she didn't want to go. In the end, she reluctantly agreed; deep down, she knew it was the only alternative we had. Under round-the-clock hospital care, she rallied. Her speech improved, her color returned and her outlook grew brighter. So did mine, and improbable hope burst through me. But it all evaporated one morning as quickly as it had appeared. In a freakish accident on the day she was set to return home, she fell again. This time she broke her jaw; surgery would be necessary. The unfairness of it all enraged me. Visiting her in that antiseptic tomb of cold tile and green walls, not knowing if she would ever be able to leave there again, filled me with a desperate powerlessness.

Although there was little communication between us, I visited every day. I spent hours, days staring at her while she slept, as each evening grew a little darker and a little more hopeless. After the doctors wired Mother's jaw, her meals became intravenous tubes of pale liquid dispensed in plastic bags hanging over her head. Nurses appeared and disappeared like revolving robots, puttering down the silent hospital halls armed with bottles of medicine that no longer had much effect. Through the tiny metal wires that held her mouth in a cage of solitude, she would occasionally regain enough energy to whisper my name. Often her fingers would reach for mine and I pressed her tiny palms to my face and smiled. Her lips moved almost imperceptibly, and I knew she was smiling back, thanking me for being there.

I couldn't help thinking what a terrible life she'd lived; after giving so much love, after enduring so many sacrifices, the end seemed a bitter coda to a life of such struggle. Suffering as a frightened child in politically shattered Russia had prepared her for disappointment, and she had known that heart-crushing emotion over and over again. I admired how brave she was; I prayed for some of that bravery now, when she needed me most.

I implored the doctors to release her. I wanted her to see her home, surrounded by the books, photographs and mementos she cherished, one final time. They hesitantly agreed. But her days of freedom only proved to me that caring for her was an impossibility. She was helpless, sequestered in silence and refused to see anyone but me. Mother became embarrassed by her condition, retreating into a world of shadows and untold memories. The only answer was to return her to the hospital. As the ambulance arrived to take her away and the white-coated men lifted her fragile body into the back of the vehicle, I felt myself breaking down. I knew it was her final journey.

I always wanted the music to play on forever. But just as the song says, had she stayed too long at the fair? "The merry-go-round was beginning to slow now," and the questions I hated to face about a future without her swept over me.

As the ambulance weaved toward the hospital, Mother's heartbeat grew unsteady, developing into sudden palpitations. I stayed beside her as she was wheeled hastily into the emergency room and then to the cavernous waiting area, where a group of doctors pushed me aside and began taking batteries of tests, tests and more tests. Her doctors told me they wanted to perform exploratory surgery—yet another trauma I hated to see her endure. But I refused to let her face it alone. As long as she needed me, I'd be there. But the enemy—time—was closing in, and I began to prepare for the inevitable.

In her room of shadows, she slept. Her breathing sounded raspy, heavy. I wondered if she knew I was there. I chose to think that she did. Occasionally, the door to her room opened and two nurses entered to adjust the mesh of tubes that led toward her arms. Doctors flew in and out, armed with thick tan folders that described her rapid decline in emotionless, clinical detail. The music of her life had grown faint. And I waited, alone with my memories, to say goodbye.

Late in the evening, she woke suddenly and tried to call my name. Her voice was barely audible, but I could feel her fear. She was intensely aware of what was happening to her. Desperately, she mumbled all the things she had wanted to say to me for years—apologizing for not providing a better life, for not giving me an easier path to follow. I certainly held no anger in my heart for her—only great love, devotion and respect. I had little to be bitter about, I realized, as I watched her grasp for words. No one could have loved me more. I touched her cheek, brushing back the soft strands of gray hair that fell across her face. She seemed cold and shivered against the pillows, unable to warm herself in the stillness of the night.

As tears filled my eyes, blurring my vision, her face dissolved into a curtain of shattered prisms, a broken mosaic ravaged by time. She turned her face toward mine and struggled to speak again. The word "sorry" gurgled up through her throat and hovered in the air. Between quick gasps, she spoke of Brooklyn, and images of my childhood flooded back, burying me in memories I'd spent a lifetime trying to forget. She told me to love Spencer, not hurt him. She said he had become a second son to her. I cried again, unashamed.

Gathering up her last reserves of strength, she warned, "Be careful of the world…all its angry people…"

Her voice broke off, a moment of silence followed, and I whispered to her that I would. She smiled briefly—beautifully— before sinking back into the bed. I looked into her eyes; they were dark pools of emptiness.

"Pray for me," she whispered finally.

"I will, I will." My throat shut.

Her breathing seemed magnified in the hushed room before she closed her eyes and went to sleep. Soon, a look of peace illuminated her face under the soft glow of the bedside lamp. As I watched her rest, the strangest image appeared. Whether caused by the shadows that surrounded us, or something far more intangible and mysterious, her face seemed young again. The suffering had vanished. For the first time since her illness, I saw her the way I had seen her when I was a child—beautiful, delicate, ageless.

Outside, the moon glowed in the inky skies and poured into the room, bathing the floor in streaks of light. I found myself repeating the same phrase over and over and over:

"I love you...I love you," choked in my throat.

I barely recognized my own voice speaking in the darkness. I no longer heard her soft breathing, only the sound of my own words.

No more pain.

No more senseless struggle.

It was over. The light slowly faded from her face, like a sunbeam that had suddenly stopped shining. I crept out of the room, knowing we would never be together again. At least not here, not now. But I also felt in my heart, as I stood alone in that cold hospital corridor, that her love was timeless. I remembered the good times, our moments of togetherness, in silence and in laughter. We had shared so much, been through so much. We were alike, Mother and I. We believed in dreams—and fought to fulfill them. Now her dreams were over. Mine were not. She had taught me well.

In our own way, both of us wanted the music to play on forever. Perhaps, just perhaps, the music does—a never-ending song that only memory can treasure, but strong and true and eternal just the same. Mother would be with me always.

I placed her in a white marble crypt that sat on a grassy hill dotted with wildflowers, and I planted a Chinese magnolia in her memory at my home. Each year on the anniversary of her death, the brown, barren branches burst into fluted pink blossoms, ringed in purest white, reminding me of her beauty and her lasting love.

Mother's death—in so many ways—set me free. I discovered, not a moment too soon, that life wasn't a dress rehearsal. This was it. All the obstacles, problems and senseless headaches inherent in my overblown lifestyle were ending. I simply refused to be caught up in the glitter anymore. Being Mr. Blackwell was not the most important facet of my existence. My personal life—and happiness— became a new priority. There were many unspoken emotions to face, important decisions to make, plans to set in motion...

Walk with Me

Spencer and I were alone now. I guess we always were, in one way or another, but now I understood that he had always stood beside me, supporting me in his own quiet and detached way. Losing Mother made me realize anew how much I needed him— and how much he had given to me. For years I had resented his reticence about displaying affection in public; it had made me feel insecure, unappreciated. I suppose his conservative upbringing kept him from being as openly demonstrative as I— but in the past, I had rarely attempted to understand his side of it. It was always about me—how I felt, what my problems were, what my opinion was. And that was one of my biggest mistakes—not being able to believe that Spencer really was there for me, believing in me when no one else did. He had loved me from the beginning, protected me from much of the world's ugliness, especially in our business. The only person he hadn't been able to protect me from was myself.

After Mother's death, I still wasn't quite sure what I had accomplished in my life. Success seemed different to me now, because my priorities had changed. Had I really succeeded? Or was my notoriety just a rickety platform for outrageous arrogance? Was success this huge white mansion, the silver gray Rolls Royce, the gold jewelry? Maybe not. God knows, none of these things had made me happy. I had spent too many years climbing a mountain that had turned into an illusion, a mirage of achievement that was never real.

Spencer and I began talking for hours nearly every day—

communicating with an openness we hadn't experienced in decades. We decided to face our problems—and the future—head on.

I soon found myself wandering about the house. It was too ostentatious for us and horrendously expensive to maintain—and, most importantly, it represented a part of my life that had ended. I remember asking Spencer to walk with me down the wide, palm-lined streets of our neighborhood. We had a decision to make. We wandered up and down the avenues until twilight crept over the city. Clouds dotted the skies like huge black umbrellas; a mist began to cover the streets as we walked back home. Turning into our drive, the magic I had once felt about this great mass of white stone and beveled glass had evaporated.

The foyer was dark. Ghosts seemed to play among the mammoth furniture and celebrated paintings. I closed my eyes and sat down on a small chair. I seemed insignificant amidst the splendor, lost in gold and crimson dreams. I wanted the fantasy to end. Spencer looked at me and smiled. I knew he agreed. It was time to leave.

I looked up at the ceiling, recalling how the rooms had once glowed with life, music and laughter. Was any of it real? I wanted a smaller home. The Windsor mansion was consuming me. Simplify, simplify, were the words churning through my thoughts—and that sentiment colored every personal and professional decision I made as the decade drew to an end. I didn't want the New York problems anymore. I didn't want the showroom, either. I couldn't imagine spending another moment in a city that seemed so different from days gone by. Within the next two years, I accomplished what I set out to do on that rainy night, sitting in my foyer, preparing for a new outlook, a new beginning.

We bought a smaller six-bedroom home in Windsor Square, across the street from the Mayor's mansion. The furniture, paintings, crystal and silver we no longer needed were auctioned off with a three night sale at Sotheby's auction house. I felt happier than I ever realized I could. The walls that had once stood between Spencer and me began to tumble down. I didn't feel so alone anymore. And I started to allow people to enter my life, those who accepted me for myself, quirks and all.

The Seventh Avenue showroom was soon to be permanently shuttered. Returning to the city to tie up the loose ends of my former life was a chore I would rather have left to someone else, but I knew I had to end it myself—with one final, elaborate show, a show that would serve as the capstone of a career by which I no longer felt obsessed. I had come full circle...From Rags To Bitches.

The Last Ride

"Are you ready, sir?"

"Sir, are you ready to leave?"

The voice echoed in my mind. A voice that had no face, a voice suspended in time. Beyond the windows of my limousine, the streets were shrouded in mist as we stopped in front of a gray apartment building. Once, many years ago, it had been my home. Not for long, just a few months. But I remembered the place well. Several stories high, with rows of small windows blocked by tattered lace curtains, these aged rooms and dirty corridors were all too familiar. Beyond those lonely walls, my devastating experience with Henry Selzer had taken place—a man I finally learned to call Dad much too late in life. Here, down those dimly lit hallways, I had discovered the truth about myself. And the secrets Mother had kept from all of us. And there, on the stone steps outside, I first felt the cold clutch of desperation as I watched Mother crying, surrounded by our few belongings, wondering what was to become of us. Now the building's entrance was blocked by great wrought iron gates, forbidding strangers to enter.

"Are you ready, sir?" the chauffeur asked again, glancing at his watch.

This time the voice was softer, kinder. My driver was watching me, looking concerned as he stared into the rear mirror, witnessing the pain that etched my face as I remembered.

A chill cut through me. I pulled my coat tighter and shivered. Curious faces began to circle the car and soon moved closer, staring into the frosted windows, just as I had done on other streets in days—was it years...damn it, decades—gone by. I represented the enemy now as the circle of strangers peered into the car. My hands clenched with fear.

"Yes," I answered quickly. "Yes, please."

Glancing down at the tufted seats, I thought of the interior of a coffin. Maybe my entire past had finally died and I would now attend the funeral of my maddest creation, Mr. Blackwell. Was I being impossibly self-destructive? After all, I had always known my greatest enemy was myself. Until now. I wanted, needed, to destroy the image—walk away from the mirror, free from the memories that blocked my path.

But there were also the beautiful moments to consider, days I often managed to forget. Couldn't I save them and destroy the rest? Edit out the heartache? Perhaps. I knew I had the power to free myself of it all now.

The car pulled away from the curb, moving slowly, progressing in fitful bursts. The street kids blocked our way and threw themselves against the black body of the limousine, jumping up on the hood, shaking angry fists at "that man" in the back. Why were they shouting at me? Why? I hadn't hurt them; I was one of them. Did I have to scream it out loud? Let me live, I wanted to say. I survived—and you can, too. Don't waste your life in useless anger. There's a way out, I wanted to tell them—all of them. One day I would.

Their eyes brimmed with scorn as the car gathered speed and drove away. I turned around and watched them standing there in the wet Brooklyn afternoon, waiting for answers that had taken me a lifetime to find. If I ever really had.

I leaned forward and asked the driver to pass the East River. I wanted to see it once again. I had dreamed about my life there on its rocky banks so long ago. As we rumbled down the streets, passing each familiar building, I could see the murky water in the distance.

I thought about my life and the story I could tell—a story that would offer hope to the lost souls of the world: If I could survive, so can you. Yes, there is always a price to pay for success, but there is an even greater price to pay for wondering what might have been. Such regrets destroy.

The ride was smooth and swift as we drove out of Brooklyn into the gleaming city in the distance. The skies began to clear; the rainy streets began to dry. I lowered my window and let the air sting my face. I could breathe, smile, be happy. I was free.

No longer would I be Mr. Blackwell. I created him, and he had performed well. Audiences applauded. The world listened— and I did what I had to do. But I refused to let him control me any longer. I was someone else.

I began preparing for my goodbyes. Perhaps the final goodbyes. I didn't know. My mind whirled with thoughts, some starkly clear, others hazy and dream-like.

Soon we would be arriving at the theater, where my models were waiting, preparing for this ultimate farewell show. I wanted to experience the lights and the glamour and the applause one last time.

Soft music filled the limousine as we sped faster. The memories retreated, and the future burst into view. I felt as if I had stepped out of one dimension and entered another. Gone now were the lavender shadows of the past. Today was the transition, the first shining step into a new world, a new life. A life beyond anything I had yet imagined. A journey lit with revived hope, undertaken with a new sense of freedom—starting here, starting now.

The Last Show

Backstage, the theater was a cavern of dim, silhouetted props, racks of clothes, drafty hallways and faint voices that gradually grew louder as I walked toward the dressing room. Beyond the mirrored maze where my models were starting their own dazzling transformations loomed the curtain—its faded burgundy velvet folds, dusty with indifference, remaining for the moment closed. On the other side, invisible to me, the auditorium was rumbling, filling up—swimming with a thousand muffled voices. I heard scattered strains of laughter, a sudden sharp cackle, the crack of crumpled paper—all set to the whining, staccato discord of the musicians tuning their instruments.

I checked off the details: lights, backdrops, microphone—all fine. My music, arranged beautifully by Richard Emmons, a friend and accompanist for years, stood next to the black concert grand piano. I could hear the rustling of charts; and a few minor chords sprinkled the air as Richard warmed up. He was a treasure—and a supreme master at covering up the myriad mistakes I made incessantly. He used to muse, after a performance, that he had no idea why my act worked so well onstage. God knows, he laughed, I certainly couldn't sing, dance or act—but like other entertainers whose talents are indefinable, I seemed to succeed on sheer chutzpah, will power—and the ability to entertain. I'd been entertaining, in one way or another, most of my life, and I had learned from the best. But after today, the character of Mr. Blackwell would only be part of my past. There was a new me and a new dream waiting somewhere out there, past this place, past these people. I wanted to find it.

I thought about the previous two decades as I stood unobserved in the recesses of the theater. Twenty years of caring, crying, wanting to be great, needing to be wonderful, demanding to be the best, wanting to like myself. The near suffocation of doubt, insecurity and isolation had darkened too many of my years, too many of my memories. This show was it for me—certainly not my professional death sentence, but an elegant way to end an era—an era that should have ended a long time ago.

I remember all too well the hundreds of shows, and each and every audience I ever had. I could always sense the mood by scanning the front row, measure the applause by a mere smile of a single woman and even smell a flop looming ahead after the first note on the piano. I remember rooms that thundered their approval, and I also knew the ice-chill that creeps up your spine when they remain silent. Some even had a lackadaisical midwestern tone—the "Yeah, partner, I guess it was OK" reaction. God, how I feared those less-than-illustrious bravos. In those days, I was onstage to save my life—still locked in fantasy, still the performer, but never the person. After this show, for better or for worse, I would be real.

Don't misunderstand. I was—and am—grateful. Grateful for creating a semblance of reality from the multihued fantasies of my childhood, and grateful for the final realization that I couldn't remain a child forever. I was grateful for Spencer. He had stuck by me—as constant as my heartbeat. And I was grateful to my clients, who had believed in me since the less-than glamorous beginning. There were those I was not grateful for—but they know who they are.

All these jumbled thoughts flew like red flags through my mind as I wandered down the backstage hallway, dark and dreary with the long forgotten relics of performances past. Above, the ugly glare of a single flickering naked bulb made me squint. I thought of the milky eye of a sea serpent, rising from murky waters toward the surface, watching me.

Standing in the doorway, I watched the models crisscross the room like shooting stars. The models who had supported me for the last best years of my career were all there. Exciting Linda Spencer, with a wondrous face and glistening golden hair. And Leno, who had grown into a magnificent woman during the three decades she had been with me. Short auburn hair and dramatic eye makeup made her very special, and adding to her wonderful position in my cast of characters, she was also my chanteuse, bringing romance to what might otherwise have been a boringly long show. And the provocative Rose Fang, the most exotic Oriental model you could have laid your eyes on--a fantasy of fashion excitement, and my audience loved her. Melinda, who has since become Mrs. Brian Wilson of the Beach Boys, was always glitteringly beautiful. And Dallas, who made the phrase sex appeal sound like a church sermon. She brought new meaning to the impossible dream as a model, and she certainly wasn't the girl next door. And there was Marit, who walked like a panther and seemed to hiss like one. I had found her as a lead show-girl at the Lido in Paris. And who could forget the magnificence of Caroline, a black beauty who walked to jungle drums, giving the audience a moment to gasp for breath. She was primitive and exciting; one felt the earth had exploded when she made her entrance. I had cast them as someone might cast a show. There they were--my girls, known as the Blackwell models.

For the moment they were unglamorously clad in a bevy of lopsided brassieres and partially fastened stockings—if they were even wearing that. Shyness is not an overwhelming trait in the modeling world. Backstage, G-strings are considered conservative apparel. Great manes of blond, auburn and jet black hair were being coifed, curled, brushed, teased and transformed into sleek chignons and ravishing gardens of ringlets, dotted with sprays of topaz and orchid petals. Sculpting the illusion, fingers dipped into jars of color, oval compacts of powder, silver and gold lipstick tubes that swiveled up and down like waxy spirals of paint, brightening lips, outlining smiles. Like master artists, my models turned their faces into landscapes of perfection. A jungle of arms, legs, hands and scampering feet greeted me. The chaos and the emotion gave me a jolt. I was in a circus of sorts, enveloped in beads and bows, satins and silks. My entire collection—all 75 pieces—hung on racks in the corner of the room, magnified by towering three-way mirrors that reflected a thousand crystal sparks as my designs swayed in the frantic, fever-pitched atmosphere. Unlike many other designers, I let the models wear what they felt best suited them; they always chose their outfits and accessories. I had learned to trust them, and they never disappointed me. I smiled at them in their pre-show madness, jeweled butterflies in flight, fluttering around me, oblivious to my presence. Reflections were all that mattered now.

I scouted out a semi-safe corner and sat down. The boisterous activity, as always, began to grate on me after a few minutes. I needed to psych myself up. I wanted to be as perfect as possible. The little stabs of pain in my stomach and back soon began—a prickly reminder that I was still as nervous as I'd ever been. What the hell was wrong with me now? Why was I feeling so scared? I should be ecstatic, but still the pervading sweat of stagefright, so omnipresent to entertainers everywhere, arranged itself artfully on my shoulders. A row of salty beads appeared on my lip. As usual, I felt myself enter one of my "moods," as Spencer labeled them. They weren't "moods" as much as moments of self-preservation. I wondered if I'd made the right decision. But there was no time for second-guessing now, I told myself. I needed to concentrate on keeping calm. I felt myself beginning to tremble. I knew words like "strange," "neurotic," "impossible" and "temperamental" would be whispered in my direction while I sat partially hidden from view by the long steel racks of gowns. The dresses represented a lifetime of work and knowledge in every hidden hem, every sequin-studded illusion. I was alone in a crowd of my own designs. That was the ultimate irony, the farewell joke.

"What's wrong with *him*?" I heard in several low whispers.

The word "him" scalded, as if molten lava had been splashed across my face. My name was Richard, not "him." Yet perhaps, in their own way, they were right. My name wasn't Richard yet. It was still Blackwell. Richard was still waiting in the wings, ready to appear. Soon. Tomorrow and in the days, months and years ahead, I would have a name.

God, I thought, realizing how my mind had rambled on. Just cool it. I reached in my pocket and took out a Valium. Just one wouldn't hurt. I needed it, I convinced myself—to quiet down and relax. I needed someone, especially on this day, to smile hello, shout goodbye or just to scream, "Go to hell!" But only murmurs and concerned stares met my view. Nothing had changed—and nothing ever would change in this world of fashionable pretense and perfect size 8s. In show business and designing, the only thing that mattered was the final product. Everything that came before was just a rehearsal. Remembering the old phrase "If you can't stand the heat, get out of the kitchen," I realized that the temperature was entirely too hot for me now. After fanning the flames of fame to scorching peaks in all my yesterdays, I wanted my tomorrows to be different—and, I laughed to myself, decidedly cooler.

In the distance, Spencer appeared from the opposite side of the stage, burdened down with piles of satin coats and jeweled headdresses. He's spent his life watching me from the wings. As the audience tittered beyond the curtains, I wondered if he'd ever sat out front as a mere spectator—and if he had, I wondered what he really would think. But strangely enough, he never had in all those years. He never once saw me under the lights.

The Valium made its quick soothing crawl up my body. My arms and legs were heavy, calm, almost numb, and my thoughts had calmed considerably. Despite the carnival ten feet away, my heartbeat grew softer, steadier. I decided to cut the Valium with an upper, which I fished out of my pocket and swallowed dry. I needed the combination of serenity and energy to get through the next few hours—but this would be the last time I'd abuse myself this way. And that was a promise I've kept—to myself and for myself. God knows I was a fool to believe a chemical could offer the peace I'd been searching for all my life.

I recall the sudden sense of detachment I experienced in that theater of memories. The pills were spinning their devious magic. The room blurred, cleared, then blurred again. I shook my head and waited for that feeling of supreme omnipotence to materialize. I could sense its arrival. My vision continued to focus and unfocus like the lens of a camera smeared by rain. The ceiling seemed to expand, bend down, then shoot back into the sky. The floor weaved. My models evaporated into a haze of hair, dense perfume and ruby lips. Mirrors buckled in the light. Distorted reflections of my face mocked me in the backstage bedlam. I held my hands to stop the shaking. My chest grew tight, then almost as quickly relaxed.

I watched one of my models hypnotize herself in the mirror—a backstage affectation she had enjoyed for years. I wondered if it worked. She spoke over and over to herself, eyes shut tight, breathing deep, then deeper. She slumped in her chair for a minute, then jumped up, fresh from her pre-performance workout. It felt good to know I wasn't the only eccentric in the room. The other two laughed and joked like teenage prom queens.

"Keep it down!" I blurted into the crescendo of giggles that spewed from their exaggerated faces. I was reminded of rouged marionettes, ready to dance across the floor. Their laughter continued to ripple through the air until I heard myself shouting again for quiet. In response, a frieze of frosty stares.

"Who does he think he is?"

"I don't have to take this, I'm in *Vogue* next month!"

Until I struck back: "All right! Don't take it! Get the hell out!"

Why did I lash out? The mounting tension was too great. I looked toward Spencer and sighed. He had retreated into the shadows, obviously disturbed by my display. I hadn't spoken to him since early that morning. I know he hadn't appreciated my impromptu sidetrip to Brooklyn to immerse myself in the past, but I had to go even if that trip revived long-buried emotions that Spencer felt should remain hidden. He didn't enjoy seeing me unhappy, frightened, angry—but what he didn't realize was that I had come to Brooklyn to save myself and start over again. For both of us.

My mood careened from delirious highs to dark lows—from a serene sense of contentment and accomplishment to sharp pangs of dread, danger and futility in what seemed to be mere milliseconds. Happy, happier…mad, maddest. The models stared and clucked their tongues in bemused recognition. They had seen it all before—but not quite. They had never seen me so severely dressed—awash in black—nor had they ever seen a collection of mine that rivaled what had been shipped to New York. These clothes were my last trump card in this business of often deadly games, filling my farewell with glamour, magic and a glittering reminder of what elegance once meant, hoping to leave an irascible memory.

As the fifteen-minute cue was bellowed from above—somewhere in the Byzantine scaffolding that hung from the ceiling like spiderwebs—I examined the gowns. My final tribute to fantasy in all its glorious, untouchable splendor ranged from emerald satin evening capes lined in ice blue moiré silk to white feather coats, gold chiffon dresses, black velvet evening sheaths studded with amethyst and ruby beads, slinky silver twenties cocktail numbers dripping in pearls and arrogance, yellow silks dashed with black sequins, dramatic veiled hats—and for the closing, the naked-illusion creations.

The illusion gowns, in many ways, like my life had been a naked illusion. The public assumed Mr. Blackwell was the real, outrageous me, stripped of pretense and outspokenly honest. I had made them think that. It was my own secret. I wanted people to believe in my fantasy—and much to my initial surprise, they did. Just like the dresses that shimmered before my eyes—seemingly revealing, but infinitely deceiving—so, too, had been my days as a designer and a performer. Richard, too, remained hidden, or at least he had until now. Reviving that long-dormant side of myself—the person who found joy and solace in a smooth river rock, a perfect smile, a golden sunset—that was my next goal. The merry-go-round was beginning to slow now, but I had to play the role one more time in the city where my whirlwind of a ride had begun.

Ten minutes to showtime. The backstage area grew tense; I didn't have to shout for quiet. My models were busily applying the finishing touches to their series of wardrobes. They looked like radiant, creamy icons of grace standing before the mirrors. I took a deep breath and exhaled wearily. The vacuum of preshow fright had been eased by the pills, but I still felt my hands sweat and my heart pound.

Five minutes. The backstage light blinked red, red, red. The house lights dimmed. Scattered applause rose from the theater in increasing, impatient bursts. I heard the drums, a crashing piano glissando—and then: "Ladies and gentlemen, the incredible, outrageous, infamous...Mr. Blackwell!"

Almost over now, I thought.

Striding confidently out into the sudden gleam of footlights, applause and music. A giant spotlight blazed across my face. And then, in a sudden crash of awareness, it happened. I saw the audience. They stared back—and suddenly, incredibly, I looked into the familiar faces of my life. Gone were the thousands of strangers that had entered this theater; instead, in a hallucinatory moment I'll never forget, I saw their hands raised to applaud—but frozen, like fossilized wood. Then I saw my brother Benson, sallow-cheeked, dressed in cowboy chaps, and stretched out beside him in the front row were the blue-coated policemen of my youth, glaring...

"Hey, kid! Hey, kid!" they yelled. "Come back!"

Aunt Bertha called out my name in the hazy mists that swept over me. Ray emerged from the side of the theater, beckoning me to follow him once again into the darkness. I saw the cold, hungry eyes of aging men as they climbed invisible stairs into dark caverns, their lips reaching for mine.

Running to the opposite end of the rotting, rank-smelling stage, through the fog that poured into the room, I confronted Cary and Randolph, sitting side by side, finally free. The Dead End Kids roared my name from the balcony as the emaciated specter of Howard Hughes appeared, murmuring the name he had given me: "Blackwell...Blackwell..."

Scattered like tombstones throughout the ghostly gathering were the hard, painted faces of the aging women of Park Avenue, long scarlet nails stabbing the air and glittering in the dust. Diamond handcuffs lay broken at their feet.

A gang member from Bensonhurst, clutching a blood-drenched knife, laughed, "We're gonna mark you now...boy."

I tried to scream, but no sound came.

A light from the back of the theater grew brighter. My eyes felt the mocking gaze of Mae West wreathed in a cloud of gold. "Turn, please...around again, please..." she commanded. Ahead of me I saw the youthful faces of Stan and Betty Harris. To my right, Jane Russell and Jayne Mansfield watched from the wings. To my left, in the brocade seats of the viewing box, sat Irving Mahler and Arthur Pines. Their sardonic smiles turned to shrieks. I held my hands to my head, unable to shut out the wall of noise.

Barbara Blakely was there too, smiling at me—but as I walked toward her, she turned her back and disappeared into the audience, which had begun to undulate before me like a great sea in a violent storm. The room roared with deafening sound. Faces spun past me as if I were in the center of a carousel. I saw the simpering sneer of John Fairchild, heard the imperious voice of Lily Pons demanding my sketches. And there was Tyrone Power, gazing at me sadly. I reached out to him, but he was gone—replaced by a thousand more passing friends and enemies—until I felt my legs begin to buckle.

The light grew brighter. Blazing white-hot shafts shot through the theater like blinding spotlights. The audience began to moan. Polished nails grew before my eyes, transforming themselves into blood-soaked daggers that clawed the dead air. I felt myself retch and double over in pain. The heat from the lights was pounding on my forehead. Sweat dripped down my face and neck. My throat closed. My eyes darted wildly about the room, desperately search-ing for a way out. But the exit had disappeared. The audience began to rise in unison, slowly walking toward me.

I could hear their harsh breathing as they drew closer, closer, their shriveled hands reaching out for me. The flesh fell from their bones, and they turned into an army of mannequins with blank, uniform, expressionless faces calling out my name as they began to climb over the footlights and onto the stage. Lurching closer, they transformed once again, this time into hideous gargoyles leering at me with lust and hatred as their nails grew into talons, clawing at me, their mouths yawning wide in silent screams of agony and accusation. Nearly upon me now, these repulsive relics of my past were coming to destroy me. I could smell the stench of their sour breath, the wet heat of their babbling tongues....

Then, suddenly, the room shattered into a million prisms, images and reflections scattering everywhere as a voice called out to me, "Mr. Blackwell?" I turned and there was my accompanist, Richard Emmons, at his piano, gazing at me with deep concern.

The nightmare was over. It had seemed to last a lifetime, but the scene that had just flashed through my mind with such cruel power had lasted only a fraction of a second. I looked around, wide-eyed, fighting to regain a sense of clarity. Standing in the wings, there were my models, more beautiful than ever, ready to begin the show. And there was the audience, rising to their feet in a burst of wild applause. They were no longer the vast wasteland of my past. The shining faces that beamed at me from beyond the footlights were resplendently real, waiting for my final show to begin. I was suddenly surging with anticipation.

The opening bars of "The Lady Is a Tramp" reverberated through the room, and I felt a surge of power shoot through me, filling me with renewed hope and optimism for a future that waited, like a present yet to be opened. I turned toward stage right and saw Spencer standing, watching, smiling. I wanted to run to him, put my arms around his shoulders and end forever this story of my life. But not just yet. I had a show to do. I had a collection I was more than proud of, and as the models sauntered out, adorned in the beaded wonders I'd worked so hard to create, the dark tides that had washed over my life had finally retreated, and only golden breezes and sapphire seas, calm and still, remained.

I closed the show with a final parade of naked-illusion gowns, then a heartfelt rendition of "For All We Know." The words "for all we know, we may never meet again" seemed prophetic now, leading me to people and places I had yet to discover, guiding me toward a new life—and a new me. The final bows were breathtakingly emotional. For the first time in my life, I believed these strangers, standing in appreciation, really, truly loved me.

And whether or not we would ever meet again, I loved them, too. They were the rainbow that let me know the storm was over.

Spencer and I flew back to Los Angeles the following morning, ready to begin again as a new decade approached. What would it bring? We hadn't a clue. But we had each other—and that, I had come to realize, was what I had always really wanted. And in the end, all that really mattered.

We had survived the long, hard climb. We had clung to the sky. We had dreamed impossible dreams. And we always would.

Epilogue

In the decade that followed, I found the freedom and happiness I had been searching for. Now, as I sit finishing my book of my life, my fantasies, my hopes, my dreams. I know now I have nothing to apologize for…even to myself.

For every road I took, every question I asked, every role I played, every decision I made, has led me to this moment.

And so, from rags to bitches, I have

No apologies.

No regrets.

Mr. Blackwell

The

Worst Dressed

Women Lists

1960 - 1994

1960

1. **ANNA MAGNANI** - The female counterpart of Emmett Kelly. One of the most distinguished actresses of our generation, who suggests Eleanora Duse playing a Shakespearean tragedy wearing tramp clothes.
2. **BRIGITTE BARDOT** - An unruly child who has acquired the bad habit of taking off her nightie before the bathroom door has been closed.
3. **YVONNE DE CARLO** - A gypsy who stole a wine red portiere from a window and draped it over her body in combination with a Kelly green couch cover.
4. **LUCILLE BALL** - One of our most gifted comediennes, she seems to bend over backward to look ridiculous, and her greatest asset in this department is her clothes. Her preferences in fashion can best be described as a sense of turmoil, because nothing blends or complements.
5. **ANITA EKBERG** - If a woman who wears a shoe two sizes too small is apt to suffer from bunions, I wonder what is the fate of one with a 39-inch bust who wears a size sixteen dress? Miss Ekberg, in either street or formal wear, provokes the idea that she dresses with a shoehorn.
6. **SHELLEY WINTERS** - The only description for Miss Winters dressed for a party is a rag doll brought to the circus and covered with pink cotton candy.
7. **CAROLYN JONES** - There is so little material between Miss Jones' bust line and the hem of her garment one wonders which will get where first.
8. **KIM NOVAK** - Lavender, like old lace, belongs in a bureau drawer, not on a torso with too great a frequency and without something complementary to offset it. She has adopted lavender as her trademark and is guilty of fabric redundancy.
9. **ANNE BAXTER** - She wears a sweater as if she were headed for the showers instead of a moonlight sail with a handsome escort. In formal attire her hair looks as if someone ran a brush through it and then said, "Oh, the hell with it."

BEST DRESSED: **Joan Crawford, Lana Turner, Marlene Dietrich, Audrey Hepburn, Elizabeth Taylor, Deborah Kerr, Rosalind Russell, Rita Hayworth, Barbara Stanwyck** and **Grace Kelly Rainier**

1961

1. **DEBBIE REYNOLDS** - If you're going to be a girl, go ahead and be one, but be one mentally. Debbie simply can't project the style she tries for in her clothes. They make her look silly.
2. **SOPHIA LOREN** - Sophia Loren, off the screen, is still the Italian shop girl she portrays in the movies. Someone should tell her that simplicity is not drabness.
3. **MARILYN MONROE** - In private life, Marilyn Monroe is a roadshow version of herself. She should get off the stage.
4. **JAYNE MANSFIELD** - Her plunging neckline has become a bare midriff problem.
5. **LUCILLE BALL** - If you can't wear it, carry it. Lucy buys her clothes without any planning, then lugs around most everything else she owns. Her appearance is absolute confusion.
6. **ZSA ZSA GABOR** - Her arrogant independence in dressing makes her look like a clown.
7. **DIANA DORS** - Nothing stylewise can be saved from this girl. Why bother?
8. **KATHY NOLAN** - She dresses for the same role ("The Real McCoys") off camera, too. I can't understand it.
9. **CONNIE STEVENS** - She wears anything she can get her hands on and it shows.
10. **SHIRLEY MACLAINE** - Looks as if everyone she knows has given her something and she wears it all at the same time. In addition to this, she is a tomboy. She romps and rolls on the floor.

1962

1. **ZSA ZSA GABOR** - Queen of the international set, she reminds me of the elephant in "Jumbo" with all its glittering trappings. Her outlandish entrances are a real farce.
2. **ROSALIND RUSSELL** - She's still "Auntie Mame," and someone should remind her it was a comedy...slacks, bangles, headbands and beads. Oh! Please!
3. **BRIGITTE BARDOT** - A buxom milkmaid reminiscent of a cow

wearing a girdle, and both have the same amount of acting talent.

4. **DINAH SHORE** - She has tried every fashion at least once and still can't make up her mind. She's always Nashville's Little Miss Muffet, tossing kisses at a grade school pageant.

5. **JUDY GARLAND** - Poor thing—apparently left all her fashionable clothes in that trunk she's always singing about.

6. **INGRID BERGMAN** - If she has a brother Joe, he must have loaned her the clothes.

7. **BETTE DAVIS** - Baby Jane's costumes aren't much different from the clothes I've seen her wearing around town.

8. **LUCILLE BALL** - Despite her great comedy flair, offstage she is a clown caricaturing an actress who borrowed her wardrobe from the studio costume department.

9. **MRS. PETER LAWFORD** - She has absolutely no fashion image, and is drab and colorless, like a poor relative.

10. **LAURA GOLDMAN** - Neiman-Marcus Gown Buyer: From head to toe, her Tobacco Road ensembles (regardless of price) make her the number one nominee for my "I can't believe it!" list.

BEST DRESSED: Joan Crawford, Princess Lee Radziwill, Audrey Hepburn, Irene Dunne, Mrs. Alfred Bloomingdale, Ethel Harris—dress buyer, Bullock's Wilshire in Los Angeles, Doris Day, Dina Merrill, Martha Hyer and Vivian Blaine

1968

1. **ZSA ZSA GABOR** - Heading the list for the second year, Zsa Zsa Gabor is awarded lifetime membership in the Worst Dressed Club. I have your Golden Needle Award, Zsa Zsa, if you care to pick it up.

2. **ELIZABETH TAYLOR** - Plunging neckline, deeper than should be legal; with plump bosoms, rounded hips, makes one think of the rebirth of the zeppelin.

3. **SHIRLEY MACLAINE** - Basically basic feathers and furs on her look like costumes borrowed from the Ziegfeld Follies.

4. **SANDRA DEE** - Words fail me!

5. **LENA HORNE** - Sings great, for Lena—shows bony shoulders and reminds one of a plucked chicken. "You can't always look good, Lena,

The Fashions Of
Mr. Blackwell

I wish you really knew him

there's so much of him inside

a man, a child, a kite set free

a ship without a tide

His world and all it's treasures

are within him, tough untold

a seeker of life's pleasures

always waiting to unfold

The veneer he hides behind

is just the shadow of his soul

like a diamond in the rough

before the jewel, came the coal

I wish you really knew him

he's a book for all to read

the binding strong

the pages soft

he is all this, indeed

If you really knew him

—Marilyn Barclay

but you could look better."

6. **BARBRA STREISAND** - All stars have gimmicks, okay! But the tablecloth bit just isn't for stars. Greenwich Village is still a sideshow. Barbra, why reject your obligation to your audience? It's a good thing you didn't set a trend.

7. **GINGER ROGERS** - When the Castle Walk is revived she'll be back in style.

8. **JILL ST. JOHN** - Jill is a beauty, accessories by Woolworth's—clothes by Bad Taste.

9. **JAYNE MEADOWS** - Looks like all the stores in town had a sale—and she bought it all; what's worse, she wore it.

10. **BETTE DAVIS** - The great lady of the cinema looks like a dowager queen from Delancey Street.

BEST DRESSED: **Doris Day, Mrs. Alfred Bloomingdale, Ann Blyth, Lily Pons, Greer Garson, Hedda Hopper, Mrs. David Whitmore Hearst** and **Mrs. Nelson (Happy) Rockefeller**

1964

1. **BARBRA STREISAND** - A tree grew in Brooklyn—dressed in tablecloth and furs. Claims she has furs for every occasion, but must be getting her occasions mixed. Her high black stockings and shoulder chain purse make one think of an unsuccessful hitchhiker.

2. **JAYNE MANSFIELD** - After appearing like a stuffed sausage for many years, Jayne has resorted to the baby pink look—between baby doll shorties and darling pink bows for her multicolored hair, groomed not unlike the sweeping end of a broom. Has she in confusion borrowed her young daughter's wardrobe? Watch out, Mother Mansfield.

3. **DEBBIE REYNOLDS** - A caricature of Zsa Zsa Gabor, who is a caricature of...well, I really don't know. Plug her in and there's your Christmas tree.

4. **PHYLLIS DILLER** - Looks like a scarecrow hung on a clothesline after a heavy windstorm. Designers' mistakes and overturned trash cans have been coordinated to make her the most ridiculously worst-dressed woman.

5. **CARA WILLIAMS** - TV's most beautiful face! Looks as though she borrowed Salvation Army discards. Total loss of femininity. Should be playing the title role of *Hello, Charlie*.

6. **PAMELA MASON** - Self-admittedly Los Angeles's greatest man-hater: bouffant hair, years outdated; bangled sweaters—a look reserved for hand-me-downs; plunging necklines revealing a comically sensuous bustline and too many yards of flesh poured into too few inches of fabric. In sum, a totally confused matron.

7. **JAYNE MEADOWS** - May I have an aspirin?

8. **CAROL CHANNING** - Painted lips, mascaraed eyes, wearing that bird of paradise. When *Gentlemen Prefer Blondes* is revived, her clothes will be in style again.

9. **TUESDAY WELD** - Looks as if she just got out of bed and grabbed the top sheet for a gown, but that's Tuesday. Maybe we should see her on Wednesday.

10. **CARROLL BAKER** - It isn't what she does with clothes, it's what she does without them. She's a sexy girl if you like Huckleberry Finn.

HALL OF FAME: Zsa Zsa Gabor

1965

1. **PRINCESS MARGARET ROSE** - A grand revival of Charlie's Aunt with a rock 'n' roll beat.

2. **BARBRA STREISAND** - Ringo Starr in drag.

3. **BRIGITTE BARDOT** - It's a good thing no one recognizes her with her clothes on because she dresses like Eve fleeing the Garden of Eden one step ahead of the cops.

4. **MIA FARROW** - Stretch pants on angel food with hot fudge frosting. She dresses like a 12-year-old and dates Frank Sinatra.

5. **PHYLLIS DILLER** - Early disaster. One look at her and birds are ashamed of feathers.

6. **JULIE ANDREWS** - Box pleats and old lavender direct from the 1940 Montgomery Ward catalogue.

7. **MADAME CHARLES DE GAULLE** - Behind every successful man there is a woman, and this one is about twenty years behind.

8. **LUCILLE BALL** - Halloween trick without the treat. Lucy, dear,

shoulder pads went out with the black bottom.

9. **BETTE DAVIS** - Whatever happened to Baby Jane? She became Tallulah Bankhead cast as Marshal Dillon.
10. **ELIZABETH TAYLOR** - In tight sweaters and skirts she looks like a chain of link sausages.

1966

1. **MIA FARROW** - A Girl Scout cookie in a martini at Arthur's.
2. **JULIE ANDREWS** - A plain-Jane Pollyanna playing Peter Pan at half-mast.
3. **ELIZABETH TAYLOR** - A boutique toothpaste tube, squeezed from the middle.
4. **ANN-MARGRET** - Marlon Brando in a G-string.
5. **CAROL CHANNING** - Fingerpaints, chicken feathers, and glue thrown into an electric fan.
6. **MARIA CALLAS** - No Italian would have ever paid for those dresses! Beware of Greeks bearing gifts.
7. **GOVERNOR LURLEEN WALLACE (OF ALABAMA)** - Next Monday's wash in a broken washing machine.
8. **LIZA MINNELLI** - Pop-art picture of a fried egg at sunrise, eaten by Auntie Em.
9. **SIMONE SIGNORET** - The Eiffel Tower without the Paris influence.
10. **MILTON BERLE** - With padded brassiere and corseted rear, the her that appears really isn't!

MOST IMPROVED: **Debbie Reynolds, Lucille Ball, Princess Margaret** and **Barbra Streisand**
BEST DRESSED: **Polly Bergen, Geraldine Chaplin, Audrey Hepburn, Merle Oberon** and **Ann Blyth**

1967

1. **BARBRA STREISAND** - Today's flower child who has gone to seed in a cabbage patch.

2. **JULIE CHRISTIE** - The great actress of the year dresses like an Al Capp cartoon of Daisy Mae lost in Piccadilly Circus.
3. **JAYNE MEADOWS** - A Barnum & Bailey circus in a telephone booth.
4. **ELIZABETH TAYLOR** - Looks like two small boys fighting under a mink blanket.
5. **JULIE ANDREWS** - A rejected cover girl for a Charles Dickens novel.
6. **CAROL CHANNING** - The blond bombshell who looks like George Sand caught in a wind tunnel.
7. **RAQUEL WELCH** - A Dresden reproduction of Charles Atlas wearing Band-Aids.
8. **ANN-MARGRET** - A Hell's Angels escapee that invaded the Ziegfeld Follies on a rainy night.
9. **JANE FONDA** - Stretch pants on angel food cake.
10. **VANESSA REDGRAVE** - A do-it-yourself kit on stilts that came unglued.

BEST DRESSED: **Audrey Hepburn, Merle Oberon, Marlene Dietrich, Katharine Hepburn** and **Sylvia Koscina**

1968

1. **JULIE ANDREWS** - A Little Bo-Peep illustration for *True Love* magazine.
2. **CAROL BURNETT** - Looks like a tornado hit the bargain basement and Carol collected it all.
3. **THE LENNON SISTERS** - Should be called the "Lemon Sisters," because their wardrobe hits a sour note. Someone should tell these young matrons they aren't vintage 1945 June Allysons.
4. **KAYE BALLARD** - Prince Valiant in a panty girdle.
5. **VANESSA REDGRAVE** - The rocket to stardom that launched Vanessa to success missed its target when she got dressed.
6. **DORIS DAY** - Has she stayed too long at the fair?
7. **RAQUEL WELCH** - She may have a heavenly body but her clothes look like they were designed by the Man in the Moon—a real luna-tic.
8. **MAMA CASS** - Little Orphan Annie in gowns by Oscar Meyer.

9. **BRIGITTE BARDOT** - Needs an architect instead of a designer. Brigitte's a real space odyssey—or is it a space oddity? We wish she would just go on her own Milky Way.
10. **JANE FONDA** - A real grown-up Barbie doll. Aspirin, please.

HALL OF FAME: **Elizabeth Taylor**
MOST IMPROVED: **Barbra Streisand**
HOPELESS AND HELPLESS: **Phyllis Diller** and **Tiny Tim**

1969

1. **QUEEN ELIZABETH II** - Everything that is out of fashion is with the Queen—Hail, Victoria!
2. **BARBRA STREISAND** - Yesterday's see-through...chemise, schlemeil, and 23 Skiddoo, and what happened to you?
3. **RAQUEL WELCH** - From Welch—you could belch!
4. **JACQUELINE SUSANN** - Tillie the Toiler gone bad in the Valley of the Falls—hair that is!
5. **GOLDIE HAWN** - A peeled grape on the end of a pipe cleaner! Has the fickle finger of fashion passed her by?
6. **CAROL BURNETT** - Looks like the last float in last year's Rose Parade. Or, a Grandma Moses painting of a petunia patch. Tacky, tacky, tacky, tacky!
7. **DORIS DAY** - Doing your own thing in blushing pink...but for thirty years?
8. **SHIRLEY TEMPLE** - The dimpled darling of the "Good Ship Lollipop" wearing "Disjointed Notions"!
9. **MAE WEST** - High camp exploding in a bon-bon factory!
10. **ANN-MARGRET** - Moisten lips...hair in flips...boots and sequins ...what a miss?

BEST DRESSED: **Gloria Vanderbilt Cooper, Princess Grace, Diahann Carroll, Mrs. Ronald Reagan** and **Audrey Hepburn**
ENVY AWARD: **Elizabeth Taylor** for the biggest diamond. And, if she gains three more pounds, she will have to hold her arm straight out to see it!

1970

1. **SOPHIA LOREN** - A 1950 B-movie costumed by Polly Adler.
2. **ANGIE DICKINSON** - Venus covered in fish net.
3. **GLORIA VANDERBILT COOPER** - Jet-set's funny folly. The all-American Gypsy!
4. **SHELLEY WINTERS** - The skinny-dip look on a stuffed sausage.
5. **JACQUELINE SUSANN** - A fright wig on a closed umbrella!
6. **CARRIE SNODGRESS** - Wardrobe by early attic and late basement.
7. **JANE FONDA** - A Tobacco Road escapee on a motorcycle.
8. **GOLDIE HAWN** - A shaggy dog on stilts...wearing Band-Aids!
9. **MARLO THOMAS** - Halloween every day!
10. **FAYE DUNAWAY** - Mulligan stew. Has Faye done-away with fashion forever?

HONORABLE MENTION: **Flip Wilson** - Looks like a basset hound in drag!
BEST DRESSED: **Princess Grace, Nancy Reagan, Lauren Bacall, Julie Eisenhower** and **Merle Oberon**

1971

1. **ALI MACGRAW** - Pocahontas wearing remnants from Custer's Last Stand!
2. **JACQUELINE ONASSIS** - Kitty of the cat pack...in tom pants!
3. **PRINCESS ANNE** - The DDT award...dull, dowdy, and tacky!
4. **DINAH SHORE** - The belle of the quilting party looking like Mary, Mary on a teeter-totter!
5. **JACQUELINE SUSANN** - Writes love, speaks love...looks like a divorce?
6. **CAROL BURNETT** - Mass confusion purchased from a Park Avenue garage sale!
7. **BRIGITTE BARDOT** - The Betty Boop of the bosom dolls!
8. **MARTHA MITCHELL** - Sun Bonnet Sue on a rainy afternoon wearing chiffon and old lace twenty years too late.
9. **SHELLEY WINTERS** - She wears anything she can get her hands on and it shows.

10. **TWIGGY** - In a strapless gown, she could sue her bust for nonsupport!

BEST DRESSED: Princess Grace, Diahann Carroll, Mrs. Charles Revson, Rose Kennedy and **Marlene Dietrich**

1972

1. **RAQUEL WELCH** - But, how do you dress a Sherman Tank?
2. **JULIE ANDREWS** - She dresses like the kind of woman every man wants for his...maiden uncle!
3. **MIA FARROW** - Around the world in eighty mistakes!
4. **PRINCESS MARGARET** - The kind of styles that make Londoners grateful for their fog!
5. **ALI MACGRAW** - Packs all the glamour of an old worn-out sneaker!
6. **LAUREN BACALL** - The epitome of drab. If you want her, just yawn.
7. **YOKO ONO** - A disaster area in stereo. Oh no, Yoko!
8. **CLORIS LEACHMAN** - Whether in sportswear or dresses she always seems to lack one simple accessory—a thrift-mart shopping bag!
9. **ALEXIS SMITH** - Her clothes have all the sex appeal of Henry Kissinger in an unemployment line!
10. **TOTIE FIELDS** - The bad-year blimp covered in sequins—looks like a Fourth of July technicolor explosion!

SPLASH AWARD: Jackie Onassis - For the swimwear that did the most for the Italian magazine industry in 1972.
WORST DESIGNER: Sonia Rykiel - For her designing of the ankle pants; **Kenzo** - For his designing of the 1900 man's bathing suit...and the Charlie Chaplin look!
BEST DRESSED: Mrs. Charles Revson, Princess Grace, Diahann Carroll, Mme Georges Pompidou, Mrs. Ronald Reagan, Ann-Margret and **Cher**

1973

1. **BETTE MIDLER** - Potluck in a laundromat!
2. **PRINCESS ANNE** - Makes her mother, the Queen, look fashionable!
3. **RAQUEL WELCH** - Trying to keep abreast of the times, with those clothes, is hard!
4. **BILLIE JEAN KING** - What a racket—with backhand fashion!
5. **JACQUELINE ONASSIS** - If pants are in, she will put them out!
6. **ELKE SOMMER** - A do-it-yourself kit with the wrong instructions!
7. **SARAH MILES** - Did she buy her wardrobe in a blackout?
8. **ANDREWS SISTERS** - "Boogie Woogie Bugle Boy" on an old clothesline!
9. **LIV ULLMAN** - Will the real thrift shop stand up?
10. **DAVID BOWIE** - A cross between Joan Crawford and Marlene Dietrich doing a glitter revival of *New Faces*!

FABULOUS FASHION INDEPENDENTS: **Liza Minnelli**, **Rose Kennedy**, **Ann-Margret**, **Princess Caroline of Monaco**, **Paula Tate**, **Mrs. Henry Ford II**, **Mrs. Fred Hayman** and **Marisa Berenson**

1974

1. **HELEN REDDY** - Isn't ready!
2. **PRINCESS ELIZABETH OF YUGOSLAVIA** - Wardrobe by Kenzo, the Big Droop!
3. **FANNE FOXE** - Too much first name showing and "foxing" around the edges.
4. **BELLA ABZUG** - A 1940's fashion intellect!
5. **CHER BONO** - Looks like a Hawaiian bat mitzvah!
6. **CHARO** - Carmen Miranda with cleavage.
7. **THE POINTER SISTERS** - Their fashion instinct is definitely pointed in the wrong direction!
8. **RAQUEL WELCH** - Still trying—fashion could give her a lift.
9. **KAREN VALENTINE** - Straight out of a Victorian scrapbook. The "Little Girl" forever!

10. **SONIA RYKIEL** - Makes them, wears them, and that ends fashion!

FABULOUS FASHION INDEPENDENTS: **Faye Dunaway, Natalie Wood, Rose Kennedy, Princess Grace, Mrs. Ronald Reagan** and **Ann-Margret**

1. **CAROLINE KENNEDY** - A shaggy dog in pants!
2. **HELEN REDDY** - She spent the year proving I was right. Should have saved her costumes for the Bicentennial explosion!
3. **NANCY KISSINGER** - A traveling fashion stew!
4. **BETTE MIDLER** - "Betsy Bloomer"—didn't pantaloons go out with the hoopskirt?
5. **SALLY STRUTHERS** - Certainly not in the "Fashion family"!
6. **PRINCESS ANNE** - A royal auto mechanic!
7. **TAMMY WYNETTE** and **DONNA FARGO** - Tied for the yearly double: country magic dressed in a circus tent!
8. **TATUM O'NEAL** - Twelve going on forty!
9. **SONIA RYKIEL** - She put the "fanny wrap" back in and out of fashion!
10. **ELTON JOHN** - Would be the campiest spectacle in the Rose Parade!

FABULOUS FASHION INDEPENDENTS: **Marisa Berenson, Nancy Reagan, Mary Tyler Moore, Rose Kennedy, Princess Caroline of Monaco** and **Diana Ross**

1976

1. **LOUISE LASSER** - "Mary Hartman, Mary Hartman"—last summer's "Tumble Weed, Tumble Weed"!
2. **MARALIN NISKA** - Carmen dressed like Sadie Thompson!
3. **ANGIE DICKINSON** - The "Police Woman" that has caught everything but fashion!
4. **CHARO** - A rumbleseat with a pushed-up front.
5. **ANN MILLER** - A 1937 screen test!
6. **QUEEN JULIANNA** - All the queen's horses and all the queen's

men couldn't make Julie look good again!

7. **LEE RADZIWILL** - Did Lee's designer go down with the *Titanic*?
8. **LORETTA LYNN** - The right dress in the wrong century!
9. **NANCY WALKER** - Vacuum cleaners have better covers!
10. **DINAH SHORE** - Wild again, beguiled again, and constantly contrived again!

FABULOUS FASHION INDEPENDENTS: **Judy Collins, Farrah Fawcett-Majors, Vivian Reed, Jacqueline Bissett, Princess Caroline, Mary Tyler Moore** and **Marthe Keller**

1977

1. **FARRAH FAWCETT-MAJORS** - Enough splits in her dress for an earthquake.
2. **LINDA RONSTADT** - Bought her entire wardrobe during a five-minute bus stop.
3. **CHARO** - Coochi, Coochi…is that a dress or a bug killer?
4. **ANITA BRYANT** - She should go to the "Queen's" dressmaker.
5. **DIANE KEATON** - Ash-can fashions from her local alley.
6. **DOLLY PARTON** - Scarlett O'Hara dressed like Mae West in *My Little Chickadee*!
7. **MARIE OSMOND** - Overdone and overdressed; "The Good Ship Lollipop" in dry dock!
8. **DYAN CANNON** - Looks like she was blown out of one in a circus!
9. **CHRIS EVERT** - If tailored is in…so is boring!
10. **MARGARET TRUDEAU** - Canada's loss is New York's loss!

FABULOUS FASHION INDEPENDENTS: **Princess Grace, Meg Newhouse, Suzanne Somers, Lady Lichfield, Natalie Wood, Contessa Cohn, Princess Yasmin Khan** and **Gena Rowlands**

1978

1. **DOLLY PARTON** - Too many yards of Dolly poured into too few inches of fabric.
2. **SUZANNE SOMERS** - Looks like she was hit by a flash flood!
3. **CHRISTINA ONASSIS KAVZOV** - Mother Earth is playing Russian roulette with her wardrobe!
4. **CHERYL TIEGS** - The three T's—Tiegs, Tacky, Togs. A moulting roadrunner!
5. **FARRAH FAWCETT-MAJORS** - Strikes a minor cord in fashion.
6. **QUEEN NOOR** - A centerfold for *Popular Mechanics*.
7. **OLIVIA NEWTON-JOHN** - The right dress in the wrong century.
8. **CINDY WILLIAMS** and **PENNY MARSHALL** - Double-feature disaster!
9. **LINDA RONSTADT** - Hits a high note in song, but a low note in fashion.
10. **BETTE MIDLER** - She didn't go to a rummage sale, she wore it!

FABULOUS FASHION INDEPENDENTS: **Princess Grace, Dina Merrill, Barbara Sinatra, Princess Yasmin, Jane Fonda, Rona Barrett** and **Carmelcita Villaverde de Burbon**

1979

1. **BO DEREK** - The "love" child of the eighties gets minus 10 for fashion.
2. **JILL CLAYBURGH** - Dresses like an African bush…waiting for her safari!
3. **LONI ANDERSON** - Gravity could be her worst enemy, and she dresses to prove it.
4. **CHRISTINA ONASSIS** - Dressed to check her oil tankers!
5. **DEBORAH (BLONDIE) HARRY** - Ten cents a dance with a nickel in change!
6. **DOLLY PARTON** - A ruffled bedspread covering king-size pillows.
7. **MAYOR DIANNE FEINSTEIN** - Looks like she is wearing the voting booth.

8. **PRINCESS MARGARET** - Most women dress to disguise their age...Princess Margaret dresses to prove it.
9. **VALERIE PERRINE** - Looks like the Bride of Frankenstein doing the Ziegfeld Follies!
10. **MARGAUX HEMINGWAY** - A Hanukkah bush the day after Christmas!

FABULOUS FASHION INDEPENDENTS: **Susan Anton, Princess Grace, Christina Ferrari, Barbara Sinatra, Sophia Loren, Nancy Reagan, Diana Ross** and **Angie Dickinson**

1980

1. **BROOKE SHIELDS** - Looks like a Halloween trick without the treat!
2. **ELIZABETH TAYLOR** - Forever Amber in drag!
3. **SUZANNE SOMERS** - Recycled spaghetti!
4. **BO DEREK** A butterfly wearing her cocoon!
5. **CHARLENE "DALLAS" TILTON** - A pin-up for Fredericks of Hollywood!
6. **QUEEN BEATRIX** - Cinderella after midnight!
7. **SUSAN ANTON** - Looks like an ad for a swap meet!
8. **NANCY LOPEZ** - A swinging fashion tragedy!
9. **PRINCESS GRACE** - Dowdy, not royal!
10. **MARIE OSMOND** - Someone should unplug this Christmas tree!

FABULOUS FASHION INDEPENDENTS: **Sophia Loren, Catherine Deneuve, Princess Yasmin Khan, Priscilla Presley, Vivian Blaine, Mary Lazar** and **Rona Barrett**

1981

1. **BARBARA MANDRELL** - Yukon Sally playing the Alamo!
2. **LYNN REDGRAVE** - In knickers her knees look like knockers!
3. **DOLLY PARTON** - An atomic jelly bean explosion!
4. **ELIZABETH TAYLOR** - She should give up looking for a designer and find an architect!

5. **BERNADETTE PETERS** - A kinked and curled kewpie doll on a hayride!
6. **CHARLENE TILTON** - Looks like Mount St. Helens erupting!
7. **LORETTA LYNN** - Up the music charts, down the fashion charts!
8. **JANE SEYMOUR** - Fashions by medflies!
9. **ELIZABETH EMANUEL** - Cinderella's stepsister waiting at the palace gate!
10. **SHEENA EASTON** - A London roadrunner dressed for the fog!

FABULOUS FASHION INDEPENDENTS: **Catherine Deneuve, Princess Diana, Lena Horne, Dorothy Hamel, Zsa Zsa Gabor, Vivian Blaine, Gloria Swanson** and **Princess Yasmin Khan**

1982

1. **PRINCESS DIANA** - Shy Di has invaded Queen Victoria's attic!
2. **BONNIE FRANKLIN** - Not Charlie's Aunt, but aunt Charlie!
3. **VICTORIA PRINCIPAL** - A Dallas Valley Girl!
4. **BETTE MIDLER** - Second-Hand Rose after a hurricane!
5. **CHARLENE TILTON** - A Victorian lampshade holding her breath!
6. **CHRISTINA ONASSIS** - Daddy's tanker!
7. **PRINCESS YASMIN AGA KHAN** - A preppy gypsy!
8. **JAN STEPHENSON** - Mrs. Miniver in a tutu!
9. **CATHY LEE CROSBY** - It looks as if she bought out a rummage sale, wore it all, and…that's incredible!
10. **DUSTIN "TOOTSIE" HOFFMAN** and **MAYOR KATHY WHITMIRE, HOUSTON** - Look-alikes wearing Betsy Bloomingdale's discards!

FASHION FLOP OF THE YEAR: **Nancy Reagan** in knickers
FABULOUS FASHION INDEPENDENTS: **Joan Collins, Lena Horne, Dina Merrill, Morgan Fairchild, Bernadette Peters, Zsa Zsa Gabor, Gabrielle Murdock, Catherine Deneuve, Linda Evans** and **Jaclyn Smith**

1983

1. **JOAN COLLINS** - Barely, bizarrely Hollywood!
2. **BARBRA STREISAND** - A boy version of Medusa!
3. **JOAN JETT** - A Bronx Pocahontas in black leather goes porn!
4. **JOAN RIVERS** - In borrowed rags she proves the House of Pancakes still has the best!
5. **TWIGGY** - Lady Godiva dressed for a Roman orgy!
6. **KATHLEEN "KOO" STARK** - A fashion Frankenstein waiting at the palace gate!
7. **LAUREN TEWES** - A shipwrecked Tugboat Annie!
8. **DONNA MILLS** - Yesterday's draperies from the Roxy Theatre!
9. **OLIVIA NEWTON-JOHN** - From toes to nose, a shredded tragedy.
10. **BOY GEORGE** - Victor/Victoria in bad drag!

> FASHION FLOP OF THE YEAR: **Ann-Margret** - For mistakenly adorning herself in a miniskirt.
>
> HOW TO LOOK WORSE FOR LOTS OF MONEY AWARD: **Cornelia Guest, C.Z. Guest** - The covered and the bare!.
>
> FABULOUS FASHION INDEPENDENTS: **Linda Gray, Caroline Kennedy, Joanne Carson, Connie Chung, Princess Caroline, Priscilla Presley, Princess Diana, Nancy Reagan, Shirley MacLaine, Zsa Zsa Gabor** and **Christina Ferrari**

1984

1. **CHER** - A plucked cockatoo setting femininity back twenty years!
2. **MISS AMERICA (SHARLENE WELLS)** - Looks like an armadillo with cornpads!
3. **PATTI DAVIS** - Packs all the glamour of an old worn-out sneaker!
4. **CYNDI LAUPER** - Looks like the aftermath of the San Francisco earthquake!
5. **DIAHANN CARROLL** and **JOAN COLLINS** - Two movie queens fighting for the "tacky taste" crown of the forties!
6. **VICTORIA PRINCIPAL** - She is everyone's "Yankee Doodle Dandy"!
7. **BARBRA STREISAND** - The Al Capone look with electrocuted hair!
8. **SALLY FIELD** - The Flying Nun takes a fashion dive!

9. **PAMELA BELLWOOD** - The living end of the endangered species!
10. **TWISTED SISTER** - A Mardi Gras nightmare! and
    PRINCE - A toothpick wrapped in a purple doily!

WORST "UNDRESSED" OF THE YEAR: Vanessa Williams
FABULOUS FASHION INDEPENDENTS: Priscilla Presley, Ann-Margret, Nancy
Reagan, Raquel Welch, Princess Diana, Jane Wyman, Caroline Kennedy,
Barbara Walters, Princess Caroline and Eva Gabor

1985

1. **PRINCESS STEPHANIE** - Her royal unisex wardrobe entitles
   her to use either bathroom!
2. **JOAN COLLINS** - One more push-up and she'll have three chins!
3. **MADONNA** - Skid Row's nomination for a poverty-party centerpiece
   contest!
4. **TINA TURNER** - Some women dress for men...some dress for
   women...some dress for laughs!
5. **MICHELE LEE** - Looks like King Kong's mother-in-law. Thank
   heaven spring has sprung; now she can wear a lighter shade of black!
6. **WHOOPI GOLDBERG** - A cover girl for *Sharecropper's Monthly*!
7. **CYBILL SHEPHERD** - Fashion's number one embarrassment—
   sneaky sneakers and a plunging neckline. Looks like a turkey on its
   way to slaughter!
8. **LISA HARTMAN** - A reject from the Shah's harem. Now she can
   remake Scheherazade! Hair by Spikey.
9. **APOLLONIA** - Living proof that every prince needs his jester. Big
   Bird bites the dust.
10. **HEATHER THOMAS** - An exploding overstuffed cabbage.

HALLEY'S COMET AWARD: **Liberace** - For his out-of-this-world brilliant array of
flashy glitzy glamour.
FABULOUS WOMAN OF THE YEAR AWARD: **Lauren Hutton**
FABULOUS FASHION INDEPENDENTS: **Jaclyn Smith, Meryl Streep, Princess
Diana, Nancy Reagan, Mary Tyler Moore, Priscilla Presley, Raisa Gorbachev,
Jane Wyman, Princess Caroline** and **Jane Seymour**

1986

1. **MERYL STREEP** - A gypsy abandoned by a caravan!
2. **VANNA WHITE** - Fashion's booby prize of the year!
3. **SARAH, DUCHESS OF YORK** - Looks like the queen of last year's English county fair!
4. **BEA ARTHUR** - Wears all the leftovers from a marked-down garage sale!
5. **TYNE DALY** and **SHARON GLESS** - Fashion frumps of the year!
6. **BARBRA STREISAND** - A shoddy Second-Hand Rose looking for a tour guide in Brooklyn!
7. **KATHLEEN TURNER** - Some people paint by numbers; Kathleen must dress by numbers, but obviously lost count!
8. **CHER** - *Popular Mechanics* Playmate of the Month. Someone must have thrown a monkey wrench into her fashion taste.
9. **WHOOPI GOLDBERG** - Whoops! Running for the leader of the bag ladies from Ash-can Alley!
10. **JEAN KASEM** - Looks like a wrinkled toothpaste tube exploding!

FASHION FLOP OF THE YEAR: **Catya Sasson**
FABULOUS FASHION INDEPENDENTS: **Jane Seymour, Princess Diana, Caroline Kennedy, Margaret Thatcher, Julie Andrews, Joan Rivers, Corazon Aquino, Contessa Cohn, Ivana Trump** and **Shirley MacLaine**

1987

1. **LISA BONET** - Dracula's idea of a good time!
2. **DIANE KEATON** - A bag lady after winning the lottery!
3. **JUSTINE BATEMAN** - A painfully stuffed sausage, unmercifully squashed in a tired old Esther Williams bathing suit!
4. **CYNDI LAUPER** and **CHER** - Minsky's rejects, still trying!
5. **PRINCESS STEPHANIE** - A gender-bender fashion frump—heaven help the Monarchy!
6. **SHELLEY LONG** - From toes to nose, a comedy of errors!
7. **JOAN COLLINS** - Dressed to chill—should be playing Baby Jane in a rib joint!

8. **SALLY KELLERMAN** - A bad drag before surgery!
9. **MEG RYAN** - Dainty Meg—the rag-bag doll of the year!
10. **SONIA BRAGA** and **SUSAN SULLIVAN** - Fashion disasters of the Shah's harem.

Bow Wow Award of the Year: **Fashion designer Betsy Johnson** - Her clothes are better suited for a cult of masochists.
Fabulous Fashion Independents: **Gloria Vanderbilt, Jr., Ivana Trump, Elizabeth Taylor, Queen Sofia of Spain, Margot Fonteyn, Oprah Winfrey, Ali MacGraw, Loretta Young, Contessa Cohn** and **Shirley MacLaine**

1988

1. **SARAH, DUCHESS OF YORK** - The palace milkmaid strikes again!
2. **IMELDA MARCOS** - An over-the-hill actress auditioning for *Evita*!
3. **DEBRA WINGER** - Winger gives fashion the finger!
4. **MADONNA** - Helpless, hopeless, and horrendous!
5. **MARILYN QUAYLE** - A 1940s unemployed librarian!
6. **SHIRLEY TEMPLE BLACK** - From the "Good Ship Lollipop" to the *Titanic*, nonstop!
7. **LISA MARIE PRESLEY, CARRIE HAMILTON,** and **KATIE WAGNER** - A trio of fashion terrors!
8. **JAMIE LEE CURTIS** - A pin-up for Second-Hand Sadie's Thrift Shop!
9. **JODIE FOSTER** - "Accused" of flunking fashion. Guilty as charged!
10. **ROSEANNE BARR** - Fashions by Goodyear, body by Sara Lee!

Worst Hairdo Award: **Barbra Streisand** and "a $250 check available to any hairdresser who would dare try!"
Fabulous Fashion Independents: **Liza Minnelli, Jane Seymour, Ivana Trump, Barbara Bush, Pauline Trigere, Barbara Walters, Christina Ferrari, Barbara Davis, Blaine Trump** and **Barbara Rush**

1989

1. **LATOYA JACKSON** - More fashion freak than biker chic. In leather and chains, she's Cher for the nineties.
2. **ROSEANNE BARR** - Barr the laughs—this bowling-alley reject is pure fashion tragedy.
3. **DEMI MOORE** - A spandex "Nightmare of Willis Street."
4. **KIM BASINGER** - This parading peep show should be banished to the Bat Cave.
5. **PRINCESS ANNE** - Lumpy, dumpy, and frumpy, she's the boring bag lady of Buckingham Palace.
6. **EMILY LLOYD** - A sweater girl for *Field and Stream.*
7. **CHER** - "If she could turn back time," she'd still be a bag of tattooed bones in a sequined slingshot.
8. **DARYL HANNAH** - The Jolly Gold Giant of the silver screen looks like a Vegas Venus on steroids.
9. **PAULA ABDUL** - This fashion gypsy dances in the light—and dresses in the dark.
10. **MADONNA** and **SANDRA BERNHARD** - The Mutt and Jeff of MTV; vampy, trampy, and cartoon campy.

> FASHION FIASCO OF THE YEAR AWARD: **Grace Jones** - Darth Vader's S/M fantasy in a Martian birdcage.
> FABULOUS FASHION INDEPENDENTS: **Geena Davis, Liza Minnelli, Barbara Bush, Margaret Thatcher, Barbara Walters, Angela Lansbury, Tina Brown, Princess Diana, Ivana Trump** and **Jacqueline Onassis**

1990

1. **SINEAD O'CONNOR** - Nothing compares to the bald-headed banshee of MTV. A New Age nightmare!
2. **IVANA TRUMP** - A psychedelic scarecrow! Looks like a cross between Brigitte Bardot and Lassie!
3. **GLENN CLOSE** - The founding frump of Nuns Unlimited! A bad fashion "habit!"
4. **QUEEN ELIZABETH II** - God save the mothballs; the

Stonehenge of style strikes again!

5. **JULIA ROBERTS** - A zoot-suit-fluke—*Godfather III* in drag!
6. **CARRIE FISHER** - *Postcards from the Edge?* Sorry baby—more like Discards from the Dredge!
7. **KIM BASINGER** - Barbie goes punk—all crass, no class!
8. **LAURA DERN** - A vision of Lust in rags fit for a truck stop!
9. **KATHY BATES** - Get the sledgehammer. Put this fashion fiasco out of her Misery!
10. **BARBRA STREISAND** - What can I say? Yentl's gone mental!

FASHION FIASCO OF THE YEAR AWARD: **Debbie Allen** - A hymn to hi-tech horror.
FABULOUS FASHION INDEPENDENTS: **Princess Caroline, Sophia Loren, Joan Rivers, Nicollette Sheridan, Governor Ann Richards, Queen Noor, Elizabeth Taylor, Sarah, Duchess of York** and **Michelle Pfeiffer**

1991

1. **JULIA ROBERTS** - Haul out the "Hook" for rag-doll Roberts! This tacky Tinkerbell from fashion Neverland...is a number-one hymn to homespun horror.
2. **WYNONNA JUDD** - The shaggy songbird of country kitsch looks like Hulk Hogan—in sequins.
3. **DELTA BURKE** - Is it Scarlett O'Hara—or just plain Tara? An antebellum atrocity.
4. **TYNE DALY** - What can I say? Tyne's a trainwreck—in Technicolor.
5. **JODIE FOSTER** - No doubt Jodie's a dazzling director—but her fashions would look better...on Hannibal Lecter.
6. **CARLY SIMON** - Little Orphan Annie meets Mr. Ed. A fright-wigged fiasco of the Carly kind.
7. **FAYE DUNAWAY** - Faye's freaky fashion follies...make her the Depressing Diva of Designer Dreck.
8. **KATHY BATES** - At Play in the Basement of K-Mart. Period.
9. **JANE SEYMOUR** - Miss Seymour should wear more—she's a paisley peep show on parade.
10. **DAME EDNA EVERAGE** - Half Norma Desmond, half Elton John...the Dame from Down Under is a mauve-topped monstrosity.

1992

1. **MADONNA** - The Bare-Bottomed Bore of Babylon…looks like an over-the-hill Lolita, sinking in a sea of sleaze! A masochistic monstrosity!
2. **GEENA DAVIS** - Big Bird…in heels! A Folies Bergere fiasco!
3. **GLENN CLOSE** - Grab the garlic and lock the door—Dracula's Daughter strikes again!
4. **DELTA BURKE** - Earthquake at the OK Corral!
5. **SINEAD O'CONNOR** - No tresses, no dresses—The High Priestess of Pretense downright depresses!
6. **SHIRLEY MACLAINE** - A carrot-topped tragedy—wrapped in reincarnated rubbish!
7. **JULIETTE LEWIS** - A corn-row catastrophe above—a bohemian bomb below!
8. **DEMI MOORE** - What can I say about The Vamp of Vanity Fair? Moore…is less. Period!
9. **GOLDIE HAWN** - In jeans that jiggle and tops that plunge, Goldie's become The Goddess of Grunge!
10. **LATOYA JACKSON** - This over-hyped horror is…is a hymn to Halloween—365 nightmares a year!

1. **GLENN CLOSE** - Forget "Sunset Boulevard"—Glenn's taken a detour down "Nightmare Alley." A modern-day Medusa—wrapped in a Hefty bag!

2. **JULIA ROBERTS** - Let's be blunt about a barefoot bride—the new Mrs. Lovett tells fashion to…Shove it!

3. **DIANA ROSS** - What can I say? She looks like a Martian meter maid—starring in a Can-Can Revue!

4. **ROSIE PEREZ** - In fish-net no-no's and thigh-high horrors, she's peerless…fearless…A fanny-flaunting fiasco!

5. **SUSAN SARANDON** - A word of warning to peekaboo Sue: In fashions this fatal…the joke's on you!

6. **LATOYA JACKSON** - In disasters that cause the world to groan, she's a tacky tragedy—from the Zombie Zone!

7. **HOLLY HUNTER** - She's speechless—and so am I! A frumpy, dumpy dirge—in the key of F!

8. **ROSIE O'DONNELL** - This ballpark bomb is in a league of her own. A fashion strike-out—from toes to nose!

9. **TANYA TUCKER** - Tanya's country-fried catastrophes are all tuckered out. She looks like a tornado—trapped in a truck stop!

10. **DARYL HANNAH** - Yesterday's misguided mermaid has taken a real fashion plunge. She's a dowdy dishrag—with a bad case of the GRUNGE!

FABULOUS FASHION INDEPENDENTS: **Hillary Rodham Clinton, Princess Diana, Maya Angelou, Connie Chung, Janet Jackson, Bette Midler, Michelle Pfeiffer, RuPaul, Cindy Crawford** and **Kathie Lee Gifford**

1994

1. **CAMILLA PARKER BOWLES** - Camilla's fashion image is way off track...she looked in the mirror...and watched it crack!
2. **DEMI MOORE** - The Diva of *Disclosure* needs an immediate fashion foreclosure!
3. **HEATHER LOCKLEAR** - From a spandex siren, to a latex Lolita, a tribute to design dementia!
4. **ROSEANNE** - An over-the-top fashion flop! Forget about Tom, Rosey, and divorce your designer!
5. **ELLEN DEGENERES** - Ellen's talent may soar...but her gender bender-bombs...simply bore!
6. **BARBARA CARTLAND** - Pass the chiffon! Campy Cartland, looks like a Victorian poodle...trapped in a pink tutu!
7. **HOLLY HUNTER** - Holly's acting is a triumph of taste...but her boring fashions...look like nuclear waste!
8. **JULIETTE LEWIS** - A Natural Born Fashion Killer! Lewis looks like a parakeet...prancing in a punk parade!
9. **FRAN DRESCHER** - What can I say? She looks like an explosion...in a paint factory!
10. **MADONNA** - The Princess of Pop is lost in a land of peroxide, powder, and paint. Yesterday's shock is today's schlock!

HONORABLE MENTION: **Shay Patterson; Phoenix, Arizona** - Send in the clowns...well, don't bother, she's here!

FASHION FIASCO OF THE YEAR AWARD: **Cicely Tyson** - The mutant caterpillar strikes again.

FABULOUS FASHION INDEPENDENTS: **Sophia Loren, Princess Margaret, Sharon Stone, Barbara Walters, Madeleine Stowe, Pamela Harriman, Ivana Trump, Princess Diana, Barbra Streisand** and **Winona Ryder**

The

Index

𝒶

ℬ

K

KABC, 288-296, 303-305
Kasem, Jean, 368
Keaton, Diane, 362, 368
Keller, Marthe, 362
Kellerman, Sally, 369
Kelly, Gene, 55
Kelley, Paul, 45
Kennedy, Caroline, 361, 366, 367, 368
Kennedy, Jacqueline, 287
Kennedy, John F., 213-215
Kennedy, Rose, 359, 360, 361
Kenzo, 359
Keppler, Victor, 168
Kerr, Deborah, 350
Khan, Princess Yasmin, 362, 364, 365
King, Billie Jean, 360
Kingsley, Sydney, 36-37
Kissinger, Nancy, 361
Kitt, Eartha, 167
Koscina, Sylvia, 356
KTTV, 183, 185

L

LaGuardia, Mayor, 46-47
Lamour, Dorothy, 167, 191
Lansbury, Angela, 370, 372
Lasser, Louise, 361
Lauper, Cyndi, 366, 368
Lawford, Mrs. Peter, 352
Lazar, Marty, 364
Leachman, Cloris, 359
Lederer, Francis, 56
Lee, Gypsy Rose, 47-48, 62
Lee, Michelle, 367
Leigh, Janet, 130

Lennon Sisters, The, 356
Lewis, Juliette, 372
Lewitsky, Bella, 48-49
Liberace, 367
Lichfield, Lady, 362
Little Tough Guy, 43
Lloyd, Emily, 370
Long, Shelley, 368
Lopez, Nancy, 364
Loren, Sophia, 351, 358, 364, 371
Louis, Jean, 191
Lubin, Arthur, 57
Lynn, Loretta, 362, 365

MacGraw, Ali, 358, 359, 369
Mack, Nila, 36
Mackie, Bob, 191
MacLaine, Shirley, 351, 352, 366, 368, 369, 372
Madonna, 367, 369, 370, 372
Magnani, Anna, 175, 350
Magnin, Cyril, 203
Mahler, Irving, 125-129, 313
Mandrell, Barbara, 364
Manhattan, 11
Mansfield, Jayne, 104, 167, 190-196, 351, 353
Marcos, Imelda, 369
Margaret, Princess, 355
Mark of Zorro, 53
Mar-Ken, 41-43
Marshall, Penny, 363
Marx, Zeppo, 156, 157, 158, 161
Mason, Pamela, 354
McCrae, Joel, 37
Meadows, Jayne, 353, 354, 356

U

V

W

Y